LIFE ALONG THE WAY

B. A. PAUL

CONTENTS

INTRODUCTION

Ages ago, I wanted to be an author. Like ages and ages.

I remember sitting at that brown kidney-shaped table in hard orange plastic chairs with my fourth grade teacher tucked into the kidney's bend, classmates sitting to my right and my left, ready for our reading group. She announced a contest that we'd be participating in. Lots of moans all around, including from me. I hated conflict of any kind (still do) even if it was meant to grow me as a human.

Then she announced the name of the contest: Young Authors.

And I was sold. I didn't even know what it was, but at the word "author" I had to check the corners of my mouth lest drool were to slip out onto my reading book and I were to become the "bullied kid of the day/week/month" (holding that honorary position for however long it would take for some other poor child to screw up life).

The teacher held up a blank book, about eight by eight inches with a clean cardboard cover and bright white blank pages. She told us we'd write our stories, then carefully copy them into the "real" book and send them to the contest. I was, however, bummed that she was going to make us illustrate them. I'm about as talented with colored pencils and crayons as I am with spatulas and skillets, but I digress...

I can't remember what I wrote. If I had to guess it was something sci-fi/fantasy—likely with unicorns or aliens. As I type this, I'm trying to visualize my little crayon pictures. I only remember the stress of the art, but the pages are smears of color on the top and penciled in words on the bottom...

I can't for the life of me remember the "real author" who showed up to encourage our tiny school's gymnasium of youngsters. I do remember the buzz in the gym from likeminded students who loved learning and the anti-buzz air of "let's get this over with and go to recess" from those students who'd rather throw spitballs than learn sentence structure.

I do remember I was a finalist. I remember tiny little Beth from the countryside riding the bouncy bus all the way to the next county to meet with kids from other schools who also "won." We walked from that school to that town's McDonalds (we had no sidewalks in the country, and no one ever got to walk to McDonalds, so I was on over-whelm). I ate my Happy Meal with "fellow authors." I remember being too shy to talk to those fellow authors, so I studied the cardboard Happy Meal Box as I ate until it was time to walk back to the school.

I remember reading out loud my story (and isn't this something... I can't remember what it was about. It's killing me...).

I remember the thrill of someone else "getting" what I was trying to say and thinking it worthy of a ribbon.

It's been a tick since fourth grade.

I don't know what happened to my book—likely swallowed up by a basement flood along with so many other precious childhood mementos, the dried flower corsage I wore to my high school prom, and my dad's death certificate.

Fast forward about three decades, give or take, and the explosion of the indie author revolution. The Kindle changed everything, and I heard "author contest" all over again.

Not that I'm competing, but that same drool response began

afresh, and after greasing the creative gears with some more up-to-date learning, I started writing again.

Then along came a blog.

And along came this book.

What This Book Isn't

Life Along the Way is not a how-to write book. It's not a how-to blog book. It's not a how-to anything.

As a matter of fact, if any of you are aspiring writers or fellow authors, it may very well be an exercise in counter examples and cautionary tales.

No marketing techniques here. The top ten trending hot-market genres are not mentioned. Eight Ways to Ignite Your Writing Passion have given over to Ten Ways to Become Distracted.

You get the point. It's not a manual.

I'm not aiming to give advice to beginning writers. This is not a do this/don't do that. Who am I to tell you what to do or not to do on your author journey?

That's not what this book is.

What This Book Is

Life Along the Way is about the beginning of my author journey.

When I started the blog, I did so because some piece of advice somewhere said readers need social proof that you're a real person and a way to connect, and proclaim, and market. (The very nature of marketing seems to involve some level of conflict and I'd rather not. But I digress...)

So I bought into that "new author" advice.

I found a Web Guy to help me because I'm about as good with tech-ish stuff as I am with colored pencils and spatulas. I found a quiet spot and wrote a few blogs. All very writing-life heavy.

And then I wondered how in the world I could keep that up week after week *and* provide something anyone would want to read. *And* still write fiction. *And* still have a day job. *And* still...

Blogging stretched me in ways I didn't know I could—or needed to be—stretched. Through the last couple of years, the blog has allowed me to vent, plan, and dream.

And, yes, it's given me a platform to announce publication dates, upcoming titles, and so on. To do that dreaded marketing routine.

But more than that...

It's taught me how to be more transparent. To own what I love. To write with *somewhat* reckless abandon.

It's allowed me to compose something and then release it for the world to see—if only to be read by dear friends and the occasional passerby. It's out there. Free. Doing its thing.

Maybe "start a blog" is good advice for authors. Maybe it's bad advice. I don't know. I only know my story and what blogging about the writing life has done for me.

Life Along the Way is a compilation of 100 blogs written from June 2018 through September 2020. The first ninety-nine of which will be taken down from the blog to "make room" for the next ninety-nine in cyberspace. So, by the time this book goes live, my blog will be a little more agile.

Any live links, websites, videos, etc., that appeared in the blog posts and that remain relevant are located in the back pages of the book so as not to clutter the text.

A list of B.A. Paul's current titles is back there, too, because, well, you know. Marketing.

I've added a little update at the end of each original blog post, along with a "Lesson Learned."

Those lessons are mine. The lessons aren't meant to be taken as a do-this/not-that finger shake. They're reminders to myself to pay attention or to change something. They can be your lessons too, if you wish. Your mileage may vary if you take any "advice" I dish out.

Many times, a blog title or idea would come to me as a direct result of scouring through stock photos, looking for ideas or cover art for one of my stories. If the content seems "out of the blue," it's likely that I found an image that tickled Little Miss Muse into action. When the image was of utmost importance to the blog content, I've described it in the update at the bottom of the original blog content.

Remember: I consider myself to be a newbie supreme compared to the long-haulers like Dean Koontz or even some independent authors who figured out their own lives along the way and made their dream a reality.

I find the publishing industry to be vast and ever-changing, and I'll likely be a newbie ten years from now.

And if I'm not considered a newbie in ten years, I hope I'm still learning (so as not to become one of those spit-ball throwing knuckleheads).

Learning craft. Learning marketing. Learning life.

After rereading 100 of my posts, I saw a pattern.

I saw my excuses for procrastination light up like an airport runway at midnight.

I saw (and on one occasion relived) the pain and grief and tragedy from recent and childhood events—sometimes shared with my readers openly, sometimes kept to myself, but these events brewed in the back of my mind, either fueling the writing machine or clogging up the works...

I was also reminded of the blessings. Writing blessings. Friend blessings. Family. Critters. Lots of blessings.

This compilation reminded me that, above all, I am blessed.

So *Life Along the Way* is part writing life blog, part memoir, and part "Beth needs to work life out in black-and-white."

My hope is that something tucked in these pages will make you giggle. Make you think. Make you roll your eyes and cringe.

And maybe inspire you to drool over your dreams just a little bit.

1. THE POWER OF STORY

Do you remember the last time you were engulfed by water? Completely, totally engulfed?

Was it an accident? Did you fall into a pool or a lake? Maybe the ocean's current pulled you where you didn't want to go—one wave held your shoulders down while the next one kept you prisoner. Thrashing, fighting.

Terror.

Was it on purpose? Were you taking swim lessons or getting baptized? Maybe you allowed yourself to sink, to be pulled toward the bottom, a blanket of water wrapping your weightlessness in quiet solitude. Floating, bobbing.

Dreamland.

Do you remember the way the water enveloped your ears and dulled all other sound? Or the sting of it when it got up your nose?

Did you open your eyes? Do you remember how long it took them to adjust to the dim? Or were you in such a panic that all you saw were scenes of your life floating by, positive that you'd never inhale dry oxygen again?

Had you forgotten about that time? Those sensations? If you

weren't reading this right now, would you have even given your last underwater moment a second thought today? This week? This year?

Stories can do that to us. Stories cause us to remember.

They submerge us, twist us, turn us, and cause us to experience memories, sensations, and emotions we had forgotten we'd filed away. A death on the page or the screen can bring back pangs of sorrow felt at a death in real life. A scene where children drink from a water hose or run through sprinklers can resurrect relics from our own childhoods.

One millisecond in a story can nudge a dusty memory from the dark, maybe even a memory unrelated to the content or plot in front of us. The storyline sets off a series of electrical impulses in our minds, firing one synapse and then another, until what was buried in forgotten fog comes into the light with crystal clear clarity. And we're there again. That restaurant. That reunion. That long-ago moment in time.

Stories cause us to notice.

A story that connects violently with all five senses causes us to feel real monsters under our beds, even if it's a balled-up sock. Or catch glimpses of that monster bent over in the backyard at dusk, even if it's the tree stump that's been rotting there for five years. A story that gently pricks those same five senses causes us to pause and make eye contact with that Monarch butterfly on the rosebush, and then we can almost hear its wings flap as it flits away.

A story that connects emotionally causes us to take notice of that old man on the bench. He's been on that bench for how long now? Bearded and shoeless. Or to realize that the guy who cut us off at the stoplight may not be a jerk. He may be rushing to the hospital for the birth of his first child. Or the death of his father.

Stories cause us to dream.

Some stories wrap us in a blanket of beautiful escape with happy endings, predictable paths or fantastical places our mind's eyes could never dream up on their own. Places where fairies ride winged unicorns, teleportation is real, and the boy always gets the girl. Places with wonder, hope.

Peace.

Others leave us exhausted and out of breath as we wrestle right alongside the characters in their races against time and evil and injustice. As if our lives were on the line. As if we couldn't simply shut the book or flip off the screen and walk away. We can't. Sometimes stories grab us by the shoulders and hold us under until The End.

Whatever your reason for seeking out the power of story, I hope the ones I create will connect with you on some level. I hope they help you escape the doldrums or tedious drama of daily life—if only for a little while.

I hope they cause you to remember.

To notice.

To dream.

* * *

I remember where I was sitting when I wrote this. I remember the sheer terror of sending it off to the Web Guy to have him post it. Gasp. What if he read it before he put it live on the site? Another gasp. What if someone else reads it? What if there was a typo (there was, maybe still will be)?

What if this, what if that.

And I remember the sweats. And I remember liking it. Sort of.

Then... What if next week's blog isn't as good as this one? Maybe this blog post, the very first one, is the absolute best I can do and I burn out as an author before I even get started because I can't write a post that competes with the first, let alone finish my dumb first novel.

What if I can't even come up with a *title* for the next blog?

Well, I did write another. And another.

Swallowed the fear. Dried up the sweat.

Finished the first novel and decided: Onward!

Lesson Learned: The more I write, the less I stress about hitting "publish."

2. MAYBE…

"The moment that you feel, just possibly, you are walking down the street naked, exposing too much of your heart and your mind, and what exists on the inside, showing too much of yourself…That is the moment you might be starting to get it right." -- Neil Gaiman

Sweaty palms. Palpitations. Shallow breaths. The shakes.

Fear.

Public speaking. Spiders. Clowns.

Death.

Some people do everything within their human power to eat the right things, move the right way, swallow the right supplements, and pay the right doctors—not to be as healthy as they can be so as to live life to its fullest, but to delay that certain deadline for as long as possible.

Because they're scared.

Public speaking, spiders and clowns don't really get to me. I don't have nightmares about those. Death isn't my hang-up, either. I know where I'll end up when I breathe my last, and I'm looking forward to that heavenly destination. I do, however, have a couple of ways I'd prefer not to take that journey.

Namely anything involving a bridge.

Why the fear of bridges? (And I'm not talking about a simple, I-don't-care-for-it fear; this is irrational, unreasonable, heart-clenching terror). Is it the height of the thing? I don't care for heights, they make my head spin. But heights only spark an extreme physiological response when coupled with a bridge.

Maybe it's the water snaking underneath. Probably not. I have the same adrenaline rampage whether the ramp of terror is over a dried-up creek bed or a concrete tangle of roadways.

Maybe it's the general lack of trust in the architects and contractors. Perhaps they showed up intoxicated on bridge-building day or used sub-par materials that will crumble little by little until the day I need to cross it and that concrete gives in to gravity in mighty chunks.

Maybe some wife somewhere was reminding her husband to bring home eggs when he should have been concentrating on that all-important angle measurement—the very measurement that holds the entire bridge together until the day I drive over it and I and my passengers end up scrambled in a billion pieces below.

Or maybe my parents held me upside down by my ankles from some overpass as a form of punishment and I buried the trauma until adulthood. My mother denies this. My father's not around to ask, so it's still a working theory...

Until recently, a bridge was the only thing that brought thick black curtains into my peripheral vision to smother out the light.

Because recently I hit the submit button and sent my first piece of fiction into cyberspace for all the world to see.

See, I wanted a pen name. A real pen name. Not because I'm ashamed of my writing or that I'm producing X-rated content and if word got out my mother would disown me. Or throw me off a bridge...

Quite the contrary. I like my stories. I have a blast writing them. They give me a creative outlet. They give me an escape from the doldrums and drama of daily life. And it's cheaper to write a story than to pay a therapist.

But what good are stories if they're tucked away in a drawer? Maybe someone else would enjoy them. Maybe something in a story could lift someone's spirits or save them money on their therapy bill. Maybe I could publish. Maybe I could build a side income—or a career—with my writing.

Maybe...

And I could hide my introverted self behind a pen name. (The reason I don't have one is a tale for another time.)

If the stories were a success, so be it. If not, I'd keep writing, change my pen name and try again, saving myself and my family the embarrassment of my failed art... because no one would know. Pen name. See?

Harder to change my real name. Harder to bite the bullet and commit to the art of it. And the consequences, whatever those may be.

My sweet aunt stopped for a visit after cleaning up my grandparents' grave for Memorial Day. As she gave me an update on the state of the cemetery, I remembered my short story "The Gatherer," which I printed for her.

"You might like it. Let me know." Then the sweaty palm thing. So I added, "If you don't like it, lie to me."

She messaged me later: Loved the story. Nearly made me cry. Keep writing.

My heart soared. Then the palpitation thing. Maybe she took my advice and lied.

Maybe she really did like it.

Maybe...

Whatever the case, the story is out there. Exposed. Waiting for judgment or accolades or neither.

Whatever the outcome, this writing journey has started. It's already taken detours, dodged roadkill, and navigated a hairpin turn or two.

But maybe, just maybe, there won't be too many bridges...

* * *

I still have the bridge thing and the burning curiosity as to the why of it all. And since 2020's ugly rearing of the head, I'm even more socially awkward than at the time I wrote "Maybe..."

Oh, well. At least I don't think everyone's lying to me about whether they like something I've written. Quite frankly, I'm too busy writing now to care about everyone else's feelings.

My family is a great support. But the fear of family emotions (whatever in the world will Aunt Sally say when she reads...") can drain the creative side of things and make writing with passion a chore.

Lesson Learned: Take the compliments, ignore the negatives—then write the next story free of fear.

3. THE POWER OF OBJECTS

Stuff. We all have it. Stuff we don't need. Stuff we don't want. Stuff we can't live without. Stuff to put stuff in...

In the last few years, we've cleaned out three estates of family members that have passed or needed to downsize.

And oh, my, the stuff.

After each clean-out, I went home exhausted and started tossing and donating *my* stuff. Thinking, if I die or become otherwise incapacitated, I surely don't want my kids to deal with it.

Then it begins:

Except that ugly yellow turtle cookie jar that was my grandfather's because it reminds me of his stories of hunting for snapping turtles along muddy riverbanks and I can still see where it lived in my grandparents' house.

Speaking of them, my grandmother found flower-shaped quartz rocks from Lake Pleasant in Arizona decades ago, so don't touch those. Or any aunt- or grandmother-made quilt. Ever. Never ever touch the quilts.

Speaking of aunts, leave those two hardback copies of *Where's Waldo* alone. I say I'm keeping them because they're tall enough to support a broken shelf on my bookcase, but really, it's Waldo, and my aunt gave them to me.

And speaking of gifts, my husband gave me a dog for my birthday ten years ago. Leave his red collar hanging on my rearview mirror, please. May the pup rest in peace.

Speaking of death, my pink marble egg that fits so nicely in the palm of my hand and is so cool and heavy, and my dad gave it to me one Easter—may he rest in peace. It was the same Easter that the sparrow flew into the house and our Boston Terriers went berserk and oh, the chaos...

And speaking of feathered things, leave my birds alone. The vintage tropical bird figurines that I really did buy at a yard sale to flip on eBay but they ended up with their own special shelf in my sunroom. And the seller was an eccentric old woman who'd collected tropical bird figurines her entire life and insisted on giving me a tour of *her* sunroom where hundreds of birds covered the walls and tables...

And as I toss and donate, I remember things that I *don't* have any longer. The corsages from prom, my wedding bouquet and a unicorn autograph book —all destroyed in a basement flood.

And speaking of unicorns, my entire unicorn collection that I sold at a garage sale when I was getting married and it was time to grow up and save space for apartment life. Hundreds of unicorn figurines amassed over my childhood. Each one magical to me at one time or another.

You get the picture. We assign memories to objects. The items aren't needed and wouldn't mean diddly squat to anyone else, but we gain comfort with them.

Some objects mark victories or terrible heartache. Think of the relics stored in museums behind glass cases, under lock and key. Permanent banners of victories, accomplishments and innovation. And around the corner, in another wing, memorials of war, death and destruction.

Think of your own banners and memorials. Your first-place

trophy versus the consolation ribbon. The wedding band you wear every day. Or the one rattling around in your junk drawer.

Triumph and defeat seem to be etched into the object's "memory." A permanent echo of the past— and only a glimpse of the object is enough to bring smiles or reopen wounds.

Fiction writing gives authors the ultimate platform to play with an object's emotional and "what if" power. Think Hemingway's six-word novel: *For sale: baby shoes, never worn.* Think of Tolkien's ring sheltering its wearer in invisibility while heightening the senses. Think of Baum's shoes and Lewis's wardrobe transporting characters to magical worlds. Think of Lucas's whip in the hands of Indiana Jones, or his glowing light saber in the hands of Luke Skywalker fighting evil in a galaxy far, far away.

But none of the objects mean anything without the characters behind them. We love Frodo, Indiana and Dorothy. We love our mothers and dads and aunts and the occasional eccentric old bird-collector. Without the character, the connection is lost and the object really is diddly squat—just another trinket collecting dust.

I love the what-ifs of objects, especially old, rusty and moth-eaten ones. What has that old camera seen? What about the globe that isn't quite round anymore? That golden cat statue guarding the flower bed —is it marking the passing of a beloved pet? Or is it stolen, a token of some long-deserved revenge? The object sparks the wonder. The characters bring it to life...

Take a look around your home. Clean out the junk drawer or the top of the hall closet. When an object causes you to pause, hold it for a moment. Smell it. Examine it. Then close your eyes.

And remember.

* * *

The turtle jar sits in my dining room. The rocks and marble egg are in my jewelry box. The Where's Waldo book still props up my shelf. I've added to the flock of birds and scored a few vintage unicorn figurines—one great-horned doo-dad I may have owned as an eight-year-old. Go figure.

Actually, everything in the blog post is right where it should be, save for the red collar hanging from my rearview mirror.

We sold that vehicle, so I finally took down the dangling reminder of Spencer Doodles and tucked his collar away in a drawer. I'll remember that pooch again when we clean or move.

I still enjoy empowering objects in my fiction stories—and I love watching how other authors do the same.

Lesson Learned: Keep special items as back-up memory storage for times gone by—just not too many, or your kids may hate you one day...

4. YOU SHOULD WRITE ABOUT THAT

When I started this journey, only a few people knew I had been dabbling at writing stories here and there—or that I had started and stopped a novel more times than I could count. I tried to hold off spreading the word (okay, I didn't want to spread the word at all), but my over-excited sweet hubby would have none of it. (And one more reason why a pen name wouldn't work.) Then Mother. Then Grandma, and the ball was rolling.

And the more people who found out that I enjoyed writing, the more bruised my ribs became.

Out to eat with friends and another patron's kid throws spaghetti on top of his head? I'd get an elbow to the ribs with "you should write about that."

Well, if it had been a grown man throwing spaghetti on top of his own head, now that'd be something to write about. Maybe.

Moving that 90-year-old grandmother from her farm of 60-plus years to a one-bedroom apartment? Another elbow to the ribs and "you should write about that" when we'd find something unusual—or unmentionable—in the clean-out.

Maybe. But only if that ancient, two-ton Gateway computer monitor had gone all *War Games* and "Shall we play a game?" echoed through the old shed—but Grandpa never wired the shed for electric. And the glowing green cursor blinked in sync with my pounding pulse, waiting for a response...

Hang on. Just a minute.

Sorry.

I had to stop the blog for a moment to file that idea under Sci-Fi. I'm back with you now.

On vacation with Amish friends for ten whole days? Multiple (very excited) elbows to the ribs and "you should write about that" or "Book material!" when we were robbed, but we weren't *really* robbed and I had to explain to two very confused young policemen—with the Amish ladies in tow—how we weren't robbed, but we did call 911, but actually someone else was the victim. Because Amish ladies typically don't know the difference between a silver Honda and a silver Volvo.

Okay. That one *will* end up in a book at some point... No need to pause the blog. Some events permanently engrave themselves in the recesses of memory.

Anyway, I suppose it's no different from any occupational "hazard" when off the clock. The mechanic investigates the clunking in his friend's Mustang, the police officer answers a dozen-and-one questions about the legalities of a neighbor's firework collection, and the healthcare worker assesses the glands of every snot-nosed kid at her family's Thanksgiving dinner.

Being a writer brings with it many elbows and people will always point out "book material." Once in a while, they bring my attention to something I otherwise would have missed, and that's cool. Or things that are significant to them, and I get to know them better for it. At any rate, I'm glad they've taken an interest in something that's important to me. It shows they care.

The Mustang, the fireworks, and snotty noses are all important to someone somewhere, but they aren't equally important or noteworthy to everyone at all times.

So how do I sort it all out when faced with so many ideas from all directions? What makes something worthy of the page? Is it the wow factor? Is it the emotional tug? Is it the relatability of a thing?

For me, an idea or topic needs that burn-a-hole-in-the-back-of-your-brain factor. A phrase, an object, or an event buries itself in that back edge of my mind, and from there, creativity starts to play.

It plays and toys with characters, settings, dialog and the "what-ifs" constantly, even when I'm supposed to be concentrating on something else—like this blog. I don't seem to have too much control over that creative bit: much like a two-year-old, it wants what it wants when it wants it—usually right now.

Some writers call it "The Muse" and name it after lovers, animals or even their mothers. Edgar Allen Poe had his cat, Catterina. Stephen King has his "Boys in the Basement." I'm afraid to name mine or give it a "shape." It may take over completely.

That creativity thing often dominates when I'm supposed to be concentrating in heavy traffic, answering mundane emails or paying bills.

Or when I'm supposed to be listening to doctor's instructions on some complicated matter, but he has the most distinct accent and a mole in the shape of an alpaca on his cheekbone. Or is it a scar? Did he do that to himself or was it done to him? Maybe he's the one speaking through the old computer in the shed...

Aaahh nuts. Hold on.

Just a minute...

Sorry about that.

In the end, if an idea burns a hole in the back of your brain, if you can see in your mind's eye a myriad of wonderfully unexpected outcomes from a "what if," if you just can't let an image go, then maybe YOU should write about that.

* * *

Actually, that glowing cursor from *War Games* is blue (I recently put Mr. Broderick's old classic on for background noise and found the error in my memory bank).

And oh, my, the line "I'm afraid to name mine or give it a 'shape.' It may take over completely" Too late.

In Blog # 34, I named Little Miss Muse. And she wants me to add that it was fitting that Blog #34 was about love. The love month. A love letter. And that's when I named her "Little Miss." Because I love her. And I do... love her. But not so much her interruptions...

(And now that I'm done kissing up to the purple imp—onward!)

Have I written the "computer in the shed" tale? No, not yet. But re-reading this blog sure moved that idea higher up into the file.

Lesson Learned: Muses demand to be named, and an idea file is an absolute must.

5. I DON'T KNOW

"I don't know." Three words I hate.

I like to know things. I like to see what's coming. I like plans, schedules, details, routine.

Ducks. In. A. Row. Please and thank you.

And, unfortunately, I've passed this need-to-know mentality down to my kids. After years of homeschooling, when Mom controlled the what's, when's and how's of each day, they really did think I knew everything. Then we'd go to church, our homeschool co-op, or some extracurricular event, and they'd barrage me with questions. Questions I didn't know the answer to. For example:

Kid asks why the dolphin show was canceled at the zoo.

"I don't know."

"Why not?"

"Because I'm not the one in charge here."

"Why not?"

"I don't work at the zoo." (Though I often *felt* like I did. Still do...)

"I thought you were in charge of everything."

"Yes, dear one. They promoted me last week from stay-at-home mom to head marine biologist. I just didn't tell you yet."

Several friends have asked me over the last few weeks where I get my ideas from. I grimace inside because...

I don't know.

The comedian Tim Hawkins puts it best in his routine: Live life. Take notes. Tell strangers.

Life provides endless material. But that material needs to be reworked into story form to hook, engage and entertain the reader, otherwise, that material is simply a "guess what happened to me today" ten-minute conversation. So where do *those* ideas come from?

I don't know.

I've mentioned before in "The Power of Objects" how I'm intrigued with dusty, rusty old treasures and the stories they may hide, so I guess some of my ideas come from garage sales and Goodwill. However, most people don't kick back after a long day of work or wrestling kids to relax with a Wikipedia, fact-only version of some concrete noun. They want action, emotion, intrigue. But how do I work those objects into a story?

I don't know.

And I touched on "The Muse" last week. That two-year-old creativity bit of your brain that gets carried away until some adult, rule, or institution comes and tells it, "No dear. You can't run down the street flapping your arms like a bird, with purple crayons hanging out of your mouth wearing only Daddy's blue checkered necktie."

Ask that two-year-old why he did that—or what he was thinking when he did it—and you'll get a shrug or an "I don't know."

At some point, though, he had the idea, acted on it, and, more than likely, had a grand time doing it. And, more than likely, that little one will look up at that big, upset adult and ask, "Why not?"

I do know, however, that I've always sought a creative outlet of some sort. Be it through writing or artsy-fartsy endeavors that came and went; a closet-full of scrapbooking supplies gave way to a closet-full of journals, then again to brushes and paints. But time constraints prevented me from fully engaging in any of them until recently.

I'd spent the better part of 15 years homeschooling, but the older my kids got, the less they appreciated the creative bells and whistles of the lessons and just wanted to get the work done. Creative outlet gone.

During that time I also worked as a medical transcriptionist where one cannot, under any circumstance, ever be creative. This work appealed to my ducks-in-a-row need, but not so much to idea generation. Because one cannot, under any circumstance, take ideas garnered through medical transcription and place them into a story. Ever. HIPAA, anyone?

When the writing bug finally bit again, I sat down at the blank screen, cursor blinking at the ready, positioned my fingers over the keyboard and....

Nothing.

Where were the ideas? I started and stopped after several attempts and everything I typed sounded like a kindergarten lesson plan or patients' files dictated to me by the doctors' voices buzzing in my ears.

So, I signed up for a creative writing course (I'll touch more on that another time). After a few weeks, those exercises oiled my rusty, stuck idea gears and I found the beginnings of my stride.

To answer the question "Where do you get your ideas?" Take your pick. Life, objects, the Muse, those two-year-old gears spinning with no adult supervision?

I'm not sure.

What if the ideas run out? Unlikely, because the last I checked, the planet's still spinning.

Why keep digging and searching and oiling those idea gears? What's the point when there's an endless pile of works out there for readers to enjoy? Isn't one more story or idea futile in the end?

I don't know.

But, why not?

* * *

I still don't know, but Little Miss Muse, at this stage, has demanded that I update this to rightly address her participation in all things creative. I should also add that those "idea gears" and "stride" have been beat half to death with more life events than I could shake a stick at. This blog originally posted in July of 2018. Now, it's September of 2020— We've lost a few folks, had a few traumas, and then, well, 2020. The gears and strides were put in the "mental attack" during these times, and each time, I've had to re-oil, readjust and repurchase Little Miss Muse's "toys" to get started again.

Lesson Learned: Just get started again. Repeated resets are not failures: They are forward momentum.

6. IT'S NOT ABOUT YOU

In the summer of 2017, I enrolled in a writing course with an established author. I wanted to get those creative gears a little more "unstuck" and get some feedback on my writing.

Not feedback from people who love me; feedback from people who don't give two rats' tails about me. My husband wouldn't tell me if I wrote crap to save his life. He loves me too much. I needed a hard-nosed opinion so I could grow and improve.

I also wanted feedback from someone who's been in the publishing industry—both the traditional and indie arenas—because I wasn't sure what I wanted to do yet. And if someone has been actively writing long enough to be firmly established in both of those arenas, they have more knowledge and practical, applicable advice to give than a lot of "writers" selling courses who've not written much, let alone have anything that resembles a career.

This author, Dean Wesley Smith (and his author/editor wife, Kristine Kathryn Rusch), were just the ticket. I had followed their blogs for quite a while and knew from their no-nonsense tones that if I turned in something that sucked, they'd tell me. They'd also tell me the blatant truth about why it didn't work and maybe give some advice on how to fix it or skills to work on.

And I wasn't disappointed. I learned more in the couple of courses I took from him than I did in all of college. I learned stuff I didn't even know I needed to know.

Then he put out a challenge last June. Write 30 stories in 30 days and turn each in to him. Dean would be the first reader and give a short critique. If you made all thirty days, you got to take two more courses from him. As of this writing, the shorts I have on Amazon and the ones you may have read on the blog are a result of that challenge.

By far, this was the hardest thing I've ever done in any of my academics. More difficult than organic chemistry. Calculus was a walk in the park, and college exams were a breeze compared to the grueling task of that many short stories in a month.

And do you know just how much "other life" happens in a month? We were flat busy in all avenues aside from this crazy endeavor.

At any rate, I logged over 70,000 words that month and completed all thirty stories. Thirty different settings. Thirty different plots. And way more than thirty different characters with all of their quirks, wardrobes, props and dialog. I think a 70,000-word novel would have been easier—at least I could've stayed in the same story world with the same group of people.

Add to that the fact that I hadn't written a short story since I was in middle school. I can't for the life of me remember doing a single one in high school.

Not all of the stories made it through the wringer, so to speak. A couple flat didn't work (though hubby thought them wonderful). A few needed a little more meat. And a few were solid novel starts— ideas too big for a short, but boy will they be great fun to revisit in a longer form.

I passed a few of them around to family members and a couple of friends. Then a strange thing happened. People thought those stories, or small bits of them, were about them or about someone we knew.

Now, remember, thirty tales in thirty days. I wasn't *thinking* at all. I wasn't thinking about mommas or daddies or neighbors or the wayward anyone. The only thing I was thinking about was the midnight deadline and would I even be able to come up with another storyline the next day.

And the next.

And the next.

I did, however, try really hard with the names of the characters. I didn't name characters (or at least in the first eight or ten stories) with names of anyone I knew personally. I think that even fell apart by the half-way point. I had to start a notepad next to the laptop to remember a cast of three during one story because all the names used from previous stories were jumbling in my head. At least two characters accidentally changed gender before the final proofing, as well.

I've also signed so many confidentiality agreements for work that I really do try not to pull material directly from other people. I try to instead work with generalities and common themes as opposed to "I know a guy who_____" (fill in the blank with something only that one guy did and the whole world knows who it is).

So did I consciously write about anyone I know? Nope. If you see yourself, or your dog walker, or college roommate in one of my stories, rest assured: it's a coincidence.

Are any of them about me? Maybe. Bits of me. Tiny moments from childhood woven into a character's world. Like in *Wouldn't You Like To Be a Red-Winged Blackbird?*, the photo challenge the girls embark on is based on a game my grandmother and I played when I was very young. The raspberry pie in *Penny's Place* and the petunias in *Green Thumb* hold a specialness for me, but they're just tidbits. A prop for a character or a detail to enrich the narrative.

And, quite frankly, my characters often didn't do what I told them to, so trying to write someone I knew into recognizable fictional form would have been a challenge without giving their address and Social Security number right up front.

But isn't that the fun part of stories? Seeing yourself, or at least little bits of you, in a character. In the way they speak, dress, move or react? Isn't that one of the ways we connect?

And even more fun—if we're honest with ourselves—is seeing our nemesis in the story's villain and being able to root for that character's defeat without the guilty conscious of doing it in real life.

And thus, creatives have to be careful, or we'll get sued.

This is why television shows and movies put that "any resemblance to actual persons, living or dead..." disclaimer in small print at the end of the credits. Books often do it at the beginning, usually just to remind us all...

No, it really isn't about you.

* * *

The shorts written for the 30 in 30 days have been bundled into nifty little collections available on Amazon.

I still take classes from WMG publishing and you can find a list of their available courses here:

And I still try to avoid like the plague writing anything that resembles the lives of anyone I know. Really.

Lesson Learned: Keep learning lessons.

7. THE LOST MANUSCRIPT

My first attempt at free, creative writing came in fourth grade when I wrote an epic space novel on wide-ruled notebook paper in pencil or, when allowance would allow, magnificent erasable ink pen. Even at that age, I had an unhealthy office supply fetish.

The cast of characters was wide, consisting of myself, school friends and frenemies (you know, kid drama—where friends and frenemies are somewhat of a fluid social amoeba). And when magic or muscle was called for, I'd throw in the occasional wise teacher along with some slightly plagiarized and/or outright stolen characters from whatever movie or TV show I was watching at the time. Warner Brothers could have so put me in jail.

The plot? There wasn't one. I can't remember what the characters' goals were. Were we escaping something, or trying to find something? No clue. I only remember that the characters came and went whenever the mood struck me.

In a fight with the best friend? Alien kidnapped her (ETA on the rescue depended on what happened at school the next day). Teacher grumpy that day? Send her through the wormhole. Bully Boy acting up? Well, even at ten years old I wrote some people out of the plot. Permanently.

I remember my mom being proud of my work. She took it to her office and made copies to pass around to her friends. And after that, probably a couple of years later, I think I stuck it in a cardboard box with academic awards and various other elementary mementos and I forgot about it.

At least I thought I did.

Until the basement flooded. I panicked remembering that notebook paper manuscript was the only thing I really cared about in that box. But after pulling out drenched certificates, report cards and photos, I realized it wasn't there. And I also realized it wasn't a good idea to store anything in a basement in a cardboard box.

Lesson Learned: Buy plastic totes.

I don't think I finished the story. I think it fizzled out. Looking back, I wished I had stuck with it. Maybe if I'd finished it, I could remember what the story was really about. Not to mention the sense of accomplishment it would have brought. Maybe I wouldn't have put off writing seriously for quite so long. Like decades. Okay, now I'm beating up my ten-year-old self. Poor kid.

Lesson Learned: Finish things.

Maybe I didn't finish it because I was showing it to too many people. A "Hey, look how many pages I got done this weekend" kind of thing. And when your work in progress is floating out there, unfinished, there's no big reveal. There's no mystery or buildup. It's like that friend/frenemy amoeba, just a blob of scribbles on paper, ever morphing but never really accomplishing anything.

Lesson Learned: Keep it secret till it's done.

That best friend that was repeatedly kidnapped? Once in a while we would collaborate on a chapter or two. I'd spend the night with her and we'd sprawl out on her bed, surrounded by pages of the manuscript and the SolarQuest game (Monopoly with planets, basically. We'd play that until we ran out of money and game parts, then we'd make our own bits from construction paper and keep going—geeks, I know).

She'd read the last several chapters and then start with ideas of her own. Some were good, and I agreed with them. Some rubbed me the wrong way. Like when she'd write *my* secret crush into a scene and he was sitting next to *her* on the spaceship. And when I got home, I'd have to take those pages out, rewrite the setups with new beats, new settings, new dialog—and another abduction.

Lesson Learned: Shelve creative collaboration—stick with board games when it comes to friends. And keep it secret till it's done.

And finish the dumb thing already.

Okay, now I'm beating up my middle-aged self. And I deserve it.

My current work in progress, which is turning out to be quite the chore, is teaching me these lessons all over again—except the "buy plastic totes." Replace that lesson with "buy quality storage drives— and *use* them."

The story is one I cooked up several years ago, started and put down. Started again and put down. I've got so many more ideas that are "better" than this particular one I've spent so much time on. But the characters are calling to me, "Don't leave us dangling like this. We'll behave, we promise." And the sting of giving up on it simply to move on to something more exciting is eating at the back of my brain.

And, doggonit. I'm gonna finish it. If nothing else, it'll be good practice. I've learned a lot since writing chapter one, and I could go back and make some of the dull parts shine if I wanted to.

Or not.

Because what I perceive as dull parts at one point *did* shine. Those parts were the best I could do for where I was in my learning and writing level at the time that I wrote them. And if I start fiddling with it, the story will never be good enough because I'm always learning and upping the skill level—this manuscript will turn into an amoeba. Ever changing but never really going anywhere.

And if I keep fiddling with it, I'll never get free to explore any of those "better" ideas.

So I'll finish it.

Because my middle-aged self needs that sense of accomplishment. Finishing is something I can control and not waste those lessons learned.

Because that ten-year-old little girl would be thrilled that I did. It's something she'd like to have read.

And because I refuse to have another lost manuscript.

* * *

The space quest manuscript is still lost. No idea.

The work-in-progress mentioned in this blog turned into Switch.

Lesson Learned: See lessons learned throughout the post.

(Eerie, the way some of these things are working out. Almost like Little Miss Muse has been with me THE WHOLE TIME. Purple glitter everywhere as she pops the cork on sparkling grape juice and toasts me. I finally understand Little Miss's ever-present presence...)

8. THANK YOU, MRS. YEAGER

It's mid-August and schools in my area will be in full swing soon. Doesn't it seem too soon? It's not the least bit cold outside, there's plenty of sun left at the end of the day, and the frogs are still chirping their nighttime melodies.

Back in my elementary school years, we started after Labor Day, finished before Memorial Day and never made up a single snow day. Ever.

Back in my grandad's day, they walked uphill in the snow both ways to school and only ate oranges for lunch—if they were lucky...

We live near the high school that I attended a couple of lifetimes ago, and the parade of buses will start soon. Ugghh. Buses. Introverts are not huge fans of buses. I wasn't a huge fan of high school, either —at least not the social parts.

I was a good student, though, a rule follower and teacher pleaser. I kept mostly to myself except for a similar group of girls who were also good students and kept their noses clean. I didn't have to study much; things seemed to come easily for me academically—and I used that academic ease as an escape from a somewhat chaotic life outside of school which was never in my control and which never came easy.

I was one of those geeky/nerdy ones who didn't mind a research paper or an essay. Big, multipart projects didn't scare me either.

But Mrs. Yeager did.

Now, mind you, she looked nothing like the photo I sourced for this blog (And, on another note, most of the photos I found when searching for "tough teacher" or similar phrases brought up wrinkled nuns waving wooden rulers. What's with *that* stereotype?).

Mrs. Yeager was a petite lady with short, blond hair and a kind voice, and one wouldn't think she'd be intimidating at all. Until she returned my first English composition paper of the semester. The composition paper that I breezed through like all of the others up until that junior year and did quite well, thank you very much.

Until I saw red.

All. Over. The. Place.

I approached her desk with sweaty palms and asked what the marks meant. And I asked how I could bring my grade up.

She smiled sweetly, told me I had comma issues and I needed to go to the computer lab and work on commas. She handed me a slip of paper and sent me down the hall.

To the computer lab.

To work on commas.

And I turned on the clunky monitor, the computer lab guy showed me where the comma program was and I worked the rest of the class time on comma exercises. Lots of them.

I hated every minute of it. I would've rather walked uphill in the snow both ways to school each day and eaten only oranges for lunch for a year. I would've rather ridden the bus with blue-butted baboons than to go to the computer lab to work on commas.

The next assignment I turned in to Mrs. Yeager turned into yet another permission slip to go toooo—you guessed it!—the computer lab to work on commas.

And the next essay? Well. Take another guess.

By the end of the semester, however, the red marks dwindled as did the trips down the hall to the computer lab. Thank goodness I was mastering the black-and-white rules of the almighty comma.

I saved those papers. Every one of them.

When I got to college and took English composition, I retyped those suckers with Mrs. Yeager's corrections and suggestions right down to the last itty bitty comma and handed them in to my professor. (Side note—don't do that today. Many—if not all—universities consider this plagiarism even if you copy your own work. You'll get kicked out for sure! But back in my day...)

I got every one of those high school junior-year papers back in my freshman college course with an A—and no red marks.

Thank you, Mrs. Yeager.

I needed that tough teaching from that sweet little lady. I wrote many papers from scratch after that and did well on all of them when I followed the rules she'd ingrained in my head.

Now I'm using those rules today. In fiction. But quite a bit differently.

I know what the rules are. I've mastered most of them.

And now I break them. Frequently and on purpose.

I'm breaking them as I write this blog with the purpose of establishing my tone and voice.

Fragments. Ending sentences with prepositions. A misspelled word. A dab of passive voice. Odd ellipses and paragraph breaks.

Writers with a solid grasp of grammar are like carpenters with a toolbox full of tools. We can play with words, structures and syntax. We can change things up. We can make characters sound like they come from a specific region. We can speed up a thrilling fight scene, or we can slowly plunge readers so deep into a setting that they lose their breath. We can paint and build and tear down. All with the tools in our boxes.

And Mrs. Yeager put plenty of tools in my box.

I don't know where she is now. I didn't look her up or ask her permission to be the subject of my blog. But I do appreciate her and the other English teachers I've had over the years. I'm sure they all put a tool or two into the box. But nothing like that blasted comma lab.

Whatever you're passionate about—be it writing or art or

carpentry—learn the basics. Instill every ounce of knowledge you can about the rigid rules of structure, composition, angles and symmetry into your brain. You never know when you'll need a particular tool...

(And Mrs. Yeager, if you're reading this, you may want to close your eyes...)

Then break those rules.

And create something amazing.

* * *

The photo for the blog on this week was of a grumpy, gray-hair-in-a-bun woman standing in front of a chalkboard.

As for the commas, I find myself being inconsistent with the Oxford one. I prefer it I think. Not sure why it's such a controversial topic, nor do I care, really.

Lesson Learned: I might need a style guide as this author adventure goes full swing. Em-dashes, ellipses, and commas. Oh, my!

9. HOOKED

I love Half Price Books.

Now, I'll shop Amazon, Goodwill, and garage sales for my favorite standby authors, and occasionally I'll even find a new writer lurking in one of these venues and fall in love with their ideas or styles.

But there's something about Half Price. Maybe it's a tad more organized. Goodwill? Not so much. Maybe it's the variety. Garage sales? You're stuck in the favorite genre of the homeowner. (I'm always a little more than disappointed when a garage sale ad boasts "hundreds" of books and every single one of them is a cookbook. Or drooled-on baby board books.)

And Amazon? I can't hold the book in my hands and feel the weight of it. Or fan the pages. Or smell it.

Yeah, I know. TMI on that last bit.

The nearest Half Price to me is about 50 miles away, which means whenever we're in a larger town and I spot one, the drooling commences and the wonder of what new half-priced gem I may be missing starts to burn a hole in my brain no matter what wonderful family activity we're on our way to do.

And someone usually notices.

"We can stop if you want." Their offer is kind.

Of course, yes. Let's ditch the zoo/concert/doctor appointment and load up with a half-ton of half-priced books.

"No, I'm good. Some other time." My refusal is equally kind (though they may not realize it), and we drive on our way as a piece of my soul hovers over the storefront.

You see, I don't enjoy Half Price with other people. Half Price is a must-go-it-alone shopping experience for me. My dear family would be at my elbow or "patiently" waiting in a corner with their noses in their phones, glancing up every thirty seconds to see how much progress I've made or how many times the pile in my arms has changed. Because at Half Price, you pick up a gob of tomes and put them all back. Pick up another load and repeat—until the titles, topics and authors are balanced just right according to the discretionary income available in the bank at the time.

And this could take quite some time. Hours. And hours.

So, I'm kind. And I don't take other people with me to Half Price.

Why not the library? Couldn't I get the same euphoria from a trip down the hill—and not spend a dime?

No.

I love our library, and I do spend quite a bit of time there, too. (And, quite frankly, many of those half-priced books end up in our local library's book sale once I'm done with them—keeps me and the hubs out of divorce court *grin*.)

But there's something about owning a book versus borrowing. Owning means I'm now invested and must find the time to consume what I've deemed worthy of dragging home or feel the sting of "wasting money." I know. Weird.

And if I do find something I love at the library, I have to give it back. And that's not fair. (Only-child issue?)

The last time I was at Half Price I found an author worth owning. His books won't end up at the library book sale. I won't put them in a garage sale, and I won't sell them back to Half Price. I'll keep them for a good long while. Collect the whole lot of them, I will, I will.

It's Steven James's Patrick Bower Series. Serial killers, twisted plots, thrilling beats, conspiracy and the occasional entirely relatable insight by the main character—or sometimes the villain—that punches me in the feeler.

Now, I've read lots of similar books by other authors, and they were okay. Crime/thriller is my go-to escape genre. John Grisham, anyone?

But there's a problem with some of those other authors. They get way too foul-mouthed and graphic for my tastes. Too many real-life, trauma-triggering issues that those elements set off, and then it's not an escape anymore—it's something to recover from.

I try to skim before I buy, but sometimes I miss the warning signs. Then I've got to skip chapters or skim even more, and I miss important bits and clues—given amongst the muck—that would've allowed me to solve the puzzle alongside the main character. So it sort of takes the fun out of it. Or I can't get past the first few chapters and it ends up at Goodwill or the library book sale. Fairly quickly.

Not James, though. I've not come across many other authors who can paint grit like he does and not get mucky in every other chapter, if you know what I mean. No foul language. No graphic bedroom scenes. And if characters are doing those things, it happens "off screen," so the reader knows the deal, but they don't have to "watch" or "hear" any of it.

I've read five of his novels in the Bowers Files, and the above has held true so far, and I hope it will continue to. He has some other series I plan on checking out when my eyes recover from the reading binge he's taken me on.

And James starts right in the thick of it as good thrillers should. No dull background dumps or meandering storylines left dangling. Which is good. Because if you give me time to get bored, you'll end up in a garage sale.

What about you? What's your go-to genre for escaping life? That novel niche that causes you to forget about dinner in the oven or, better yet, steals your hunger altogether.

And forget about sleeping...

Hop over to the Facebook page and share some suggestions!

* * *

I much prefer the weight of a book in my lap to the glow of an e-reader. But times are a changin' and when the libraries and book-stores are on COVID-closures and garage sales are few and far between, what is one to do?

Half-Price is still going strong, or at least it seems so on the surface. Curbside pickup and limited-capacity in-store pickup is available as of the time of this update. I hope they make it through to the other side — of the pandemic and of the great falling-away of traditional brick-and-mortar bookstores.

Finished the whole Patrick Bowers series by Steven James and read his others. Still like him. Still appreciate the escape without the smut. The newscasts and the Walmart parking lots give us plenty of the other all day long...

Lesson Learned: Wearing a mask in Half-Price books makes me buy more books because my glasses fog and I can't see how tall my stack really is. Oh, well. *Shrug*

10. THE TOP TEN WAYS I GET NOTHING DONE

Here they are, in no particular order. The ways I procrastinate writing. Reasons or excuses. Legitimate or imaginary. Out here. In public.

The things I need to change or reprioritize (Well, maybe not number 8. I'm not the only one with a say in that matter):

10. Say yes. Saying yes to one thing means saying no to everything else. Including what's on the to-do list. Saying yes to everyone all the time is a real time killer. Free for lunch? Yes. Catch a movie? Yes. Come fix my...? Yes. Want to see my new puppy? Absolutely yes. And on and on it goes.

9. Netflixing.

One.

More.

Episode.

Especially when the hubby's home from work and that's what he'd like to do as well.

8. Own a fifteen-year-old cat with a poor digestive system. And who sheds his weight every third day. His companionship may outweigh his maintenance on certain days, but others—not so much.

7. Wait for the perfect moment/environment. I tell myself I have to have a clean area to write creatively, but when I take the time to clean up piles of mail and tackle random to-do list items, I end up on that time-consuming trail of solving the "pressing" issues hiding in those piles instead of writing. Writing can wait until morning when the desk is clear. But morning typically brings all new piles—real or imagined.

What I've found is that I'm waiting for the planets to align where all of the areas of life (motherhood, wifehood, granddaughterhood, businesshood, churchhood, etc.) are totally quiet and calm. With all of their respective problems solved.

Ducks. In. Neat. Rows.

Never going to happen.

6. Work in front of a big window.

Squirrel!

All it would take is for me to turn my desk toward the wall, but that claustrophobia thing kicks in and I'm back watching the leaves blow in the wind again. And oh, look! The mail truck came. Time to make another pile on the desk...

5. Hop down the social media rabbit hole. I'm not a big Facebook user outside of this blog, but I came across this post and, bless the heart of the one who put this where my eyes could find it, now I see it everywhere. Best two minutes and twenty-six seconds on the internet. When you're done reading the blog, come back up here and click on it—but only if you have time to watch it to the end. The bird on the right represents most of my friends. Me? I'm so the bird on the left—it's not even funny. And yes, when I searched for the link, I let the video play and smiled all the way to the end.

Another two minutes and twenty-six seconds swallowed whole.

4. Lose four hours of sleep in the middle of the night on a regular basis. This one is a creative energy killer and ties directly to external chaos and life issues.

3. The office door doesn't lock, and those I reside with aren't trained to read the "Do Not Disturb" sign.

Or they think it doesn't apply to them. Because they're special.

And they are. Special.

Or they don't think their "quiet" presence in the room bothers me. But I can hear them. Breathing. Hovering. Waiting with loud, oxygen-sucking thoughts as they scroll on their phones. Except the cat. We took his phone away a while back...

So why bother with a locked door or a sign? Everyone ignores them anyway.

2. Blog about it. If you're blogging about your hobby, you're likely not engaging in said hobby. None of the words I write for this blog count toward any fiction progress at all. The energy and time the blog takes are not recoverable. Would I be better off working on my work in progress? Probably. But, alas, here I am. Doing the introverted marketing thing. Writing while not writing.

1. Devalue the writing. Writing doesn't pay the bills—yet, and the publishing world moves slowly, so what's one more day of lost writing time? But those days turn into weeks. And then into months. I push the writing aside for *everything* on life's to-do list or when chaos strikes. Then I tell myself there's no energy left for creative thinking. But, I do have the brain cells for sarcasm and whining about the thing that squeezed against my writing time. And honestly, sarcasm and whining take as much creative energy as sitting down and making up stuff for other people to read. I'm just doing that other bit out loud as opposed to on a laptop...

So those are the big ones. My reasons/excuses/self-imposed limitations. And nearly every one of them I can work on. And nearly every one of them would go away if I solved number one. Except number 8. He keeps respawning his nine lives.

Solving number one. What a cool realization from writing this blog. I didn't intend on learning anything when I clunked this list onto the screen. It was to be just one more blog post...

I need to value my writing. It needs to be important enough to be a stable fixture in the day. A priority. And fun.

A fun priority.

A fun priority that keeps me out of the therapist's office and out of my pastor's sermon illustrations.

What about you? What's your "fun priority" that you can't seem to get around to?

Make a list of your top ten or fifteen hinderances. Then hunt for that one thing on the list that, if solved or rethought or restructured, would solve most of the other points. That one thing that you absolutely *can* control (without ending up a headline on the six o'clock news, mind you).

Then go have fun!

And if all else fails, click the link in number 5.

* * *

Well, dear old Cosmo, may he rest in peace. Grandma, too. Great cat. Great grandmother. Both very ill at the end, but neither are forgotten.

We do, now, though, spend a tick of time vacuuming up after three rescues who shed their weight in hair every third day. I think we'll keep them, though. Little Miss Muse has grown quite fond of spooking them. And no, our three new critters do not tolerate closed doors, nor do they respect "Do Not Disturb" signs, either. That struggle continues.

And instead of granddaughtering, I'm neice-ing and daughtering and daughter-in-law-ing. It's all good though (though my attitude fluctuates greatly when they triple-tag-team me with competing medical issues).

I've turned my desk to the wall—at the expense of a crick in my neck to strain and look out the window at every little sound. It'll likely be flipped around view-side-front before long, per chiropractor orders.

And that video is still the best of the best.

I've learned to value the blog. I enjoy it. It's fun. I've figured out lessons and processes I didn't know were happening—and probably never would have—had I not taken the time to rant about them publicly. So, though no fiction progress is made during those blog-writing stints, I am making other kinds of progress, and that's okay.

Lesson Learned: Value your writing enough to shoot the ducks—they never line up anyway.

11. ACCOUNTABILITY

Following up on last week's Top 10 list. The one where I startled myself while writing it with that goldmine in point number one. On why I've been so "stuck"—and how to fix it.

To start solidly down this path, I'm enlisting all of you (or if no one is reading this, some scavenging info-hoarding bot on Facebook will do just fine—because Facebook nudges me to post something on my page every single day) to hold me accountable. Accountable to deadlines and word counts. At least for a while until the habit is as ingrained as anything else I do on a regular basis.

I find I don't need this level of accountability for many of my other responsibilities—the nature of most everything else I do has an inherent deadline. Work clients need their content turned around in 72 hours. Grandmothers need their pacemakers checked every three months. Bills are due once a month like clockwork.

There's a rhythm to the rest of life. But not the writing. Because, as I discovered last week, I've not placed it in high enough priority. I've treated it like a hobby.

But I want more.

And I think that's okay, since I'm a fairly responsible adult and I'm fairly certain I'm free to want more. And I'm fairly certain I won't damage family or friendships if I spend a little more time a week sitting at my desk making up stuff (isn't that a fun job title?). I'm fairly certain I'll still cook the occasional dinner (don't cook much anyway —that's a blog for another day). I'm fairly certain the cat will be fed and the bills will be mailed and the pacemakers will be checked. I'm fairly certain my motives are harmless.

I'm absolutely certain I want more.

I've mentioned that I participated in a short story challenge last summer. That challenge squeezed more productive words out of me than anything I've ever done. It had deadlines. Daily ones. With enough words to build complete universes filled with characters and conflicts and twists—thirty times over.

Thirty days I wrote. In a row. The rest of life went on. Bills got paid. Work got done. Pacemakers got checked. Didn't miss one church service that month. Didn't skip any obligations. Cat didn't die. At that point, I even had a special-needs Schnauzer demanding walks, medication and cuddle time.

How did that happen? How is it now that I want more, I can't seem to produce? I think it's because last summer:

Someone was waiting (Dean).

Someone was dangling an attractive carrot (Dean, with his extra class offers).

As much fun as that challenge was, I'm not going to enlist in that again. So Dean can't help me this time around.

So, I'll use you guys. You'll all be the "someone waiting." So number 1 is taken care of.

Now for the carrot.

Winning the carrot means setting a goal—a slightly uncomfortable goal or it's not worth doing. A specific goal with a deadline.

Starting today, September 3, 2018, through the end of the month on the 30th, my goal is to write 30,000 new words on my work in progress and three additional new shorts. New words—not rewrites or redo's—brand new, forward-progress words.

And three shorts. Complete with their respective cover art.

Thirty thousand words and whatever number of words it takes to create three new short fiction stories in 28 days. Blog words don't count, but so far I've not missed on the one-post-a-Monday streak, so I'll keep that going as well.

I'll post my progress every third day on the Facebook feed and give a final tally on the evening of the 30th.

If I "win" my challenge, I'm going to buy a shiny new orange fountain pen for my growing collection. Fountain pens are awesome, and I don't have an orange one. Orange because it'll represent the carrot (corny, I know—but fun!).

If I "lose" my challenge, I'll be words—and maybe a story or two —ahead. So I still win. Just no orange fountain pen.

And, as I'm about to hit send on this post, I know what will happen. The crystal ball in the back of my head just lit up like a white-hot firecracker, sending up warning flares and blaring sirens.

Fear takes hold. Because any time I try to do something big or, heaven forbid, write something in ink on the calendar...

Life happens. Bad stuff. Good stuff. Everyday mundane stuff. Anything and everything to push and steal time and bring guilt and procrastination.

You name it. It will happen.

But it'll be fun to see if the challenge works in spite of life. Because I want more.

And thank you in advance for keeping me accountable.

* * *

Ouch. That hurt to read today, nearly two years later. I still get stuck. I still need accountability (and I've tried several other methods. Can't seem to find that magic carrot just yet, though the stack of my very own paperbacks and the hard-copy publications that have a few of my words tucked between the covers does help).

Little Miss huffing at me at three a.m. helps sometimes, too.

In the midst of life (currently three cats, three elderly/medically complicated ladies (one with another pacemaker—go figure), and a flare-up of my own sciatica, I know I can get the words down. I did it before. I can do it again.

Lesson Learned: Revisiting past "failures" can be painful—but re-framing your mind around what did get accomplished is a breath of fresh air.

12. IMAGINARY FRIENDS

What do Wonder Woman, Mister Rogers, and an unnamed teenage girl I met playing in a creekbed down the road from my childhood home have in common?

They all became fixtures in the imaginary universe I created when I was young.

Call it boredom. Call it only-child syndrome. Call it psychosis.

Call it whatever, but those figures (some borrowed from others' creations and some all my very own), spent countless hours with me padding around after my Boston Terriers, lazing in my room or swinging—alone, but not alone—on the rickety metal playset in my backyard. You know, those old swing sets where that one pole always left the ground once the swing hit a certain elevation, twisting the entire top support beam into a squealing pretzel...

A precursor to that epic space adventure I scribbled, these characters would come and go as I needed them. I was the center of their universe. How cool is that? Mister Rogers and his entire neighborhood gang all mine—right down to the mailman. All mine to have whatever adventure I could muster—including a trip to the Crayola Crayon Factory through his magic Picture Picture.

And Wonder Woman never had to use her lasso of truth on

Mister Rogers—only on the rotten kids from my class that would also show up in the yard or in the living room. She'd kick their bully butts and we'd be off to lasso up another adventure. Superman showed up occasionally, too. Wonder Woman constantly had to save his rear end from the first-grade bully bearing the kryptonite crayon. (See any themes to my madness?)

Adventures. Day in and day out.

Alone, but not alone.

I can only imagine (no pun intended) what kind of adventures I would have had back then if the Marvel movies of today played in theaters in the '80s. [And I just deleted two paragraphs of wonderful what-ifs to file away for another writing session. Although, now that I understand copyright infringement better than my six-year-old counterpart, I'll proceed carefully.]

Looking back, I know my parents must have seen me talking to myself. Or maybe they thought I was singing to the pudgy Boston pups who were never far from my heels. They had to know, right?

But I distinctly remember the day I knew I'd been "caught."

My dad built our house, and he routinely did maintenance on the place himself. On this particular day, he was running wire or plumbing or something in the crawlspace. He took me into the dusky damp underbelly of the house with him, and I got to take my own hot pink flashlight. (The things we remember...)

The access to the crawlspace was through a small, partial basement the size of a closet that always had about a foot of water at the bottom. He dropped a ladder in as there were no stairs, leaned it against the wall, and once he was set, he one-armed me through the air, over the mini pond, and through the access door. The space was big enough for me to walk hunched over. I handed him some tools as he slithered on his belly and tinkered with the project. Then he dismissed me to explore.

Imagination fodder! (Way before the days of my claustrophobia, clearly.)

The nameless girl from the creek I'd met a few weeks before showed up in the crawlspace. (I'm not quite sure why I latched onto her so tightly. She was kind and played with me—a real person, to splash and be splashed with, maybe—but I named her Alice and we had great times together though I never actually saw her again.)

Then Wonder Woman appeared. I got miffed at Alice for hogging all the attention, since it was Alice's own stupid fault she got herself stuck between the floor joists and needed rescue. Superman showed up—in the form of Clark—to settle things diplomatically. My pink flashlight lit the corners and crannies with a pale yellow beam, showing the characters where to go and what to do next.

And then it happened.

"Who are you talking to?"

I froze. I remember that heart-stopping sensation where the seconds don't move. My dad was incredibly intimidating most of the time, so I wasn't sure if I was in trouble. Lie or tell the truth?

Lie.

"No one." Well, maybe it wasn't a lie. There was no one there.

Truth.

"Sounds like it was someone." I whipped my flashlight toward him, he scolded me for shining it in his eyes, but he was grinning. My heart started beating again and I turned back toward the corner where just seconds before Alice had gotten hung on the floor above us.

Diana Prince, Clark Kent, Alice.

Gone.

Alone.

I tried to be careful from then on. I realized talking out loud meant letting others afford a small peek behind the curtain—a curtain I didn't want real people to look behind. Because it was *mine*. I think I held on to that world a little longer than most kids. My daughter's imaginary friends (a boy named Tyler and a cat named B.I.) moved out after she started preschool. My son never had any that he let me know about, but then again, he had a sibling. I did not.

Maybe I eased into writing that epic space story as a way to add layers to a universe where I could control things. I could stop talking to myself and eliminate the risk of getting "caught." (Though, as I age,

I find that I'm talking to myself at an increasingly alarming frequency, but at least it's to *myself*, not Clark Kent...or Tony Stark.)

I could write in solitude for as long as I wished. Alone, but not alone.

Call it boredom. Call it only-child syndrome. Call it psychosis.

Call it whatever, but the drive to create and write (and, yes, to control something in an otherwise uncontrollable and unpredictable life) still burns inside me. At any given moment, I have entire paragraphs of dialog running in my mind with descriptions of settings, beats of action and twisted plots.

And that little girl with the hot pink flashlight is having a blast again.

Occasionally my inner critic will boom out, "Who are you talking to?" The voice that threatens to halt heartbeats and freeze time.

So I summon Wonder Woman to kick butt.

And I move on.

Alone in my thoughts. But never alone...

* * *

Little Miss would like to add that she is now my Wonder Woman (the little purple imp is insanely jealous of my childhood superhero. Not sure where that came from...).

I do talk to her now, Little Miss. I guess to outsiders it sounds like I'm talking to myself. So, dear reader, please keep that to yourselves, lest the van with the straight-jacket brigade show up in my drive and haul me away from my house in lavender puffs of smoke.

Lesson Learned: Dream—out loud or to yourself— no matter who's watching.

13. WHAT DID THE AUTHOR MEAN BY...?

I hate that question. I've hated that question since the very first time I saw it on a standardized test. I'd read that question and go back and reread the "selection" from whatever writer the test had chosen to torture me with. Then I'd read the question again...

"What did the author mean by the use of the pink ribbon in little Sally's flower bouquet?"

What the heck? I don't know what the author meant. Maybe pink was his favorite color. Or his mother's favorite color.

Maybe just before the author wrote that scene, the mailman showed up on the doorstep wearing pink socks because the mailman's wife washed her fire engine red blouse with said socks the night before. So pink it is.

If the mailman's wife had been more careful, maybe Sally's ribbon would've been white.

Or black. Who knows?

Unless that author gives a clear reason for pink in the story, or he gave an interview explaining why the pink, or there's a primary source indicating what he intended, the answer could be anything. But "What the heck. I Don't KNOW!" was never a choice on the bubble sheet.

I can't tell you how many stories were ruined for me in school because of dumb questions like this. A perfectly fine novel or play (that I likely would have enjoyed had I been left to discover it on my own) ruined with the threat of test questions and reading some dead author's mind. Always looking for the "meaning."

Can't it just be a cool story?

I eventually mustered enough gumption to ask one of my teachers about it. I produced an argument, similar to the one above, but not nearly as creative.

The response was less than satisfying: "You're smart enough to know what the test is asking for. Give me the answer the test wants." Meaning she had no clue either and I was right.

So I filled in the "right" bubble. Or bull-crapped my way through an essay. Assigning meaning where there may have been none.

But it still bothered me because I'm sure the test preparers didn't take the time to call up that author (if he wasn't dead or otherwise unavailable) to ask, "Why did you give Sally a pink ribbon?"

And if the preparers *did* take the time, the author probably didn't know why, couldn't remember the ribbon, and, by the way, who's Sally? He likely wouldn't remember a detail that mundane. By that time, he's probably even forgotten about the mailman in the pink socks.

So the test makers—not willing to accept the author simply used the pink ribbon as a prop—ask the dumb question, making up intent and placing a deeper meaning when there is none. On a pink ribbon in a little girl's bouquet. Because it looks good on a test. And college placement and scholarships and financial aid hang in the balance.

That's asking a lot of pink. And poor Sally. And ribbons in general.

Something similar happened with "Your Friendly Neighborhood Pharmacy."

I have an editor who I simply adore. He's thorough, honest, and points out errors I would've never seen in my drafts. He also gives thematic synopses about theme, flow, etc. and helps me write the blurb copy.

I was reading his notes on "Friendly" when I was smacked with the realization that even something as mundane as a short story written in one evening for a challenge could hold any meaningful depth.

In his summary, the editor made a connection between the occupation I assigned to the main character, Tristan, and his plight in the story. A connection that I hadn't intended.

What the heck? I reread the story and there it was. Assigned meaning. An unintended thread that wove an unintended theme into the storyline.

I laughed out loud. Because I had made a list of occupations and chose one at random with no forethought whatsoever. If I had written the story one day later or one day earlier in the challenge, Tristan wouldn't have been an investment manager—he'd have been a movie director or a retired plumber.

Part of me wanted to agree with the editor's observation. Take the credit. Own it. Or at the very least give my "muse" credit for cleverness and nod and wave and smile and...

But I simply found it amusing. I had fun writing it. It was due in an hour.

It was a cool story.

Don't we all do this, though? Assign meaning where there is none? We see people whisper and think it's about us. We listen to someone yack about their weekend, and we hang on their words, not because their weekend was so great, but because we're searching for some euphemism or double meaning to make life more interesting.

Sometimes life is just what it is—simple events transpiring during the earth's spin on its invisible axis until the sun peeks over the horizon the next morning.

Other life events do mean something. Love. Losses. Wins. Sorrow. Peace. War.

But why make every event, conversation, or story into a test question of utmost importance with four right-or-wrong answers from which to choose? That's a lot of pressure to put on said event. And because meaning can be so entirely relative.

To some, the pink ribbon means everything—a lost spouse's favorite color, the hope of adopting that baby girl, or a battle with breast cancer. And that's okay.

To others, pink is just pink. Equally okay.

Better to ask, "What does the pink ribbon in Sally's bouquet *mean to you*?"

And let it be an essay question. No rights or wrongs. Assign meaning if you want. Or don't.

And let it be okay if the student answers, "Nothing. But it was a cool story."

* * *

As I reread this today, I felt my dander rising and anger tickling its way up my spine. This keeps happening. This "meaning" thing. Good grief, folks. Take a chill pill...

Lesson Learned (again): Let good stories be good stories. Let escape fiction be just that—an escape from the heaviness of current events and crisis and chaos. Let it be.

14. RESET

Happy Fall and thank you for hanging with me through the writing challenge. Instead of trying to wax eloquent about the beauty of the season (which I did attempt at the start of this and deleted several times over, each time sounding like everyone else's blog this time of year), I tried something different this week.

I've had a love/hate/angst/excitement relationship with this blog for some time now. Should I, shouldn't I, etc., etc.

But "Reset" wouldn't exist without it. For that, I'm grateful.

Neither would thousands of new words, potentially. And again, I'm grateful.

And I'm grateful for all of you! Have a blessed season!

The rain pats the window. An unexpected shower trumps the bright fall rays.

An interruption is imminent.

The keys clunk and click as the author pounds out his manuscript, just a few more lines...

A small child runs to the author and presents him a dripping bouquet of fall. She asks for—no, *demands*—lap time. So the child can plunk and plink at the keys.

He rolls the current page of his manuscript out—only half done —and lays it aside. He feeds a fresh, clean sheet into the machine.

She wiggles onto his lap, legs dangling against his shins. He smells her hair, slightly damp from the rain, but the warmth of the autumn sun in her brunette locks hasn't yet faded from her outdoor adventures.

She begins to push and fumble with the keys, her tiny fingers barely strong enough to hold them down long enough for the hammer to make an imprint. The author shows her tricks with the shift button, unlocking a whole secret code.

The space key brings a smile, and the girl watches the roller move the paper several inches before she tires of its function. She prods along as nonsensical black marks appear on the paper. He takes her hand and pushes it against the return lever, sweeping the carriage to the starting position.

He shows her which letters to push to make her name. She grins when he winds the paper up so she can see what she's created.

He winds the paper down again. Swipes the return bar.

Reset.

Twice she pushes too many keys at once and the hammers jumble together above the roller. Twice he untangles them, squares her on his lap and she starts again.

Reset.

He shows her which letters to push once more. Letters to create a *whole entire sentence.*

She does so, and every time she pushes the correct key, he tickles her ribs, causing her to bend away from his fingers with delightful squeals, kicking him in the shins.

But he doesn't mind. He squares her again and again on his lap.

Reset. Reset. Reset.

He remembers a similar little girl long ago with brunette curls and tiny fingers and...

After the last letter, he points to a key, and she slams the period onto the page with flare. He rolls the paper up and shows her the masterpiece. He reads the sentence she so confidently typed under his direction. She giggles and slides from his lap, skipping away and yells back, "I wuv you too, Gampaw."

The session is over before it begins.

These sessions always are.

The author smiles as he holds the child's work in his wrinkled hands. Her name nestled between strings of nonsense.

The "I Love You." at the bottom.

He runs his thumb over the phrase and feels the indent that final period left in the paper.

He gathers the still-damp leaves and the child's paper and sets them to the side of the typewriter next to the pile of pages comprising his manuscript.

The dedication page faces him. Always.

He glances through the door where the child plays with the calico kitten on the braided rug in the next room. All giggles and squeals as the kitten chases her feet across the rug.

He rolls the current page of his manuscript into the machine as he reads the two-line dedication—a ritual he performs each time he loads a new page.

For my loving daughter and her husband.

I vow to love her forever.

The author brushes a tear, takes a deep breath and starts plunking and clinking the keys exactly where he left off before the glorious interruption.

Reset.

* * *

After it appeared on the blog, I reworked this flash piece to send into a contest. (No, it wasn't a winner, but I did have fun revisiting it.) It's now a part of Spunk and Spice Volume I.

Lesson Learned: It's harder for me to "rework" existing words than to spin a fresh tale.

15. THE DEATH OF A CHALLENGE

I told myself so.

I told myself as soon as I made this crazy writing challenge public that something unforeseen—and very likely untoward—would hinder my efforts.

I knew we had a trip planned to DC when the Accountability blog was posted. Turns out I did some of the best writing of the challenge in the early mornings while the guys were getting ready for the day. Sitting on the balcony overlooking the courtyard of our Airbnb apartment building, listening to the big city waking itself up for the day's adventures. That was quite a nice change of pace.

I also knew that there'd be bumps and days of low word counts. But overall, I figured I'd average a good amount of writing time around those bumps.

Ha. Bumps.

Oh, please, please, give me back the bumpy days. Turns out , bumpy days are easy.

What we had in September was the Everlasting Gobstopper of bumps. Multiple Gobstopping bumps.

Two hospitalizations (we crammed the DC trip in between those hospital stays at the insistence of the entire family that we not cancel our plans), lawyers, case workers, skilled rehab facilities and the wait-ing. Endless waiting on someone—anyone—to provide us with answers of any sort at all regarding our loved one's progress or lack thereof. And the footwork it takes to find paperwork for these matters was unreal. I logged more steps around town and the hospital than I did in DC—at least the emotional toll coupled with the stress sure made it seem that way.

And the roller coaster of emotion. Wow. When you're swimming in doubt, regret, anger and fear, there's little room for joyous outlets. I think—no, I know—that I boohooed in more public places last month than in the last twenty years. Really weird places, and I got caught by total strangers and vague acquaintances.

And the scenes I wrote—or tried to—those mornings after a dark day were all antagonist scenes. Dark ones. A few I deleted because the cynicism and gloom spilled over into scenes that didn't require such darkness.

Then things started happening to other people I care about. Really awful things. Things that made my Gobstoppers look less like slender, evil hands reaching from dusky corners to choke the creativity out of me and more like bumps. Goosebumps at that—simple and nothing to complain about.

Perspective.

I found the perfect image for this blog. That balloon cracked me up. The challenge is over. Dead in the water and no orange fountain pen for me. But that balloon. Bobbing with just a bit of hope and lessons learned and, yes, a little morbid, but it matched my mood.

I learned perspective—a lesson that I am forever learning. Likely none of us fully learn it nor do we keep it at the forefront of our brain because perspective always seems to hit us in the face in the middle of a whine fest.

I did get words in. I did make progress that absolutely wouldn't have happened had the challenge not existed—otherwise the writing would have been the farthest thing from my mind in September. Likely October, too. So, I'm happy with that, and I'm on sort of a roll with the WIP. No short stories, but that's okay.

I gleaned story fodder. A myriad of bits and pieces to weave into backgrounds and lives of my characters. Tiny details like how the streets around the apartment in DC filled with dogs pulling their owners to the nearest tree or hydrant after the all-day rain finally stopped.

Emotional details like how it felt to write my grandmother's name in her clothing as I was stocking her room at the rehab facility. Which turns out to not feel one bit like writing my kids' names in their clothing when they went to church camp...

Sensory details like being too tired to sleep—and when sleep does come, it serves up nightmares of future outcomes—or terrors of the past.

And that day ten people followed me into the elevator—and someone says we could fit four more—and the sweaty palm thing happened. White and blue sparkles flashed in my periphery warning of impending doom. When the merry riders cleared the doors on the first floor (as if nothing at all terrifying had just transpired), my feet were firmly cast in concrete blocks and it cost much effort to exit to the air...

Yeah. Not a fan of the claustrophobia details. But there they are. Gobstopping fodder.

And I decided I'll try it again. Another challenge.

An orange fountain pen for winning.

Another "Dead Balloon" graphic and a pile of lessons learned if I don't make it.

Taking a breath in October. Cleaning up messes and adjusting to a "new normal." Reset. Reset. Reset. Boy that flash fiction piece from last week rings true, doesn't it?

November? NaNoWriMo? Maybe. Maybe you'd like to join me... We can dodge Everlasting Gobstoppers together...

I'll keep you updated.

* * *

The image referenced was that of a "corpse" (a posed stock photo image, mind you, not a real corpse) on a table covered in a sheet—save for the feet—with a blue balloon tied to one of the toes.

And most of those exhausting gobstopping moments turned into simple goosebumps, at least in hindsight. Our family has had that happen in several more waves since this writing—such is the nature of elder care and navigating the still awful healthcare system, let alone the challenges the pandemic created on top of it all.

Lesson Learned: So what if you failed? You failed forward. Go at it again.

16. FLUSH AND DELETE

We spent most of each week in September in public. Hospitals, business offices, restaurants, memorials, museums, etc. Mostly the hospital.

Which means we spent a good deal of time searching for and utilizing public bathrooms.

I spent so much time in one particular building that I knew which stall to avoid. Because a very sensitive automatic flushing toilet resides in the second stall from the right on the first floor near the elevators (the same elevator I almost died in—see last week's blog). Two visits in a row it surprised me, and I made a note to remember the stall so I could avoid it on all future visits.

Until the next trip into the building, and all the other stalls were filled (probably by employees or frequent visitors who also knew about that particular toilet's temperament).

But it was one of those moments. When you gotta go...

And the impatient porcelain potty flushed on me TWICE before I was ready for it to do so.

"You've got to be kidding me," I said rather loudly to no one in particular after that second flush, and the other ladies giggled.

Then there's the confusion that comes from automated, semi-automated and not-automated-at-all hand washing stations. Will the soap squirt out with a wave of my hand, or do I have to do it myself? Water? Toweling? I found myself waiting on (or beating on) various dispensers because who knew if the automation was on the blitz or if I really was responsible for rolling out the paper towel for myself.

That confusion followed me home. Sometimes I stood in front of my own sink, hands under the faucet, waiting for the water to come on automatically. Sometimes I waited for the plastic bottle of Dial soap to squirt out a portion, but alas, I had to pump it myself.

Confusion (read: exhaustion) and waiting capitalized massive amounts of time in the last few weeks. I checked the stuff I wrote during those bits once I had two seconds...

Some scenes were decent. Some too dark. And some were total confusion. Revisions (read: deletions) will be needed before the piece ever hit the editor's desk. At one point I had the main character in two places at the same time (which is how I felt, so I knew how he felt, but it doesn't make for good story flow). One scene I wrote for the work in progress belonged in another story altogether (which is also how I felt last month). I swapped character names a dozen times (also something mirrored from the chaotic weeks).

Oops.

But the great thing about all those writing problems? There's this small, rectangular key with slightly rounded corners in the upper right-hand side of my keyboard, "Delete." He has a friend, "Backspace," that I'm fond of as well. "Select All" is also a powerful tool, especially when coupled with "Delete." I can scroll up and insert bits and details to make the story flow, then scroll down to add in new structures, dialog, moods and beats. No harm, no foul. And if I hadn't told you about those bad apple scenes, you'd never know.

I remember when my dad got a typewriter that actually had backspace with erasing capability. That was a huge deal, and I was mesmerized by it. Before that, Liquid Paper was his friend, along with a few choice words I'd hear him sputter from the table as he had to line up the roller just so to undo a mistake—after he waited for the correction fluid to dry, of course.

Don't you wish life came with editing capabilities? Ones that could help you orchestrate events just so? Oh that we could "Select All" and rewrite the events leading up to a bad decision—ours or someone else's?

And don't we all have that great comeback line that didn't come to mind until the argument was over? Wouldn't it be cool if we could scroll up and add that sucker in there?

Alas, we don't get even get a 0.74-ounce bottle of White Out for life. Some people have selective memories and can "White Out" the awful or regrettable, but most of us aren't wired that way. Truth be told, if we did get a bottle, we wouldn't be patient enough to let the fluid dry before we tried to rewrite, ending up with a gummed-up mess of illegible ink.

We'd be like that toilet in the second stall from the right. Flush, delete, flush, delete. And we'd never move forward for fear of getting life "just right."

My temptation will be to fiddle and fuss with the story until it's "just right." Flushing and deleting repeatedly, but not moving forward to the next thing.

Our temptation with life is often the same: to make it "just right," resulting in confusion, exhaustion and a constant state of overwhelm.

There is no "just right" life, just like there's no "just right" story.

There is the only next decision—and it's our choice to make the wisest decision with the facts we have at the moment in spite of confusion and exhaustion.

There is only the next scene—and it's my decision to make it the best I can with the abilities I possess at the moment in spite of confusion and exhaustion.

Then leave it be.

Move forward.

And always, always avoid the second stall from the right.

* * *

Here it is, nearly two years later, and that toilet STILL isn't fixed properly.

And, by the way, where's my White Out for 99.9% of the year 2020? I'd even take an old-fashioned gum eraser and go at it like in grade school when I erased a hole clean through my math paper.

I have since updated my laptop. At the time of its demise the backspace and delete buttons had no more lettering on them. When I undo something, I must do so with flair!!

Lesson Learned: Delete until the letters wear off your keys: It means work is happening...

17. ASHES TO ASHES

Another morbid post.

Sorry. It's the phase of life we're in right now. It's been a long chapter and doesn't look to close anytime soon.

We've been thinking a lot about the hereafter and how to transition from the top side of Planet Earth to below-the-ground status.

Funeral and ceremony planning has filled the days for those close to that transition — and for those not so close but destined to take that journey someday unless the good Lord makes other arrangements...

Lessons learned through this process:

Dying is expensive.

Dying requires lots and lots of paperwork.

Living is expensive.

Living requires lots and lots of paperwork.

Pre-planning (and pre-paying) your end-of-life choices takes a huge burden off your family—or whomever may be responsible for your affairs when you no longer need affairs.

I've been teetering between a couple of ideas for myself. Until we went to DC, my main wish was direct cremation. No viewing. If you must have a ceremony, make it a happy, geeky, corny one. When the ashes come back from the crematorium, don't put me in an urn or shove me in a box (claustrophobia issues, remember?). Buy some cheap, purple flowers of some sort or another, take the flowers and bag of remains to the local river and dump me in—but don't drop me from the train trestle (bridge fear, remember?) then be done.

Move forward and make more life and more memories.

After we went to DC, however, I had another idea.

One that would take some forethought and planning, a bit of money, and is quite possibly illegal, but that won't be *my* concern when the time comes...

The Library of Congress.

My favorite spot we visited in all of DC (and we hit almost all of the main ones). Drop-dead (no pun intended) gorgeous architecture with meaning and intention packed into every nook and cranny. If you ever go, take the thirty-minute tour. Well worth it, free and informative, then walk the tunnel to the Capitol building and have lunch in their cafeteria. Interesting desserts there, but I digress...

I love the National Treasure movies. Plotting and planning and problem-solving with codes and cyphers, and... well, that's just plain fun.

My gang may need to hire Nicholas Cage (or the script writers, at the very least) to hatch a plan to get my dusty old self past security and into the stacks of ancient tomes to discreetly spread my ashes. And the National Treasure gang already "hypothetically" broke into the place once (with the President's help, of course), so the groundwork is laid...

Thomas Jefferson has an impressive book collection he sold to Congress after the city burned. Neat story. That would be a cool place to rest. And the fact that old Tom raised his own geese so as to never run out of writing instruments adds to the appropriateness of the space. But one would need an exceptionally good reason to be in there if not on a tour.

The main rotunda would be awesome. One would need a library card to access the room, but dropping bits of me out of a holey pocket under some massive desk wouldn't be too difficult.

The marble staircases, worn and uneven from years of foot traffic, adorned with little boys (putti, not cherubs) depicting all manner of trade in early America is breathtaking. One could pose as a photographer while sneaking some of me right into the relief up and down the steps.

At the bottom of those stairs were two lion heads (I believe, didn't get too close) which used to be water fountains. One could stuff me inside and I'd bet I'd hang around for a bit. The fountains don't work and I doubt the interiors of those get dusted much.

The list could go on and on. At that point, I promise not to be too picky. Just pick a spot and don't get arrested. Or pick multiple spots and don't get arrested. Then move on.

Make more life and more memories. (Though getting arrested would certainly be memorable...)

Maybe at that point, I'll have a tome or two of my own hiding in their stacks.

Move over Jefferson.

Now wouldn't *that* be cool?

* * *

I'm not sure about you, but the Library of Congress plan still feels solid to me. Yes. Yes. I think that's my wish.

Lessons Learned: The making memories while you can bit also seems a solid plan. Folks are fragile. Some more than others. Grab those moments.

18. DIME UPON DIME

A while back (a long while, actually) my grandmother presented my son with an empty two-liter soda bottle and five dimes. She said if he'd fill it up with nothing but dimes, he could save $700.

That would be 7,000 dimes if my math is right. And if they all fit? Some sources say it would be closer to 5,500 dimes, but nevertheless...

She's been faithfully saving her dimes to give to his project since then.

We've been faithfully adding dimes to that thing for months and months. The bottom is barely covered.

Now, the main problem with this challenge is that we don't carry cash very often, so procuring dimes on a daily or even weekly basis is a rare thing.

We've also been tempted to cheat. To appease Grandma, we could buy rolls of dimes and empty them into the container to show more "progress."

Or we could add a few quarters in the mix to use up the volume in the bottle and speed things along.

But we haven't cheated—yet.

And we've not made a dent in the available volume.

The dime challenge feels a lot like writing a novel. One word at a time. One sentence. One paragraph.

How many words will it take to get to "The End"? More than 7,000. Likely more than 7,000 paragraphs.

And some days, I just don't have the "cash" to churn out words. Life moments and Everlasting Gobstopper bumps demand I spend mental energy elsewhere.

Some days I'm tempted to cheat—to just slap words down in haphazard form, meandering from one paragraph to another. Puff up the volume a bit.

But that would take away from the craft and art of it.

There are no "word banks" to cash in poorly thought-out narratives for shiny, concise storylines. Well, I guess there's plagiarism, but that's generally frowned upon. Probably like spreading human remains in the Library of Congress...

But, someday, that two-liter bottle will be full. Don't know when. Dime upon dime, month by month, the empty space will fill up with tiny little Roosevelts. Someday, we'll take that sucker to the bank and cash it out. Smiling all the way home.

Then we'll probably do it again.

Someday that novel will reach "The End." Don't know when. Word upon word, sentence upon sentence. Someday, I'll publish that sucker. Smiling all the way home.

Then I'll most definitely do it again.

* * *

The novel won the footrace between words vs. dimes. And with 2020's "Great Change Shortage" here in the States, well. That two-liter bottle's been gathering more dust than cents.

We still haven't cheated yet. Grandma would be proud.

Lesson Learned: Little by little, a little becomes a lot. The Tanzanian Proverb rings true.

19 BONFIRE

A creepy little flash piece to wrap up this month. Stay safe and smart this week!

I don't want to be here.

Not here in this barren field with these people.

Neither does the eight-legged arachnid dancing at the edge of the flames by my feet. No doubt forced from his once-safe home, he creeps around the edge of a log, his new reality not quite sinking in. He twice attempts to edge to the underside of the log. Embers twice send him out of the heat's grip.

He's pushing it. He needs to let it go.

Merry voices, skewered processed meats and sugared desserts dot the circumference of the bonfire. I should be enjoying myself.

But I don't want to be here. When she texted me the location for tonight's gaiety, I cringed.

Because I was just here last week.

But *she* texted me, so I make an appearance.

Someone offers me a brownie. Someone offers her one, too. She accepts with a giggle and bites into it. Makes a face. Tosses it into the flames.

"That's awful." She goes for a marshmallow, puncturing it with a stick and holds it inches over the flames. She smiles at me. I smile back.

The spider darts another inch from the flames when the brownie catches fire and smolders.

I look at my brownie and decide to drop it under my camp chair. No one would know the difference. Maybe the ants will be grateful tomorrow when the ruckus dies.

"How's work?" One of the older ones asks me. Small talk.

"Good. You?" I don't care what the reply will be. My focus is on the fire and what lies beneath.

What I put there last week.

I glance at her. The firelight highlights her cheekbones and auburn streaks in her hair. She looks just like her mother. She catches me looking and brushes back a lock.

I focus down again. On my friend at my feet. I wonder if he knows. I wonder if he senses what I did here just a few days ago. Maybe that's why he made his home where he did. Maybe that's why he won't give it up. He takes a couple of cautious steps toward the heat.

I can't blame him. It's mesmerizing. Flames dancing, sparks popping. The yellows and oranges birthed from the pale blue flames at the bases. He decides to back up once again. Do spiders see in color?

"—next week, would you like to go?" A guy whose name I don't know speaks to her. Deep in my thoughts, I missed the first part of his question, but I already know it doesn't matter.

She smiles. "Absolutely."

He grins like he's won the lottery. And since she's said yes, he has.

He's pushing it. He needs to let it go.

I study him as he studies her. Tall. Blonde. Muscles.

Confident.

That's all she sees. Too young to discern.

I see more. Low morals and lower intentions.

A piranha.

She doesn't see that part. She didn't see that part with the last guy, either.

A heat to challenge that of the bonfire swells inside me. I stretch out my foot, tapping the log where the spider contemplates his next move.

I make the move for him. One final tap and he topples onto the edge of an ember. Four slender legs curl and disappear. A tiny sizzle —but only if you're really listening for it—followed by the curling of the other four legs.

Gone.

Tall and Blonde strides away.

She shrugs up her shoulders and whispers in my ear, "What do you think? I think he likes me, Daddy."

I smile at her and brush away that same stray lock.

I glance back to the log. Another spider, twice the size of the first, explores the log.

There's always another.

"Well?" She prods.

"Give it some time. If he sticks around, maybe..." This satisfies her. She turns her attention to her girlfriend sitting opposite, all silliness and whispers.

I help the second spider along his way. He can share my secret lying beneath the bonfire.

Legs curl. Sizzle. Gone.

I lock eyes with Tall and Blonde. I smile at him. He smiles back.

Sizzle.

I'll be back here next week. To the cold, ashen bonfire in the barren field where I'll double my secret.

I'm glad I came tonight.

Gone.

* * *

This was another piece I reworked for submission to a third-party publication. Again, the flash bit came much easier than the reworking of the thing. The new, somewhat longer version is available in Mystery Minutes Volume I.

Lesson Learned: Really, leave the flash alone. Write new.

20. OWN IT

Some people are just too sweet.

A couple of weeks ago I insulted my culinary skills in front of some acquaintances. They said I shouldn't talk that way and that it couldn't be that bad. That's sweet.

But my cooking *is* that bad. And I own it.

I hate cooking. I hate the mess it makes. I hate the planning, shopping, prepping, and whatever else goes along with trying to take a set of ingredients and concoct something semi-edible at best. My meager attempts have kept body and soul together, but those attempts are mostly of the chew-and-swallow variety. If it can't be swallowed (or chewed), peanut butter or takeout are always the backup plans.

My dear husband says I do just fine. One of those sweet people, he is. But he comes home famished after work, and everything tastes at least okay when you're that hungry. After twenty-plus years, I think I've burned out all of his taste buds. Poor thing doesn't know any better.

I find myself asking the recipients of my efforts the same question nearly every meal: Is it edible? I'm not looking for praise in that moment. I'm gauging whether I should cancel my plans for the rest of the evening and take said recipients to the nearest ER to have their stomachs pumped.

Two days ago I tried something new. The tomato-y pasta-ish soupy mess didn't get the chance to boil past a few seconds before the smell smacked me upside the head and I tossed it over the fence— still smoking (umm, smoldering)—for some poor raccoon or opossum.

Come to think of it, that may be what happened to the half-bloated, half-flattened raccoon on the side of the road not far from my house. He partook of my mishap and decided to stand in traffic.

Give me a twenty-step chemistry experiment and I can pull out a textbook-perfect result right down to the last molecule and write you a crisp, clean lab report complete with graphs, tables and diagrams— and not blow one thing up.

Give me a three-step recipe and I "forget" I'm cooking. I boil junk over. I slop stuff on the floor. Burn. Smolder. Undercook.

Smolder *and* undercook—now *that* takes talent.

You name it. All in three miserable steps.

There've been recipe errors that my poor Schnauzer (may he rest in peace) wouldn't even eat. And he feasted regularly on Legos, dirty socks, and those metal bits that hold erasers on number 2 pencils.

And may the dear Lord help me if I have to cook for strangers. There's just not enough Prozac.

I own my culinary inadequacy. I also own that I don't care to get any better at it, either.

I own my claustrophobia. Steel-covered bridges and crowded elevators. Crowds of any sort, actually.

I own the love/hate relationship I have with my 16?-year-old cat. He's been at the threshold of death's door a couple of times now, but he keeps spawning lives. As I type this, he's rubbing his face all over the corner of the laptop screen, demanding attention. How sweet he is. Until I try to pet him and he decides in that millisecond between sweetness and my hand reaching his cheek that he's now a demon-possessed cougar and wants to eat my flesh. Love/hate. On both our parts.

I own my love of unicorns. I recently had one made by a dear friend. That sucker is lavender infused! On particularly rough days, I bury my nose in its mane, breathe in deeply and visualize its real-life counterpart galloping along a peaceful stream at the base of a majestic mountain. Where there are no phones. Where there is nowhere else to be and time pauses. And where there are definitely no people to feed.

What I haven't owned yet is calling myself an author. Or a writer. Someone asked me about my blog the other day. "So you're an author?" I froze. I had no idea what to say. No? Yes?

Sort of?

"Well, I *sort of* play around with words."

That's bull crap. I've written stories. Some I really like. Some probably should go stand in traffic, but hey. Unlike the soup mishap, I had fun and I learned something while writing those duds.

"Sometimes I make things up and stories *sort of* spill out."

Bull.

I'm working on a book. I've written stories. And blogs. And flash pieces. Many have sold on Amazon and a few are under consideration to be published "for real."

But somehow saying "Yes" and leaving it at that seems arrogant. Not sure why. If I asked my plumber if he is a plumber, he'd say yes and he'd show me his license if I asked to see it. If he answered "Sort of," he's not touching my pipes. If I asked my nurse practitioner if she is a real-life nurse, she'd say yes and show me her degree. If she answered "Sort of," she's not touching my pipes, either.

So why is it when people ask me if I'm an author—or call me an author to another in the conversation—I get all wonky weird and socially awkward, yanking away as if these good-natured people are about to hiss and draw blood?

I haven't owned it yet.

Something to work on. I may need to inhale that lavender mane a few more times before shouting "I'm a freaking AUTHOR!" from the rooftop. Or I could start here.

Beth, you're the worst cook on the planet, AND you're a freaking author.

Okay. That last phrase just sent me into a hot flash. Off to snort my unicorn...

* * *

My cooking still sends the random nocturnal critter into the street, begging for the end. I'm truly sorry about that, but over-the-fence with the disasters is better than burning out my garbage disposal...

My aversion to being called an author/writer is pretty much over. Yup. That's what I do. I'm good with it now. It took a few minutes, though.

My unicorn still smells like lavender. I still snort its mane.

Lesson Learned: I'm an author. So there.

21. FORWARD THINKING

Spend time with little kids long enough and you'll realize they're hardly ever content with their age. I asked my niece, four years old at the time, what she was most looking forward to.

"Being five." No hesitation. No emotion. And she'd just turned four, so nearly a year to wait.

Five looked much better than four.

Third graders itch to be in fifth grade. The fifth graders are drooling all over themselves to be the top dogs in middle school. Middle schoolers would chew their feet off to be in high school.

It's in high school that this dynamic splinters a bit. Pardon my stereotypical split, but when I was that age, the percentages were about 50/50. It's probably not too far off today:

About half want to plunge into adulthood, fully forward thinking (or so it seems)—college or career bound. Or maybe familyhood is calling.

The other half would give anything to pause time and stay in the echoing hallways, musty gyms and drama-filled homerooms until life dumps just the right opportunity into their laps. Maybe this group is doing less forward thinking and more forward worrying (not that the other group isn't terrified—they're just better at hiding it).

Or maybe they're not thinking at all, content to be carried passively right up to the gates of adulthood—and then some.

Either way, the future is barreling down on them, and it's decision time. Because unless some odd arrangement has been made with the faculty, the school likely won't let them hang around the campus for an undetermined number of years like so many adult children twiddling thumbs in the corners of their parents' basements do.

I was no different through most of my growing-up years; I always wanted to bust through to the next stage. I don't think I was bratty or vocal about it, but I do remember frequent discontentment.

And I'm doing it again. To the point of not enjoying the moments. And now I'm, let's see, I'm how old? [pause here while I do the math, I don't keep track of my age anymore...2018 minus 1970-something... Gulp.]

Well, I'll just keep that medium-largish number to myself, okay?

At any rate, several facets of life are unpleasant at the moment. A couple of those are self-inflicted and some exist simply because the planet still spins. I want those chapters to be done now, please.

Over. Gone. Let's move on with it, already—see what the next chapter has. Because the next chapter will be nice, clean, and stress-free, right? [insert every eye-rolling emoticon ever created here]

But when I really examine the last few years, good things happened. Lots of them. Lots of blessings. Lots of celebrations and milestones. Lots of moments...

And shame on me for not living in those moments when they came around because I was too busy "forward thinking" to the next task or season.

I do that with my writing. I want to be over the "learning" stage and on to the next "proficient" stage as quickly as possible.

However, and I'm not sure who to credit this to, there's a theory in the writing world that says the first million words anyone writes are pretty much crap. You're learning. Growing. Fine-tuning voice and style—and I'm nowhere near one million words.

I'm in the fledgling stage. Back to the third grade, you impatient [insert medium-largish number]-year-old.

This wasn't supposed to be another sappy, lightbulb-moment post, but alas!

I guess consistent, patient contentment while striving for the next goal is the goal for the season. No matter the trials or chapters.

Capture the moments.

Batten down during the storms.

Then strive for the next goal.

And hopefully I won't end up in my mother's basement.

* * *

My same tendencies hold—even to the point of taking classes that I've no need of yet. I'll have to take them again when the time comes to do marketing, or audio books, or whatever…

I do hope I'm slightly more effective at capturing the moments, but I know that needs work.

I've reached 480,000 words, give or take a jot or tittle. So not a million, but a good plenty more than I had in 2018.

Lesson Learned: You're closer to "proficient" than you were two years ago.

22. NEVER TOO OLD

A while back, I accompanied my 91-year-old grandmother to our public library. To say she's an avid reader would be a gross understatement of fact.

I'm an avid reader.

She blows me out of the water.

Now, granted, she's retired, and I'm not. She lives alone, and I don't. She cooks for one, and I wallow in misery trying to cook (if you can call it that) for three. So, she's got the time, and I don't.

We moved her to town from the country this past spring, and I signed her up for a card, showed her the stacks she may be interested in and left it at that. She'd been taking herself to the library weekly since then—sometimes more than once a week—until pneumonia drug her down this fall and she needed a ride.

I'd thought about signing her up for the book mobile that comes to her neck of town. But, quite frankly, they don't come frequently enough and there wouldn't be enough books on the bus for her liking.

Before she moved, I'd load her up twice a year with flats of books from the library's used book sale. Flats of them, like twenty to thirty per box. And she'd buzz through them at breakneck speed.

Then I thought, well, maybe she's not really reading them. Maybe she's skimming or "not getting" the story.

But I was wrong. I'd probe her about the plot or characters and she'd school me every time—as if she were living the storyline right along with them. So, yes. She was reading every word and "getting" the stories.

At any rate, she had difficulty remembering which titles she'd checked out. I told her to put a tiny mark somewhere in the book, like on the back cover—her initials or some symbol—so she could keep track.

We went to her favorite author's shelf. The first ten books Grandma pulled had her tiny star in the back cover. It was a real struggle to find something that she hadn't read. Then she only wanted to pick out two because she was still feeling tired.

I made her choose four, and she finished them all within the week. The library should give out some sort of a trophy for readers like her.

The takeaway?

I hope the stories I write inspire readers to grab the next one. And the next, and the next.

I hope I write enough tales that people have to put their initials (or tiny little stars) in the backs of tattered, taped-together copies.

I hope I'm never too old to enjoy a good yarn.

I hope I'm never too old to write one, either.

* * *

On my next trip to the library after rereading this blog, I visited that author's shelf. I pulled out a few books. All of them had my grandmother's tiny initials in them.

I cried.

Lesson Learned: Don't forget the small things. Like 91-year-old initials inside tattered covers.

23. THINK ABOUT IT

A few weeks ago I allowed myself some meandering "me time" once things sort of hit a new normal with our family's medical drama.

I meandered through the library and the library's book sale.

I meandered through the shelves of donated novels and textbooks at Goodwill.

I even spent waaay too much time meandering through Amazon's selection of books—paper and electronic.

I ran into several hard copies of *Gone With the Wind* in all three locations. Never read the book. Only remember seeing bits and pieces of the movie when my parents would watch it because it was the only thing on TV. But I did a little digging and it got me thinking...

That sucker is over 410,000 words long. All done on a manual Remington typewriter. It's rumored that Margaret Mitchell would place each completed chapter in a manila envelope, and, once she was done, the stack stood taller than she did.

I bet so.

And remember the "first million words are crap" advice that's floating around now that I mentioned in an earlier blog? Well, probably not many authors would care to risk wrist and thumbs to pound out that many words on those clunkers.

And think waaay back to the fountain pens the poor blokes like Shakespeare and Homer used. Feather quills? Pretty prolific writers for pen and ink. I don't know. Maybe they had it easier. Maybe not.

But that's all they knew in their time.

I remember playing around with my dad's manual machine when he'd drag the beast out of the closet to type up something for the high schoolers he taught way back when. He'd let me mess around with it until I'd get the levers hopelessly gobbed together and he'd have to undo them.

Then I remember how different it felt when I used a keyboard for the first time at school. Much less work to press those keys down. No messy levers, either. And the laptop I'm on now? Barely any effort at all.

I do think if I had the chance to type a short story out on an old machine, I'd try it. You'd definitely think more carefully abut word choice because each letter takes so much effort.

On the up side, you wouldn't have to remember to save anything... (This being noted after MS Word decided it needed a nap a while ago and I had to start this blog over.)

Then I got to thinking, maybe technology has writers at a disadvantage. If an EMP goes off and all electronics are wiped out, we'd have to dig out the clunkers and hope someone hoarded ink cartridges.

Or go back to pen and paper.

I've tried to write on paper—and I love it for outlining and brainstorming—but going from point A to point B? I'm totally spoiled to my MS Word (persnickety though it can be). At this spot in the blog, I've cycled back through the piece at least five times and tweaked/deleted/added text.

Do you know what that mess looks like on paper? Like someone handed a baboon a ballpoint pen and said, "Have at it."

And trying to do that on a manual typewriter? Not likely going to happen. That's where the image of wads of paper strewn all over the floor comes in. Start, stop. Nope. Unroll. Wad.

Repeat.

At any rate, I'm spoiled rotten to the backspace key and cut/paste options.

If you're reading this, you're likely tech-spoiled, too. Better find a hobby that will carry your sanity through until the emergency responders can restore power after the EMP dissipates. And Martial Law is lifted. And until Best Buy can import their newest batches of electronics from across the sea.

The next time you're in a room full of books, think about it. What did those authors do to get those thousands upon thousands of words out of their brains and coded into little black marks so someone else can read their minds? Not to mention the hoops and tricks and time it took to get the finished piece into the hands of a publisher.

Hemingway probably said it best:

There is nothing to writing. All you do is sit down at a typewriter and bleed.

* * *

Since this blog posted, I've published several short story collections and a novel. For each book, one must decide fonts, size, headers, chapter heading styles. On and on and on.

Lesson Learned: Take a second to appreciate and notice the finer details of the printed word. There's a lot more to those e-books and paperbacks than a passing glance can afford.

24. MOWER LINES

A while back, a friend of mine injured her arm. I asked her if there was anything I could do, and of course, there wasn't. Most of my friends are like that — stubborn and won't ask for help.

I even offered to mow the grass for her. She gave me a distrusting glance. And then I remembered: She likes her lawn mowed as if it were a major league baseball field. Stripes in perfectly patterned rows. Engage the blades, kill the blades, in just the right rhythm and at just the right time to make a picture-perfect yard.

Come to think of it, I have several friends like this. I think they're strange.

My husband is like this, a nice and careful cutter. I also think he's strange and way too preoccupied with the state of the yard.

Now, don't get me wrong. If that's your thing, fine. Stripe it afresh everyday all week long if you'd like. And I don't want our grass to be so tall that it harbors snakes or varmints or squatters. Or that it needs to be raked and baled between trimmings.

I say mow it. Then be done.

'Cause in a few days, those nice, neat lines you spent so much time fussing with will be gone.

Just mow it.

Then be done.

No need to converse about it. No need to analyze it. No need to bring it up five times that day that the grass looks so good. Is it mowed? Great. Probably looks like everyone else's lawn up and down the road—or pretty darn close, striped or not.

[Disclaimer—We did have that one neighbor who mowed their grass once a year whether it needed mowed or not. You could've hidden Tomator and Jimmy Hoffa in that yard... Not a fan of that, either.]

Now, I enjoy mowing grass. Always have. It gives me time to think. The vibrations and hum of the engine and occasional blade-against-the-mole-hill spurt lulls me into daydreaming and release of tension. But the deeper I daydream and disengage from reality, the crazier my "mower lines" become. Meandering. Wiggling. Bending. And sometimes, I forget to disengage the blades on my way back to the garage and cut another swath diagonal to those wiggles. But hey, it's mowed. It's done.

And if I know the following week will be busy or rainy, I put the deck down as low as it can go and scalp the grass. Hey, it'll grow back. Eventually. And it gives me a few days' buffer between cuttings.

When I mow, the lawn definitely doesn't look like anyone else's. And neither does the look on my husband's face look like anyone else's when he analyzes the job I've done. His jaw clenches, his eyes go bloodshot, and he gives a subtle nod, silently vowing to get off work earlier the next week to beat me to the mower.

That's why my friend gave me that look. She knew—or at least suspected— that I am no careful cutter. So I've never offered again. Because her grass would be short, but it wouldn't be pretty.

Driving through neighborhoods in the summer when everyone has mowed their grass on the same day irks me. Sameness. Stripes here. Stripes there. The job is done, but there's no uniqueness. My husband admires them all. Conformist, he is.

Like Grisham's *Skipping Christmas* (with the Kranks). Everyone doing the exact same thing. And when I try to break free with my curvy, wiggly lines, someone comes chasing me down the street, beating me with their bigger-than-life Frosty the Snowman.

Same thing happens in the fall. I love seeing fallen leaves just after a rain. The blanket of color beneath the tree matches the leaves that held on through the storm. Perfect. Until someone comes along with a mower, blades whirling and mulches away the beauty. Back to the nice, neat stripes. (And if the tree isn't done shedding, you've gotta do it again, so why not just leave it be?)

Did you know you can't hide Easter eggs in a nicely striped lawn? They stick out like sore thumbs.

And you can't jump into a pile of leaves if you've mulched them to shreds with the Husqvarna. Just try it sometime. Takes all the crispy, crunchy fun out of the event.

What's the point?

A young lady asked me to proofread her scholarship essay a few weeks ago. She did well. The content was great. But the passage was just like every other high schooler's scholarship essay I've read. Perfect five-paragraph essay complete with intro, meaty middle with all the appropriate transition words at the start of each paragraph, and a nice, tight conclusion. Each paragraph had the same number of sentences. We tweaked a few things.

I begrudgingly left the structure because I know this form is what they teach in school. It gives a standard to evenly measure everyone by. Helps to organize thoughts, etc., etc.

She emailed me, thanking me for the help, and that she'd gotten into the scholarship pool's next round. Told me she wanted to be an author. I asked what kind. She said fiction of some sort. Because this paper was so easy for her. She could write just like that each time and make a nice living. And would I like to proofread those stories when she's ready.

Oh dear.

I gave her the mower lines analogy. I encouraged her to learn what they have to offer in English class— then forget it all (forgive me, Mrs. Yeager).

Otherwise, she'll end up with a street-full of perfectly mowed lawns. There's no room for treasure-filled egg hunts or crisp, fall dives into reds, yellows and oranges. Just sameness story after story.

I don't think she liked my answer. I haven't heard back from her. She's probably inflating her Frosty...

* * *

We still argue about the yard. Probably not so much the trees. Not this year. A July 2020 Indiana pop-up Great Wind Event took out two of our massive leaf-producers. I'm quite sad about that. Loved those trees.

But alas! My Web Guy also does woodworking. He's making me consolation coasters and a desk organizer from the fallen timber. The equivalent of those "I survived 2020" T-shirts.

Lesson Learned: I'd so get fired as an English teacher.

25. MAKING A MESS OF THINGS

Have you ever made such a massive error—either in judgment, timing, or craft—that it took way more energy than it was worth to back up, track where things went off the track, correct, then go forward?

I can think of several such instances in my life. Sometimes with a project (Cross stitch pattern off by six rows? That teddy bear now has a crooked ear and a tooth where an eye should be). I learned to count more carefully. And that I needed glasses.

Sometimes with a wrong turn down a poorly identified country road in the middle of winter in the days before GPS (yes, I'm showing my age to all of you young'uns out there). I learned to memorize the map before I left the house. And that investing money in a GPS wasn't a bad idea...

Sometimes in relationships (you know, the ones that you think are worth it, but aren't, because the other party is an idiot—or you're the idiot and didn't deserve the other person to begin with). I learned to be careful who I trust. And then to trust someone until I couldn't (hardest Lesson learned by far).

I could go on, but you get the point.

I made such a mess of my first novel attempt that that poor piece has been started and stopped more times than New Year's diet procla-mations in the collective United States.

The idea came about during a creative writing exercise years ago when I was trying to train my brain to turn off the medical transcrip-tionist/editor voice and turn on the muse. Shake the gears loose, so to speak. I loved the idea (based on objects at the time, not on charac-ters) so much that I dove right in with reckless abandonment.

I cast my characters complete with photos taken of people from the internet to have a concrete way to describe them accurately and to put faces to my names. The cast consisted of two boys on the brink of high school, two elderly men, and two millennial villains.

That was my first issue—but I didn't know it at the time.

The characters' ages made my target audience unclear. Was I writing for upper elementary kids? Young adults? Adults? Who knew. Most heroes for elementary audiences are twelve years old. Most for young adults are upper high school. And adults? Well, would they even tolerate my immature main characters long enough to fall in love with the old men in the cast?

Part of this problem, I figured, was that I was on the tail-end of finishing up homeschooling my kids. I had been absorbed in that world for so long—reading and pre-reading their school's material—that I think my brain jumbled what I really wanted to do.

My second issue was rooted in content. Not so much the storyline, but how I decided to "move" the boy's parents out of the way. They weren't front-and-center nor important to the plot, but the way I went about it wouldn't do for elementary kids. Secondary problem: Extri-cating the parents was woven and brought up several times through the story, so massive edits would be needed to correct it.

Third problem? I set the story in a time where corn stalks needed to be taller than the kids, but it was late spring in the novel. Hmmm. Over-eager farmers planted corn in January? Tweak the weather? Extend the school year because of a horrible winter the season before? Magical corn? Oh my word.

Fourth: Pickup trucks, especially the exact same pickup truck, cannot be in more than one location at the exact same time. Neither can people. Unless the world you've created is magical. Mine is set in real-life earth with a few magical objects and maybe a slightly supernatural villain. But no time-bending, space-shifting stuff. So massive issues—and I did both with the pickup and a secondary character.

So, I'm cleaning up the messes, looking hard at my target audience and deciding which bones and ideas of the story are worth fixing, polishing and moving on with. Tossing around ideas for a couple of sequels, as well. Massive swaths of chapters and scenes have to be cut or reworked.

But, boy, am I learning a few things:

Finishing something that I started when the creative writing urge took hold of me by the throat and wouldn't let go is huge for me. I've a thousand and one other ideas I'd rather put energy into, but this is important. To finish. And I won't forgive myself if I don't.

I'm learning about audience. Tone, style, pacing.

I'm learning about keeping track of who's on stage, who's off stage and who shouldn't be in the book in the first place.

I'm learning it's painful to cut scenes that I was emotionally "close" to, but that sometimes it makes the story stronger. Tighter. More elegant.

I'm learning more about writing by finishing this disastrous first attempt than I've learned doing almost anything else.

I've also learned what I need to keep working on.

Take a look at the current mess you may have—in judgment, timing, or craft—and decide what to keep. What to rework. What to delete to make life more elegant.

What to keep working on...

I promise it will be worth it.

* * *

Little Miss Muse has piped up, irritated, and reminded me in a purple huffy puff that she's not a "machine" to be turned off and on. She's an above-me entity with real feelings.

(Hold just a moment while I dig in my desk organizer for that last piece of purple bubble gum. She's such a diva...)

Man. That corn height vs. school year problem would've been solved with a pandemic—little did anyone know. And no. I'm not placing a pandemic-related anything *anywhere* in those Oliver Andrews books.

Lesson Learned: Since wrestling with that first manuscript, I've learned to let it be. Write the best you can, fix the major issues, then QUIT FIDDLIN' WITH IT. And move on.

26. BLANK SLATE

Every end-of-year and start of a new one brings the same thing for most: Resolutions. Goals.

The glorious Blank Slate.

The proclamation from the rooftops (or maybe a subtle, silent one known only to yourself), that this coming year, 2019, will be different.

And by 2020, I will have:

Gained something...

Prioritized something...

Lost something...

or

Achieved/Accomplished something...

Mostly, we just want to have

Changed...somehow.

Whatever part of our lives is most uncomfortable—that part that bugs us, bothers us, hurts us, keeps us up at night—tends to get a good looking-at near the end of December.

But February rolls around, and most of our haughty proclamations or silent promises have been replaced with distractions, work, life, or simply maintaining the status of our comfort zones.

Or, sometimes, just surviving a crisis will knock us off course.

And then we stay off course.

Our blank slate of hope becomes muddied, marred, and mundane.

And the calendar is merciless, flipping page after page until there's only one page left. That last one with its red and green title signaling happy holiday parties, family gatherings, end-of-semester activities, and OH! That last week of December. Let's take a good look at...

Then comes the guilt at the end of 2019 when you realize you've let yourself down again. Or maybe let someone else down.

I got tired of that roller coaster years ago, and haven't made a New Year's resolution in quite some time. I have goals, dreams, etc., I just tend to map them out when the urge hits and go from there, no matter what the calendar says.

The OCD part of me would like to start all of these activities at least on the first of any given month, but I gave that up too.

Sometimes I don't even start on a Monday. (Three of my well-placed ducks just flew off the pond...)

Case in point: I started healthier eating on November 5th. Stupid month to do a major diet change with the holidays and birthdays barreling down, but I couldn't take it anymore. All the running and stress and fast food during the weeks prior with my grandma's crisis had made me physically miserable. At the time of this posting, I'm down several pounds, tugging at my jeans to keep them put, and I have more energy.

I'm glad I didn't wait another 57 days to coincide with January 1. I'm that much "further ahead" than if I'd waited for the infamous Times Square Ball Drop.

Another stupid timing case in point?

That dead-in-the-water challenge I failed back in September due to "bumpy" times? I'm attempting it again starting this month with a few tweaks to match the "new" normal of "nothing is normal, and the day flips on its head every time the phone rings" status of our family. And I'm giving myself a little extra buffer to allow for edits on my WIP. Still a challenge, but not unreachable given life at the moment.

Orange fountain pen on the line and all.

By March 1ˢᵗ, I'm shooting for 50,000 new fiction words to include three shorts (with covers) and a DONE WIP middle-grade novel first draft. (And here I just heard my very loud inner critic shouting, "Get on with it, Beth. Stop screwing around with it. You know how the dumb story ends, just FINISH, already!")

With more energy, healthier eating, and the majority of footwork for banks, lawyers, and insurance portions of caretaking done, my thinking was much clearer at the end of November, and I didn't want to wait for January 1 to start the challenge. I'm starting sometime this week (as I write this, it's the week of 12/10).

I'll post weekly updates on Facebook if you'd like to see how this one goes. About 80 days at 625 words per day average. I produce more words than that through the day making lists and reminders for myself...surely to goodness I can handle 625 a day.

Why not just wait until after the holidays? Start on January 1 like any sane person? Because that's too much pressure to put on January 1. And because I left sanity a while back. And...

My blank slate starts when I say it starts.

Not when the calendar says it does.

And so does yours, quite frankly.

* * *

Well, time to take another piece of advice from myself—with that healthy eating thing. Again, bad time of year, but, again, family drama and chaos has me on the road more often than not, and packing fresh food vs. remembering the loved one's medications... guess which one wins?

Lesson Learned: Sometimes I give myself good advice. I should listen to it more often. Just sometimes, though...

27. WISH LIST

This season's wish list. Short and simple, and I highly doubt Santa has any of it in his pack...

1. I wish the Christmas season would start December 14th and end the 26th. That gives you a good thirteen days. Twelve days to get from the Partridge-In-A-Pear-Tree right on down to the Drummers. And one day to clean it all up. Scrooge, I am, I am—and I may have lost all my readers just now. But the real meaning of Christmas (you know, the arrival of the King, and believing in something more important than yourself, and bright hope for the future, etc.) gets lost in shopping and commercialism and marketing and, and, and... And Christmas music in October? Please.
2. I wish those who have the means and ability to make Christmas magical for someone less fortunate will do so. Without reserve. Without fanfare. Quietly and in secret...
3. I wish for the removal of ugly sweaters from the mass market. Isn't half the fun of "ugly sweater parties" to sport Aunt Agnes's well-meaning attempt at love, or to at least

hunt something retro or vintage from the local thrift shop? All you gotta do now is shell out twenty bucks—no effort or imagination needed. And on the same note...

4. I wish the mass market of unicorn items would stop already. Unicorns are rare and magical. They shouldn't be EVERYWHERE. (Our local Walmart sells an ugly sweater with a protruding stuffed unicorn front and center. What have we come to?) Unicorns should be just a tick hard to find, so when you finally come across one, you do that giddy little jump-and-squeal move and race toward that single, unique likeness of majestic-ness.

5. Finally, I wish you and yours a multitude of giddy little jump-and-squeal moments throughout 2019.

Keeping it brief and snarky today.

Seriously, though...

Wishing you all a bright, peaceful Christmas and a happy, productive New Year.

* * *

The ugly sweater thing is so out of control—the phenomenon has spawned a short story that'll be available sometime in 2022.

Lesson Learned: Don't be embarrassed to do a giddy little jump-and-squeal. Be ridiculous with it. Those moments can be few and far between these days.

28. ANOTHER DIMENSION

Did you ever make plans a few months or weeks ahead of time, then when the day comes barreling down, you're just not prepared? Even if it's a simple 24 hours away with some favorite people? After lining up care for the elderly grandmother and elderly cat (who needed a sitter, which required me to have a semi-clean house) and clearing off work, and something else that I can't quite remember now but it was super important on that day, I was beat before we ever got in the car to leave. I've never worked harder to leave the house for such a short period of time.

But we made it. We got to the Airbnb, and I tried to shake off the day's frenzy and enjoy jawing with a friend while the others in our group trickled in.

Just sitting, yacking, and absorbing the old bed-and-breakfast-style home near downtown Indy.

When it happened, I was in mid-sentence.

Sparkles appeared in the periphery of my vision, and I tried to whisk them away with my hand. As if a hoard of lightning bugs hovered just to my left. Floating. Dancing.

Then again.

"Did you see that?" I asked.

"See what?" replied the friend with *that look.*

Uh oh. That's always a bad sign. When no one else sees what you see. My friend assured me there was nothing floating through the air. No sparkles. No spots. No glitter.

Just air. And just *that look* on her face.

Great. Water, crisp fresh air outside on the porch, and food. Maybe that will help. And it did. All the pretty lightning bugs faded into the background then, poof. Gone.

Fast forward a few weeks to Halloween. In an attempt to be a team player, this introvert came as a unicorn to our kids' program. Silver horn, face paint and all.

And glittery hair. Now that's a funny one. I thought I bought a can of white hair paint with glitter in it. I'd actually bought pure spray glitter and went overboard because my hair wasn't turning white, and I couldn't tell anything was happening.

It was. Happening.

Glitter and sparkles everywhere. I did have enough sense to do the spraying outside, but this brilliant unicorn shed all over the house, especially the bathroom, and all over the vehicles (we had traded cars with a friend. Who hates glitter. I felt bad).

The next morning as I was brushing my teeth, it happened again. All the pretty sparkles. But alas, this time it was real glitter left over from my dumb-butt stupidity, sent flying in swirls around me by the furnace. Okay. That was real. No issues. Just vacuum out the vent, Beth.

Fast forward to November. Our vehicle tried to putz out on us on the way to Thanksgiving dinner, and hubs insisted it was time to call a lemon a lemon and get new transport. Holidays are stressful enough, then add car shopping on top of that and I was a mess. I test drove the new SUV to church in thick fog. Sparkles everywhere. Glittery against the dense ground cloud. Some bright like tiny camera flashes and some muted like white Christmas lights covered in snow. All moving and dancing. Everywhere.

"Hey guys, isn't that pretty? I've never seen fog like this." Me. Being a seriously oblivious idiot.

"What are you talking about?" Hubs.

"I don't see anything." Son.

Then *those looks.*

Uh oh.

There's nothing wrong with me. I'm not having a stroke. I'm not stressed. I'm okay.

I lied to myself. To make myself feel better. (And don't sit there all smug, wrapped up in your fuzzy robe while sipping your coffee and judge. You lie to yourself too. We do it all the time.)

And I lied some more:

What's really happening is that I'm SO SPECIAL that I'm the ONLY ONE who's developed the unique ability to see into another dimension, but this current reality keeps pulling me back before I can get a true glimpse of where the glitter and shimmers and lightning bugs are trying to take me.

Maybe a waterfall. Maybe a mountain. Maybe the ocean is spitting up white shimmering sand and if I get a little closer I'll be able to smell the moist saltwater air.

Maybe my unicorn spirit animal is just beyond the glittery veil and all I have to do is keep walking/driving/moving toward the lights.

All the pretty lights...

But alas, in my current reality, naggy and concerned loved ones have *that look*, so I went to my Eye Guy. After torturing me with Satan's slit lamp, Eye Guy said there's nothing wrong with my eyes and that the spot that had been on my retina many years prior had disappeared. I asked him the date of that last crazy vision episode I had, when that spot had turned up on my retina. And guess what?

That previous visual issue, which boasted psychedelic colors and trails of leftover images (and occasional lightning bugs) happened during a different massive stress event about eight years ago. I'm sensing a pattern...

As I looked back at my calendar for 2018, I'd say our family hit massive stress in early spring and promptly left *that* station for sitting in the corner, rocking back and forth and not knowing what day it is around late summer. It's been downhill from there.

Eye Guy, with *that look*, sent me to Primary Care Woman who smiled sweetly with *that look* and told me that I'm likely stressed. And the great thing about it? *I paid her money for this particular news flash.*

And guess what? Not one single thing I can do to remove the current stressors. Just gotta wait them out. And maybe take a little pill so my ticker doesn't explode. And so the pretty glitter will go away.

Now to work on my response to the stressors. Like pray. Walk. Fresh air. Hydration. Healthy food. Write more. Take the good moments when they come and wade through to the other side of the stressor. But not to the other side of the shimmering veil where the lightning bugs dance and sweet ocean air calls my name... Okay. Not ready for *that* trip just yet...

So, evidently, glitter is my warning sign. Or a sign that I may have over-sprayed my unicorn mane, but since that glitter is mostly cleaned up (can you ever really clean it all up? It was seriously every-where), I'll stick with "It's a warning sign, stupid. Go chill out," and not a unicorn calling from another dimension.

I'm okay. There's nothing wrong with me.
I'm not even stressed.
Now where'd I put that little pill?

* * *

Little Miss Muse would like to add that she had nothing to do with this episode. At all. The glitter was white, not purple. And she's not a fan of me being stressed. I'm no good to her in that state.

I still have the same Eye Guy and Primary Care Woman. Together, they keep me ticking along, eyeballs and heart muscles doing as they should. But I do still lie to myself—and on a daily basis since February 2020. I'll let you check your own calendars to see what was happening in that month...

Lesson Learned: Keep the appointments. Do the healthy things. Keep the white glitter away.

29. CAGED IN

Freelancing. Ahh, the good life, right?

Hahaha. Maybe. Some days.

Some days it gives you the freedom to be places you couldn't otherwise get to during "normal business" hours. Like brunch with a friend or time with aging loved ones. Some days it gives you the freedom to work in your pajamas and avoid traffic or slick roads.

And a big plus for introverted freelancers is that, normally, there are no people in your actual space. Only in cyberspace. Faceless emails and screen names. But no whining, drama, or fit-throwing takes place in the comfort zone of working from home (unless you have small children, teenagers, a spouse, and/or an elderly cat, then all bets on whining, drama, and fit-throwing are off). All client fits, customer complaints, or otherwise unhappy work-related instances happen behind the glowing screen.

The ultimate goal, the infamous five-year plan (or howmanyeveryearsittakesalready plan), is to stop the freelancing gigs and just write. No more checking for work. No more pooled jobs, where if you don't "keep swimming" you miss out on income. No more making clients and other freelance writers happy. Just making this writer happy. *Grin*

I'm blessed in that I have a supportive husband who encourages this plan and cheers me on—albeit he doesn't know how to read the Do-Not-Disturb signs. Some may never be able to quit their day job to pursue a dream. I'm spoiled rotten, and I know it. (Even as he stands here telling me that he doesn't read my blog and doesn't even know how to access it. Baby steps, itty bitty ones.)

But in the meantime, I'll keep swimming, editing, and, occasionally, I'll take up a gig that requires writing to spec.

Which means writing nonfiction to specification. Following someone else's directions to the letter, dotting each little i and crossing each little t, no matter how insane their wishes may be.

My very first spec job was an informative blog article about the care and keeping of bearded dragons. This required substantially more research than what the job paid me to do, and, in the end, I did *learn* a lot, but I didn't *earn* a lot.

I've taken gigs writing product descriptions for a gardening company. They wanted 175 words about each of their differently colored rose bushes. Go ahead. Try that. Put your word counter on. See just how many words 175 is AND make each product description different from the other—even though it's the same blasted bush in five different colors.

What I wanted to write was "Here's a rose bush. It's pretty. It'll smell nice. Don't kill it." Or "Here's the same bush as item #133, but in pink. It has thorns. Wear gloves when you plant it. Or, live on the edge and don't wear gloves. Knock yourself out."

175 words of pure fluffy bull content that, like the bearded dragon piece, took way too long to write and paid way too little.

All the pieces I've written to spec (including landscaping articles, pest removal services, medical and legal blogs, and all those blasted product descriptions) are now copyrighted under some company's name—it's in the contract that writers give up rights to those pieces upon submission. It's how the content-creation game is played. I'm not even to speak of the specific companies I've written for. That's okay. They can have those pieces because I won't need them where I'm going.

But I did learn something very valuable. Writing to spec takes pieces of my soul (or at least my creative energy) and those pieces don't grow back right away. It takes them a bit to regenerate...

Those writing jobs put me in a cage. No creativity allowed. Only the black hole of precise formatting, search engine optimizing, and metadata nightmares. I'm typically a black-and-white thinker and you'd think that I'd thrive under such specific directions and requests, but when it comes to *creating* something—even nonfiction —I don't appreciate those boundaries.

After spending a morning or afternoon writing content like that, I've got no juice left. My Muse is in her cage and won't come out and play no matter how many ways I try to unlock the door. She stomps her prissy little feet and whines, "You've done gone and wasted the words on someone else. We'll never seeeee themmmmm agaaain!!!!"

And it takes her a good long time before she's ready to talk to me again.

The real kicker—when I switched to editing content instead of writing it—was when a company from overseas asked me to write product descriptions.

For mail-order brides.

I left that particular platform and never looked back. And no. I have no content copyrighted under anyone else's business having to do with the sale of people.

I won't edit those types of pieces either, no matter what the pay. Good grief. With the close of a tab, I sent that jaw-dropping ridiculous assignment back into cyberspace.

At any rate, I'm thankful for my current gigs. And I'm learning that my creativity works best in the morning hours, so I'm making it a priority to get words out before the gigs take over and slowly cage up the Muse, bar by bar.

About the time I'm ready to turn in for the night, the bars loosen, and she slips out of that cage and starts to tickle the far corners of my brain. Gee thanks, girl. Can we put it on hold until tomorrow morning?

Sometimes she lets me. Sometimes not. I at least try to jot down ideas to satisfy her and not lose the gems and sparkles she points out.

Sometimes I force her back into the cage for the night in exchange for much-needed sleep. But only sometimes. Because if I ignore her too often, she gets even. She stages a jail break during my REM stage and I end up sleep walking in the hallway, holding the hand of an aunt I haven't seen in years, or dreaming of thorny technicolor rose bushes floating above my head in hi-def.

Do what you need to for your day job, but let the Muse out to play once in a while. It's not worth your sanity to keep her caged...

* * *

When I contemplated this project, the thought occurred to me that I wasn't entirely sure when Little Miss Muse started showing up in the blogs. Yes, I've mentioned the muse generically, but when, in the course of this blog, did Little Miss start to have a personality all her own?

This was it. The first time she showed herself a little more clearly.

Little Miss would like to reiterate that she's ALWAYS BEEN HERE. I just didn't have the correct brain cells in the correct alignment to see her.

Now... as I keep reading, I wonder when I named her? Ahem. When she told me her name, I mean.

Lesson Learned: Time to retweak that howmanyeveryearsittakesalready plan. 2020 doesn't count, you know.

30. SOMETHING NEW

January is happening, and most people have already planned out their year. But, I've blogged about being a rebel to the calendar and New Year's Resolutions and Holidays in general...

At any rate, I do want my 2019 to be different from any other year.

I want to try some new things. This isn't a new desire for me. I've been whining and barking about it to my poor hubs for a while, but "doing life" keeps getting in the way of "trying the new," and we don't make it a priority. And I'm not getting any younger, so the bucket list is starting to knock loudly on the back door. Better let it in soon...

I don't have it all figured out yet, but that leaves room for new opportunities later in the year.

I want to:

DO something new. An activity never-before-tried. Nothing to do with bridges or crowds, please. Start a new tradition of some sort? New board game with a few good friends?

LEARN something new. A hobby? (I have to be careful with the hobby thing. I tend to go big or go home, so I'll likely end up with two closets full of "only the necessary supplies" and then ditch the hobby two months later.) A new writing technique from a different teacher? A skill, like plumbing? So the next time my hot water line blows under the sink spraying scalding water all over my legs, I'll be prepared. (Some things are probably best left to experts, but hey. YouTube reigns!) A new recipe? (Hahaha. I've blown up the water line and a microwave in the last couple of months cooking *old* recipes. May end up with a whole new house and some angry friends in the fire department if I try a new thing...)

And

GO somewhere new. Exotic? (Not really my speed, but it would be new.) Local places I've missed? (There's a wolf rescue/preserve not an hour from my house. That's on the bucket list, actually.) Writing retreat? (Also high on the bucket list).

Some of these may blend together, but that's okay. Once a quarter, I'd like to check off that I'm not letting my brain rot in sameness. That gives me until the end of March to figure out a new thing and DO IT ALREADY.

Put a few new folds into the old gray matter. Give the Muse more ammunition for creativity.

It allows me to branch out so my characters can branch out. We write and discuss and think best about the things we KNOW. And you can't really KNOW something unless you've at least dabbled in it. And the cool thing about dabbling is it lets you FEEL. FEEL is as important as KNOW on the page.

If you don't KNOW something, you're WONDERING. Wondering is fun, but it doesn't set a clear stage on a fiction page because someone out there, some wise or experienced reader, does KNOW. And then they'll point it out or leave your story for someone else's who actually KNOWS what they're talking about because their scenes not only have the facts right, but they got the FEEL part right, too.

That's why my first novel is set in a rural-ville farmland. There's a field within spitting distance of my house, and there were fields within spitting distance of my childhood homes. I've experienced and felt corn in all of its stages. I know and remember what it FEELS like to wander into the field far enough that the stalks tower above and you can't see landmarks. And I've been sliced by the green leaves enough to know those leaf blades are sharp and the cuts bleed and bleed.

I could look this stuff up, but Wikipedia only takes one so far. Wiki can provide the FACTS, but not the FEEL. [1]

That's where DO, LEARN and GO come in. Real-life experiences. To KNOW. To FEEL.

To EXPAND.

* * *

Board game tried: Catan. That was cool. I won, sort of. The rules were a bit shaky depending on whose family you listened to. I'd like to play again and win for real according to the black-and-white instructions in the box. Nerdy, right? We added Farkle to the mix when we were shut in. Brainless, time-passing game. We burned out on it pretty quickly.

As far as the new hobby/skill: I'm still waist-deep in writing classes. I've left Hobby Lobby, hardware stores, and recipe books for others more capable than I.

New place: Las Vegas. For a writing workshop.

Planned: Alaska Cruise. For our 25th anniversary. Then... COVID. No thanks. We canceled the cruise, then the cruise canceled the cruise, so...

Lesson Learned: When re-tweaking the schedule, I need to plan out some DO-LEARN-GO adventures. COVID or not.

31. A FEW CLICKS OFF

A few weeks ago, I mentioned my rather emergent visit to my Eye Guy. I like the guy. He's personable, thorough, and has served me and my family well through the years.

Since we homeschooled, he'd always given us a discount on our kids' exams because they weren't getting the free screenings they would have gotten in a public school setting. He also patiently put up with one of my kid's insistence that he was nearly going blind, even though he wasn't, and walked us through that process quite well.

Not to mention the multiple unscheduled trips because that same child seemed to end up with a dog toy to the eyeball at least once every six months for quite a stretch. Unreal.

He also graciously endures my near-terror stricken response to having drops placed in my eyes. He knows better than to ever suggest contact lenses. Armageddon would break out in my bathroom whenever it would be time to put in or take out those devilish disks.

Eye drops are of the devil as well. But because I have this history of crazy little spots on my retina, every year we have to go through the sliding-down-out-of-the-chair-while-holding-my-eyes-open-long-enough-to-put-in-the-dilation-drops-don't-punch-the-Eye-Guy routine. If someone would video that, Eye Guy and I could make a few bucks. It'd go viral.

At any rate, several years ago, we were doing the standard vision exam where he'd flick, slide, and flip different strengths of lenses in front of me, and "what's the smallest line you can read?" deal. You know. Is it clearer with lens 1 or 2? 3 or 4? Until my eyes go blurry and I can't tell which lens was better. Because I know the eye drops are coming and I'm starting to shut down all mental processes…

After this particular exam, he told me I didn't need new lenses because "you're just a few clicks off normal."

I stared at him.

Then I laughed.

"Only a few?"

It's likely a phrase he uses with people all the time, but I found it hysterical.

A few clicks off.

Well, that explains more than just my blurry vision. That explains a lot, actually.

It explains unicorns in adulthood. It explains bridges. It explains the extreme introversion. The geekiness.

The writing.

I'm not sure anyone who spends a significant amount of time making things up is normal. They have to be just a few clicks off, else the characters wouldn't talk to them. The dialogue wouldn't snap. The settings wouldn't sparkle. We wouldn't have such places as Narnia, Asgard, or galaxies far, far away.

We'd have no characters. No Jack Reacher, Jack Sparrow, Jack Bauer, or Jack and his Beanstalk. Not to mention Mickey Mouse, Oscar the Grouch, or Paw Patrol (okay, I know a few parents of young ones who wouldn't mind a break from that last one, but you get the point).

Even the music we enjoy would go dull or altogether silent if the artists were zeroed in on being normal.

I imagine in "normal" humans, the Muse is properly caged

behind opaque black plexiglass. Going blind and suffocating. Probably happened when "real life" or "adulthood" took place with the realization that you have to grow up. Do things the way they've always been done. Keep the status quo.

If you think about it, no child is "normal." Every single kid I've met has a "click" or two or fifty that some adult is trying to snap back into place. To make the child "normal." To make things clear and crisp. And proper.

Let them be a few—or many—clicks off. Simply teach them how to "dial it back" in social settings so as not to give Aunt Agnes an embolism during Thanksgiving dinner. Or so as not to disrespectfully blurt out during a lesson time or during moments which require decorum.

Then let them dial it up. All the way up.

Provide them the materials they need to create and play and dream and imagine. Instruments (of the store-bought variety and also of the upside-down pots and pans with wooden spoons variety). Notebooks and fountain pens, word processing programs, crayons and markers and scissors and BLANK paper—not those coloring books where they must conform to someone else's lines. Encourage them to make their OWN lines.

Being a few clicks off may just work to their advantage someday.

Or at least to their Muse's.

* * *

Little Miss firmly agrees that dialing it back is very bad for muses in general. And that blank paper and large purple markers are the best. Permanent markers, please. Brand name. Because she likes the high she gets off the—

And now, I've sent Little Miss to the corner to play with her bottle rockets with a stern scolding regarding the sniffing or huffing of anything with a fume.

Lesson Learned: Watch how children play, and talk, and interact. Take a few of these smallish folks out for ice cream. Drop a "muse bomb" into the conversation and watch them mold it into something amazing.

32. BUBBLE WRAP DAY

It's the last Monday of January. And you know what that means?

It's National (yes, *National*) Bubble Wrap Appreciation Day. It has its own day.

Who knew it had its own day? To be appreciated?

I appreciate it. I like popping those satisfying pockets of air just as much as the next person. When the kids were little and a package would come with the wrap, they'd fight over it. I'd have to get out the scissors and split it evenly or war would ensue.

We especially had issues if the "jumbo" bubbles came. Those sounded like cap guns, and you'd be careful to spread the joy through the day because there weren't as many to pop.

I had a friend growing up who'd pop every single bubble in line, never skipping one. Never randomly darting or searching for an unpopped button, until the whole sheet was a withery, limp mess. Once I came up behind her and popped a bubble at the edge of the sheet she hadn't reached yet. The outcome was not a peaceful one.

I didn't do *that* again.

If you'd like a bit of history, here that is.

In my very brief, what-am-I-going-to-write-about-today skim of the internet, I came across apps. Ones that mimic bubble wrap popping.

Are you kidding me?

There's an app (or a game, or a simulation) for everything. There shouldn't be nearly as many apps as there are, especially ones that mimic or replace real-life, touchy-feely experiences.

I'm guilty of using something similar. It's called White Noise. I prefer to sleep with a real, wind-stirring fan in the bedroom. Hubs freezes to death, so we compromise. But I'd still prefer the fan.

Apps vs. real life. Like the difference between an ice-cold Diet Coke and a lukewarm sugar free can of a knock-off brown cola-soda.

And never buy generic Mac'N'Cheese. Get Kraft. Relive childhood with the blue box and neon yellow cheese dust. (Although I believe the recipe has changed to make it "healthier" which is a bit disheartening. All those preservatives gave it its uniqueness...)

And read real books once in a while. Smell the pages and feel the weight of the thing in your hands. Keep the libraries going.

At any rate, go out and get the real wrap. Walmart sells it by the roll.

Pop until your heart's content or you drive your cohabitants crazy.

Then ship something to someone (in the unpopped portions if you're kind; if you're feeling snarky, use your withery mess) and spread the joy.

* * *

Okay, for what it was, this blog post didn't turn out as badly as I had remembered. I do remember grasping for something to write about because we were neck-deep in drama and death and disease. It just wasn't a good time, and I needed some "happy" to play with.

Bubble wrap still makes me happy.

Lesson Learned: Enjoy the little things. App-free.

33. IT'S JUST A RANT

Above is the last photo I took of our 16-year-old Cosmo. He always loved lying spread-eagle across papers, laundry, game board boxes, fuzzy blankets. Anything he could assert his catliness over. "These are mine, and these are mine, and these and these..."

Who am I kidding? The *whole house* was his.

RIP, buddy.

He "helped" me on this snowy day. Keeping me company as I edited and untwisted that tangled tale I started weaving years ago. The edits moved along just fine—much better than the dread I danced with had led me to believe.

See those blue notes? That's my timeline—I found problems with weekdays and continuity of things like weather and sunrises by doing those.

Those yellow ones are chapter summaries, point of view references, and my Muse saying, "Hey, idiot—don't forget to wrap up this promise, or clue, or here's something for book 2..."

The pink ones are plot holes. A couple of them are plot pits. I managed to find the character that "walked off the set." I found the bit where the same pickup was in two locations (and no, not a magical truck), and I found several issues I didn't know I had.

Some people, those who've never written or prefer some other hobby or way of unwinding, won't understand the time and effort and why I care so much about this endeavor.

"It's just a story."

I do know that it is, in the big scheme of things, just a story. I've written lots of "just stories." And hopefully this will be just another story someone reads and likes, or doesn't. And maybe recommends to someone, or doesn't. And the end result, the readers' reactions, I can't control those. But I can do these bits of notes and edits and thinking before the tale leaves my care. To me, at this stage, it's more than just a story.

It's an escape and de-stress from the doldrums and drama of life.

It's a way to spend a snowed-in afternoon.

It's a way to stay out of a therapist's office—or depending on the drama, stay out of jail.

Most importantly, it's a way to dream.

But from others' perspectives, I know my writing will be just a story or just a hobby. From my perspective, if my "real life" responsibilities are handled, what's it matter to anyone else if I spend time or —heaven forbid—actually *make* time for spinning fantasies and mysteries and misfit characters and putting them in print?

I have—and will continue to—put this endeavor on hold in times of others' great needs. But sometimes I won't hold it off. I'll keep writing, and it will seem selfish and others will rant "It's just a hobby..." or something similar. And I will rant back, "It's my oxygen mask when the plane is crashing."

Let's turn it around for a minute. What's your "just a"? And, for the sake of argument, let's say it's sports. Your team loses (whether you're watching professionals play on TV or you're on a team yourself). I say, "It's okay. It's just a game." Punch to the gut, right? (Full disclosure: I do this to my poor hubs all the time. It really ticks him off. But we're married and I have this almost 25-year-old piece of paper signed by officials and witnesses that says it's okay if we fight like a married couple, so...)

But saying this to a ten-year-old after he's lost his Little League tourney game would be cruel. Saying this to a grown man (who's not my husband), who may have gambled next month's rent and car payment on the success of a pro team may earn me a punch in the mouth.

I know that as the news spreads about Cosmo's demise, I'll get *that line*. That awful "I'm sorry, but he *was* just a cat. You can always get another one" line. Though I'm sure it'll be meant in all kindness —insert eye roll here.

Do me a favor. Keep that "just a" line to yourself when someone loses a fur (scale, feather, hairy) baby. To them, in their moment of grief, they don't want to hear their beloved pet was just a cat (dog, horse, lizard, bird, guinea pig, fish). If you must say this line, if it's your go-to line and you can't help yourself, for the love of all things great and glorious, please say it behind closed doors to your significant other or to the four walls. Don't say it to the grieving one.

Or, maybe, you'll get a firm punch right to the mouth.

And if that happens, don't say I didn't warn you.

And don't worry, either, because it's *just* a tooth.

You can always get another one...

* * *

In the photo, I had laid out my hardcopy draft chapter by chapter on our hardwood floor. Then Cosmo spread out over as many chapters as he could. The draft was dotted here and there in color-coded Post-Its. Later that snowy day, we realized it would be the last weekend with our dear fur friend.

Can you guess what was said to me during this season of loss? About the writing? About the loss of a pet? Go on, guess. I dealt with it using snark in public. I dealt with it through tears in private.

Unfortunately, I find myself guilty of the same thing. Devaluing what others value because I don't truly understand.

Saying "It's just..." or "It's only..." can be some of the most hurtful words.

We all have opinions. That's okay. But most of the time, others are best served when we sit down and shut up. In others' grief journeys, our opinions mean very little.

Lesson Learned: Swift to hear, slow to speak. It's a continual, ongoing lesson in kindness.

34. YOU'RE MY "YOU"

Can I write you a letter? Can I pour out my heart to you? Can I write just for you?

My *You*. If that's okay.

You who've watched me fumble and fit and mostly self-doubt and occasionally celebrate right here on the blog.

You.

You're my why. I don't know where you are or even *when* you are. Maybe my you is someone five years in the future who stumbles across some link somewhere and clicks out of sheer boredom.

Or strolls into some bookstore and picks up a second-hand copy of a random anthology one of my stories is tucked in.

But I know *you* are there. Somewhere.

Maybe you're watching. Maybe waiting. Maybe neither watching nor waiting—not quite yet.

I don't know what you look like. Sometimes you have a face or a form. Most of the time not. A face that isn't and that is always changing.

Someone, though.

Some vague someone, but yet not vague at all. Someone unique, and yet just beyond my mind's eye's ability to see your features.

My Muse likes to play and pretend and tells me that "you" is a twelve-year-old kid. Other times, my you is my 90-year-old grandmother. Sometimes, my you is nothing like a kid or a grandmother, but some middle-aged man in Colorado riding a horse up the side of a snowy mountain. Little Miss Muse needs to stifle it sometimes...

Maybe you're someone that clicks a link and lands here. Someone that maybe clicks another and lands on Amazon. Someone that waits for the first Friday of the month. Or maybe *you* don't, but another you might someday.

I don't know what you look like. Not necessarily. I try not to put a face to my "audience" even though the Muse does her best...

If I did, then the "audience" would influence the next thing I do, and I don't want that. I don't want to write what *all* the "yous" expect. I don't much care about other authors' yous, that's the other authors' responsibilities. I want to surprise myself, so I likely won't write to mass market. And I want to surprise *my* yous. My yous are the most important to me.

I want the words I write to move you to feel something. Something like joy. Maybe tears (well, maybe not that, so much, but it's been known to happen a few times to a few yous.) Maybe to give you a temporary escape from the mundane. Open a world where nearly anything is possible. Mostly to move you to dream and imagine. To shock sometimes.

I think about you quite often. Probably more than I should, given the fact we may not have met. Maybe we never will.

I think about you when I need to escape. I think about you when life gets rocky and the thought of you gives me great comfort. That you're out there. Somewhere. Waiting. Or someday will be waiting for our next adventure.

And the thought that I can be where you're at and not even know you is incredibly cool.

Have you ever thought about that? That when you read something, the author, in a way, is right there with you. In your head.

That's an intimate experience. That I can put thoughts into your head. That, if I've done my job correctly, I can put feelings into your being that you weren't experiencing before you opened the book.

Or clicked the link.

I've thought about you so much that there's this connection now. That I can use words to paint scenes and people and events into your imagination that wouldn't have been there otherwise. And for a moment—hopefully many moments—it's just you and me and the world I've created and we do this intricate dance that transcends time and space. With just little black-and-white marks on the page and imagination.

You and me. Me and you.

And if we, the authors, are lucky or skilled or whatever enough, you won't be thinking of us too much, per se, but you'll nonetheless allow us to seduce your brain into suspending disbelief long enough to take you on a journey. A journey we've taken with our story multiple times during the writing process, and now we share it with you and you're there with us. With our characters. With our ideas and dreams and hopes.

I wrote a blog early on called "It's Not About You" where I explain that I'm not trying to put anyone I personally know into my stories. That all characters are made-up people.

And that's true.

But it is *for* you. My audience. My readers.

If it's not about you, you and me together for a few moments of escape, then what am I doing this for?

Thank you for being you. The you right here in 2019.

The you who stumbles across this in 2024.

The you who will someday find this work in some format current technology has yet to dream up.

The you who went old-school and found it in paperback.

To all the yous.

Thank you for being my why.

* * *

Wow. Massively sappy. True words and a solid concept, but wow. I tend to blog on the side of snark. I must've been feeling all the feels over Grandma and the cat and the season we were in.

And there it is! The first instance where Little Miss Muse is named. With proper capitalization and all!

Little Miss is doing the happy dance and laughing so hard her chunky cheeks jiggle. "You put me in a love letter." And now she's on the floor. Rolling. Literally. She's gonna get cat hair all over her wings...

You see, Little Miss Muse and I don't do so well with romance and sap. We play our best word games with the twisted and "out there" ideas. So the love letter thing is, well, quite comical.

Lesson Learned: Appreciate those you work for. And don't forget to laugh at yourself.

35. VOILÀ!

Don't you love it when you hit that "groove" of whatever it is you like? If you're a chef (and I can only imagine this because a chef I am not), maybe it's that moment you've pulled the cake or truffle or soufflé out of the oven and it's perfect. You spent some chunk of time tossing ingredients into a bowl (in my case, I'd hope for the best and stand by with the fire extinguisher), and your hard work's paid off. Voilà!

Maybe you're a woodworker or carpenter. That pile of lumber and raw materials now has shape and form and function. Where before it was just a pile. And not just anyone could do what you've accomplished. It took a tick of skill. Voilà! (As with the baking analogy, woodworking endeavors would require a standby fire extinguisher and EMS team fully stocked with goodies to stop arterial bleeds...)

My recent writing challenge produced a cool short story. One that fits into another world I have some other shorts in that I've named The Recruitment Saga. These won't likely appear in the free fiction Friday section here on the blog because they'd not make too much sense as standalones—well, they do and they don't. I spotted a common theme among them, added a pinch of fantasy and dash of doom and Voilà! A series was born.

The most recent, *The Dragonfly*, (still in editing) is the first in the series that crashes some of the seemingly unrelated characters together and we get a sense of what might be at stake. I have a feeling The Recruitment series will be *sort of* like the Star Wars saga. No, I'm not comparing my skill or imagination to Lucas. Not in the slightest. Nor to the talent that writes for the more recent Episodes (but doggonit, Harrison? Really? That was my childhood flashing and falling and dying before my eyes right there on the big screen...) I haven't brought myself to watch Solo yet. Real life happened when that movie was out, and I'm still bitter about Mr. Ford.

Anyway, Star Wars has prequels and sequels and has been presented to the audience in an out-of-order fashion. You could choose to watch the Episodes in the order they were created or in the order of "story timeline." Or you could watch just one and have fun. Some stand alone, others don't. There my comparison to this far, far away universe ends.

Little Miss Muse is dishing out The Recruitment Saga to me out of order. Old, young, past, future. The first Recruitment story I wrote over a year ago, "The Recruit," is written in time future. I thought it was a one-and-done sort of deal. The next one I wrote, "The Biblio-phile's Curse," takes place before all the others, time-wise. At least for now. That might change as I revisit characters' backstories. At the end of "The Dragonfly," the main character meets the star of "The Killing Jar," and the Wolfe lurks from Bibliophile, and we can vaguely see the thread that binds the stories together.

My goal is to smash them all into an anthology once I have enough to warrant a full-blown book.

I have fun writing in this world. I like the idea of subtle other-regions colliding with our present-day world—most people being oblivious to their existence, but a chosen few must embark on some epic quest to save one or the other of the worlds. And these chosen ones must keep the rest of humanity in the dark, because, well, humanity as a whole has never done a fabulous job of caring for itself. Humanity, as a whole, rarely has Voilà moments.

I've realized something interesting while writing Recruitment. I have an obsession with siblings. I knew this only vaguely before I started writing, but it's grown. Being an only child is rough in the relatability department. I can't quite fathom the bonds between brothers and sisters. I watch them play out in families I know and in others' portrayals of them in books and movies, but I don't get it. I've never experienced it.

I never understood my own two kids—why they wouldn't get away from each other when they were younger. Why they seemed to thrive on fighting over the dumbest things. My husband (the baby of three) assured me this was completely normal.

When I write about siblings, I must imagine hard the love/hate/bond/betrayal, etc. because I've never felt that.

Twins and multiples and uber large sibling groups intrigue me to no end. What must it be like to have someone be there all the time, from the very beginning? Yeah, yeah, your parents or guardians are around, but multiples? They shared a room from the time they were one cell tall. And multiple kids, like more than two? (Two is my number, so anything more is "big" to me.) How do you ever keep the laundry clean or the bellies full? I think the managers of those households are superheroes.

I'm also terribly fascinated with the relationships in adoptions and fostering situations. These instances show up frequently in my stories as well. And, I'm not writing what I know at that point, I'm writing what I guess or imagine is the case. I've got nothing to base them on.

I'm not adopted. I don't think. Though sometimes I wonder... Nevertheless, I have to guess what these kids feel and think when I write about an adopted character. Some, I imagine, are grateful. Some may not even know the story of their beginning yet. Some may be resentful, full of hurt and loss and abandonment. Some may be grateful and resentful at the same time. What a gloriously difficult burden to bear.

I've never fostered or adopted a human. Furry, four-legged things and one winged thing, but no babies. I know what it's like to have a doctor hand me a squirming child of my own making, but I've no idea what emotions must flood over parents who bring home an infant or toddler or teenager that isn't biologically theirs, but *theirs* nonetheless. To love and nurture and hope and dream with. And to struggle with.

A huge shout out to those with adopted or fostered kids. You've chosen to make something amazing out of a seemingly mismatched set of people—yet not mismatched at all, perfectly perfect for your world. You've chosen to take someone else's blood and make them part of your everyday life. Part of you.

Voilà! You've created a family.

You have my undying admiration.

* * *

Recruitment Saga Update: I may can this idea, at least for a moment. Because "The Dragonfly" sold to Ellery Queen as a mystery. And now I'm royally confused. Maybe that very faint line of similarity is a bit too thin... I'm still mulling over that.

You can, however, read these tales in the various collections linked at the back of the book.

Lesson Learned: Plan projects in private. Don't announce them on the blog unless they are available already!

36. FOG

Last month, I trodded through the backyard thirty minutes before sunrise. We border our high school's property, and they have some impressive aged pine trees. Beyond those is a stretch of road and then a field.

It was the fog's fault. Or Little Miss Muse. (I guess that's her name now. Little Miss. It fits.)

I'd stood at the kitchen window and thought how cool it would be if I could capture the early morning fog with the tree and the road and the rolling field. It'd make an awesome book cover. Since most of my stories have an element of death or drear in them, it would fit somewhere.

I had on my slides but was otherwise dressed for church. By the time I crossed the backyard, the hems of my pant legs were muddy and my socks were soaked with melted frost, but for a few minutes, I was alone. Surrounded by the damp and cool, accompanied only by one screeching crow—also fitting for the setting and elements in many of my stories. I took a couple of shots and was aggravated because no matter where I stood in the yard, the power lines and sewer grates showed up. And I'm not at all adept at Photoshop.

I walked further and further away from the house to find a clear enough section (that wasn't smack in the middle of the road—we have crazy drivers near the city/county line) to aim and not have to edit too much.

If we weren't leaving soon and I didn't have to change clothes, I'd have stayed quite a while, watching the light play with the fog. Maybe capture that angry crow in midflight. Sit still enough and wait for our family of deer (our family, like we own them or something) to show themselves in the tree line across from the field. Each spring we have turkeys that waddle their young ones into our backyard for whatever reason. It'd be cool to sit still enough to have them pass right by me. Close enough to see them wink.

Then it struck me. Maybe this is what Max and Marie felt in "Red-Winged Blackbird." Or what the kids felt in "The Sunrise Project."

Alone but not alone. In the quiet and solitude.

In an earlier blog, I mentioned wanting to learn/do some new things this year. Something different. This is one thing I'd like. Out before dawn, before the world starts moving and honking and hurry-ing. Take a walk or leave a camp chair out behind our fence so I can drag it over to the pine tree and watch the sun come up. Learn how to capture those sunrises/sunsets/weather phenomenon in my own backyard.

I might take a drive an hour before light and find an old cemetery or river's edge. Or farmhouse. Watch the light. Wait for the right moment and snap.

With no filters needed.

* * *

I've done this a couple of times. But I've realized I'm no photographer —I enjoy it, but not enough to invest the money and time to make those amazing shots that the stock photo companies have.

The stories mentioned in this blog can be found in the collections mentioned at the back of the book.

Lesson Learned: Use stock photos for covers... not those from your camera roll.

37. IN MEMORY (OF GRANDMA)

On Thursday, February 7, 2019, my grandmother, 91 years old, went to Heaven.

She'd been declining since September after a bad bout with pneumonia. Another round with a sinus infection, a stomach bug, and severe weakness, and her body just gave out.

She'd rallied the weekend before. Got a snazzy new haircut that took about ten years off her face and looked great. She was able to go to church that Sunday and even sang in front of the congregation—one of her favorite things to do.

Monday she was wiped out. Tuesday was worse.

Wednesday something was different.

The evening before she passed, I'd gone to spend the night with her. When the end is imminent, you just *know*. Somehow.

I cooked up her last meal request (though I wasn't entirely sure it would be her last at the time). She couldn't get it down. I offered to take her to the ER and she snapped back, "I can die in my own home better than I can die in a hospital."

Well, okay then. Passing away in her own home on her own terms had been her wish for many years, a wish she reiterated weekly over the last few months. And she promised me she wasn't in any pain.

I helped her get changed for bed, said goodnight for the last time, and stayed with her as she breathed her last breath.

She was in her own bed in her little apartment that she adored. On her own terms.

Thursday morning, the skies over Indiana split open and drowned us. I don't think Heaven was quite prepared for her grand entrance through the pearly gates.

After the thunder had rattled our utility room lights for the third time, I teased with my son that God was scolding, "Sit down, Lois. I can handle this." No doubt she was stomping around in a brand new, feel-good, weak-no-more, worry-free existence. And a whopping two hours in, knowing Grandma, she was likely telling God how to run things.

Because Grandma was never short on opinions.

Politics? Want a rundown on everyone in Congress? Need up-to-the-minute status of the world? Just ask her. The Fox News anchors were her second family. (I kid you not, she knew their names, ages, and kids' names. I can't even remember how old I am.)

Religion? She'd likely read through the Bible more times than the Pope himself. Maybe all the Popes all put together.

Family? If everyone would just do it her way, we'd all get along better.

Food? Cook it her way. Country style. Liberal with the bacon grease (an aside: how are these old country cooks living into their 90's eating their weight in bacon grease??). Don't throw away the leftovers. Not even after they've started growing black beards—if you give them a good shave, they'll be perfectly fine to eat. And to prevent family from tossing perfectly good food, hide them in old butter tubs or cottage cheese containers. (In Grandma's fridge, you never knew if you were gonna open the margarine, like it said on the container, or be greeted by three-week-old salmon. She once saved my toddler's grape juice in a sippy cup for our next visit. Bad weather struck and it was a few weeks later. She'd turned the juice into wine and was furious with me because I wouldn't let him drink it.)

Others' appearances or preferences? If it popped into her head, it slid out of her mouth. I once had to tell her what I told my kids when they were little: "When we're in the car with the windows rolled up and the engine running, you can say anything you want to me. But please *don't* say it in public!"

No, we were never short on opinions.

Neither was her family ever short on her outpouring of love. Even though she forced six-year-old me to eat scalloped potatoes to get raspberry pie for dessert, but turns out the pie was blackberry because she didn't have her glasses on, and I despised blackberries. Even though she force-fed nine-year-old me chili when I had the stomach flu and, years later, tried to fry us all fish when *my* kids were puking. Even though she beat my shins with a broomstick the day the mouse tried to hide behind my legs down in the cellar. Even though she threw hickory nuts at my head. When I asked why, she said she didn't know I was downhill from her and that those nuts had worm holes in them. Thanks, Grandma.

Over the years, she was one of my biggest supporters in any endeavor, whether something of utmost importance like motherhood or the mundane like trying a new craft. She would be the first in line to cheer and champion me on. I think I could've told her that I wanted to sell *intergluteal clefts* (Do you like that crossword puzzle word? She was a big fan of words...) to plumbers, and she'd be on board with the idea. Probably even buy one herself to show how much she cared.

My writing aspiration was no different. When we were cleaning out her papers, I came across printouts of some of my short stories that I'd given her to read. They were worn out. Some looked like they'd been dropped in a mud puddle. She'd read them and likely passed some of them around to others. "I want more stories," she'd say. So I'd print off another one or some of my blog posts for her to read.

"I think you're gonna be an author someday," she'd said with tears in her eyes.

"I hope so," I said.

"I know so."

Thanks, Grandma.

* * *

As I was working through these blogs, copying and pasting the text and writing these little followups, I knew this one was coming. I debated on stopping at #36 and letting the project just sit for a while. I debated on skipping #37 and doing it at the very end.

But, plough through, is what Grandma would have told me. So I did. And, as life would have it, I've a close friend this very minute who sits at the bedside of her 101-year-old grandmother in that lady's home. Saying goodbye.

So it's bittersweet for me. Thinking about my friend and knowing what she's feeling. Reading about the stress and upheaval of the few months before Grandma died. Reading about Cosmo's death. Reading what the public saw through the blog, and knowing I didn't even cover a microfraction of what was going on in our family. Some things are private and will stay that way.

Lesson Learned: Cherish the moments. They slip by very quickly.

38. MEET STELLA

As promised, here's the new addition (well, new as of January). She's settled in quite nicely. About three weeks later, my son decided to adopt a cat from the same shelter, so Amara came to live with us, too. When he starts his blog (insert eye roll here) he can introduce you to *her*.

Stella came one day after Cosmo passed because I had a flip-out-hairy-fit episode over not having a pet in the house for the first time in nearly two decades. I'd have preferred a dog, but I don't currently (and definitely didn't then) have the time to train a pup. I figured a cat wouldn't care if I was MIA for long stretches caring for the aging one.

So off I went to shelters (I originally heard of a little girl who was available from an 80+-year-old, but when it came down to it, the old lady wouldn't cough up the kitten, and I had to go hunting). Any other time, if my quiver had been full of cats, there'd have been needy felines dripping from tree branches all over the neighborhood. I could've had my pick. On this particular panic-filled day, however, not a stray in sight.

I found Stella at a local pet store which displays shelter cats for potential adoption leads. Stella pushed her feathered, red flannel catnip fish toward me and patted it as if saying, "Do you like my fish?"

"Why, yes. Stella. I like your fish very much." We greeted each other through her cage's wires. I told Stella I'd take her home. I think I fell in love with her whiskers first. She's all whiskers. Then I fell in love with her uberly hairy toes.

Turned out, I had to visit the actual shelter who took her in, the Animal Care Alliance, and fill out the paperwork there. And Oh. My. Word. She was one of 40 cats available. Cats everywhere. One-eyed cats, three-legged cats, inexperienced ones, ancient ones, one-eared cats, gaunt ones, obese ones. In all colors and body styles imaginable. Most of them loose and running through two gigantic rooms filled with food dishes, litter boxes, toys, towers, and beds. And 90+ percent of them actually getting along. We were stunned.

And the staff there. They know most of them by name. They know their personalities and quirks. Many staff members foster the animals until the kitties are well enough for the Cat Room.

And my little girl, freshly back in the Cat Room after her pet store journey, was cowering in the corner hissing at the other cats for getting too close. She'd had enough. I could relate. I don't much like people in my face when I've had enough.

I signed the adoption forms. They gave her an updated dose of meds and handed her to me with a "Smile for Facebook"—because the Alliance posts photos of the adoptions on their social media feed. We smiled for the photo, then she right-hooked me in the lip—twice, drawing more blood than I've shed in a long time. She leapt from my arms and hid in the corner. I think they thought I wouldn't want her after that. They swore to me she was one of the gentlest cats they had and that she'd never ever acted that way.

But I understood why she did it. Travel weary. Poked. Prodded. Stella had had enough. Stella had been found under someone's porch after she'd birthed a litter of kittens (which we got to meet, so that was cool). The Alliance took her and the kittens after a stretch with a foster family. And, oh, by the way, she's been SHOT! The pellet is still in her back, but I've been assured it's harmless.

So before the ripe old age of three, Stella was: Abandoned. Shot.

Pregnant. A momma. Fostered. Spayed. Separated from her kids. In The Cat Room. On display. Adopted.

I think I'd right-hook someone too.

Stella is mine in more ways than one. Jayden's cat is totally different.

Amara likes to be cuddled up close and personal.

Stella does not. Because she's mine.

Amara likes all visitors and wants to sit on their laps and lets them hold her like a baby.

Stella does not. Because she's mine.

Amara waits patiently for attention when we're busy.

Stella does not. Like to wait.

Amara is laid back and meanders through the day.

Stella is not laid back and is always on a mission. Because she's mine.

Amara is quiet and not pushy.

Stella vocalizes/dirty looks/body languages her opinion whether we want it or not. Because she's mine.

Yesterday she was lying on my manuscript pages. I tried to take them from under her. She gave me that "glare over the spectacles" look and put her paw on top of my hand—her claws weren't out, just a little "I'm not done yet" warning. I remembered the burn on my lip the day she boxed me.

I decided I didn't need those particular manuscript pages just then.

Stella needs her space. I can relate. We're still bonding. But of all the 40+ cats in the Cat Room, I think I picked the best one for me.

Okay. Who am I kidding?

I picked *me.*

* * *

So the timeline of this rocky road: Cosmo died January 7, 2019.

Stella was adopted January 8.

Amara happened February 5 (Amara happened. She was not adopted. She's not to be owned. Much like Little Miss Muse...).

Grandma passed February 7.

The grand illusion that we'd have some "down time": February, end-ish of the month (after Grandma's services were held).

Actual down time: Two weeks.

Next Life event: Mid-March.

Next breath of air: TBD...

Update on Stella: She's still me. A touch-me-not, impatient being that needs space. But she's settled in very nicely and has the sweetest personality as long as things go her way— still like me. She's very happy to be happy and "off duty" from motherhood-under-the-porch, stray-status, and Cat Room participant. Her bullet in the back hasn't moved and doesn't seem to bother her in the least.

Update on Amara: Jayden's cat is now not patient, not laid back, and not quiet. She's a bully, brute, and ring-leader of all things loud and forceful. Turns out, Amara bamboozled us. She's a velociraptor in the shape of a cat. Sometimes we're afraid of what she might do to us while we sleep...

Lesson Learned: The next "life roll" is always on the horizon (so cherish the down times), and cats are such liars.

39. THE FORMULA

Ready for some mind-boggling math?

There are two sides to every story.

If the above statement is true, logic dictates there's my version of events and yours. If we were the only two "there." For sake of illustration, let's say "there" means at the library when the book stacks caught fire.

And let's say *you* sat the stacks on fire. (Sorry, someone's gotta be the "bad" guy, and I don't think I'd have the guts to burn books in the library during business hours). You though, I wouldn't put it past you...

So now, there's my eye-witness account (which is clouded by my high emotional state and my perception of you, not to mention smoke inhalation), there's your story (clouded by your emotional state, your perception of the events, and smoke inhalation), there's Mr. Librarian's side along with two other patrons' versions, equally clouded by their elevated emotional states, their perceptions of you and me and the library, and, no doubt, smoke inhalation.

Now how many sides are there?

Five people in a setting that's on fire.

Five sides to the story?

Or are there ten? The version that each actually experienced with their senses—no filters or emotions attached (you came in, you burned the stacks) and the OMG! I just about died version (the one where they swear you were ranting and raving and giving dirty looks, and, and, and...)

Even if one were trying to be objective, there's the trouble with the five senses. Not all five are firing at optimum capacity for each witness at any given moment, so maybe those sides of the story aren't worth much. Someone forgot their glasses or turned down their hearing aid. One patron came to the library to sleep off an all-night bender so his wife wouldn't yell, so none of his senses are reliable.

Let's just take me. My version is skewed because I'm ticked at you for burning the stacks. I'm also scared out of my mind because you nearly set us both aflame, and I can't think straight because I'm having trouble breathing. But maybe you're my best friend so I'll fabricate an additional storyline to tell the fire department because I don't want you to get in trouble. Even though I thought it was over the top that you would use arson to make a point to Mr. Librarian who dumped you, my best friend, on *Valentine's Day* even, to go out with the technician from the CDC (who's in town to investigate a biological hazard in the school across the street from the library). I get why you're ticked. I mean, those two just met...

In only *my* head, there's what I think I saw (which may differ from what you actually did), what I'll tell everyone else I saw (a version of the story, but perhaps not a totally accurate one,) and last but not least, the version I'll tell myself so I can sleep better at night (perhaps the oversized water bottle in my backpack would have doused the situation before it got out of control. I just won't mention that I had the means to stop it lest I'm implicated too...).

That's three stories in one head. How many do you have? Three? Two? One? What about the librarian? His version of what happened must be skewed because now he's afraid you'll show up (or send me since you're likely going to jail) to burn his house to the ground while he sleeps...

Maybe he's so afraid of you, that he'll tell the fire chief that *I'm* the one that set the stacks on fire. And since I was standing so close to you when you did it, I'm covered in evidence, so the story would fit.

Or maybe the angle was off from the point of view of one of the patrons. And they saw Mr. Librarian in the stacks last. And that patron overheard Mr. Librarian talking with his boss about how upset he was that he didn't get off work early on Valentine's Day to take Little Miss CDC to a nicer place to eat.

How many sides are there to every story? As many as the human mind, emotional state, and motive can muster. This makes for great fiction. Thrillers and mysteries and dramas would run cold if there were only one side.

For real life (and I've had fantastically more than my share of real life lately), I wish there were a formula. Plug each eye witness's tainted memories, emotional baggage, and skewed motives into one side of the equation, and out pops absolute truth on the other. Then everyone knows "the rest of the story." But alas, we're left to wonder and ponder and lose sleep over drama and dilemmas with no answers.

Meanwhile, what no one knows is that you did it because Little Miss CDC was a terrorist who'd unleashed a biohazard virus into those stacks and you sat the library on fire to kill the deadly bug and save thousands of lives at the expense of a few books. But your fire destroyed the evidence of that bug, and you're now sitting in jail because everyone else's versions fit better.

And Little Miss CDC gets away.

But you're very happy that I didn't douse your flame with my water bottle before the fire overtook the stacks. Because thousands would've died a horrible death.

And because I didn't use that water bottle, I'm now the hero of my own twisted tale.

At least that's how I'll tell it if anyone should ask.

* * *

Disclaimer: The CDC/biohazard virus thing was written waaaay before I knew anything of COVID. Good grief.

This blog was inspired by real-life issues that kept coming up. Drama and loss and chaos seems to not only cloud people's judgment, but also their retelling of the facts, no matter what the topic is. This piece was my way of venting in public about very real issues behind the scenes. Many, many issues.

But alas, the rule holds: The specific piece was not about any one person or event in particular, but more about noticing a larger pattern of human behavior.

And now, enter 2020, and wouldn't we all like that "Formula" for an accurate read on all things pandemic, political, and public welfare-related???

Lesson Learned: Real life is stranger than fiction. Story fodder all day long...

40. NAMING SPACES

Last year, my grandmother decided to move from her country home of nearly 60 years to an apartment in town closer to us. Her declaration surprised us all. We'd thought we'd have to blast her out of that home with a dump truck full of TNT when the time came. But she was slowing down considerably and, I think, a little scared after a couple of minor incidents with her health, and so we went on a big journey. Her 90 years old and me feeling like I was 90 years old.

We spent many days going to Grandma's house to clean, sort, box, and toss decades of living packed into her three-bedroom home, garage, and two large outbuildings.

And that's what we called that space in the country: *Grandma's house*. Or for short, just *Grandma's*. Even when Grandpa was living, it was Grandma's house. Maybe because she was always in the kitchen and he was always in the yard or in one of the outbuildings. I don't know why, exactly. It was just *Grandma's*.

Back in town, we signed the lease for the apartment and learned when trash day was. We readied the apartment with the essentials like toilet paper and a shower curtain before she came. On moving day, the apartment was filled with helpers and her old Corelle dishes in Butterfly Gold and her country furniture. And that's what we called that space: *The apartment.*

Until she arrived at the apartment, never to spend another night at *Grandma's house.* Then the apartment became *Grandma's,* and the farmhouse became *the farm.* Just like that. Decades of country = Grandma's... gone.

I returned to the farm several times to clean things up and keep the yard mowed. The two-story white cinderblock home with green shutters became more and more of a shell for foggy memories than a home, the life sucked right out of it. It was simply a structure that needed upkeep.

Within a day, maybe even hours, of her moving, the name of the spaces changed to match the occupant—or the lack of one.

Within a day, or maybe even hours, of her death, we started calling her apartment *the apartment* again. Something that needed cleaned and purged and it, too, became a shell of memories, some foggy like the ones that run together because an activity happened every day like the rundown of Fox News reports or what she ate for breakfast, to more vivid ones like putting up her last Christmas tree or playing the last game of Scrabble.

We had no roundtable discussions on these nuances. We didn't plan it. But all of us adopted the name changes quickly.

They just happened.

What's this have to do with writing? I'm not sure yet. I'll likely use this phenomenon in a story someday and worked it out here on the blog. Noted it down for future reference. Or maybe I'm still grieving.

And remembering.

Trying to hang onto what the farmhouse smelled like during canning season and memories of rolling down the cellar hill with the neighbor kids and climbing the apple tree with a book in my hand, trying not to get stung by wasps and picking daffodils (before I was allergic to daffodils) to arrange in a glass vase to take to the morning church service on spring Sundays.

Or helping her buy curtains for the apartment and teaching her how to use her new library card and fixing the remote control for the tenth time in a month.

Maybe it's to give myself permission to name that space inside me brimming with memories and full of all things Grandma a name: *Grandma's.*

* * *

Okay, #37 was a breeze to get through compared to this one. I managed that one with no tears and just moved right on to Stella.

But I'll need a break now. Time to allow "all the feels" of walking memory lane do their thing. Time to throw one of Grandma's quilts onto the bed and have a minute wrapped in memories. Time to cook her famous mac-N-cheese for lunch and try to not blow the kitchen up.

Time to check on my friend who still sits in vigil of that last breath of her own grandmother—likely walking down their family's decades of lane-building.

I've not written a story based on this yet. I think I need to, though. Even Little Miss with all her rambunctious rambling sits in somber respect as I let the tears slide. The cats are quiet. The crows, angry for the last half hour, have moved on. My microfraction of the world pauses for just a moment... and I'm thankful.

Lesson Learned: Grief knows no time constraints.

41. NEW CHAPTER

As I write this, it's mid-March and I'm recovering from the loss of Grandma and all that her death entailed during that chapter of our journey.

I'm also looking back on some goals that I'd made late last year and earlier in 2019. Some don't apply any longer. Some got turned upside down and wiped out because I either hit them already or I'm no longer interested.

(Turns out, living in a state of constant motion and caretaking of another human lends itself to some strange and often unrealistic ideas. Caretaker syndrome, I think they call it. I did resist the urge to run away from home, get a tattoo of a prancing unicorn on my fore-head, and quit my productive day job in lieu of working for a trav-eling circus. I'll take the wins where I can get them. I did, however, manage to sign up to help butcher chickens later this summer because it sounded like a good idea at the time. So..., yeah.)

At any rate, I'm preparing for a time of rejuvenation and reset. A time to focus in some peace and quiet and without the Oh-Look problem. "Oh, look. The laundry needs switched." "Oh, look. That window needs new curtains." "Oh, look. That cat needs pets."

Or, my favorite writing/goal-setting procrastination line: "Oh, look. I should sit down and write five more blog posts."

So I'm doing a few posts ahead to be clear of the excuse to do them while I'm away.

I'm dangerously close to finishing my first novel. I say dangerously, because finishing is terrifying. What next?

This novel has been an Oh-Look problem as well. Want to write something new? Try out a different style? "Oh, look. That story needs piddled with." "Oh, look. This chapter has to be redone." "Oh, look. Let's change the point-of-view character."

When something major has been hanging over your head for so long and then it's not any more, there's a hollow that must be filled with something. Because no hollow stays hollow. Something will crawl in there accidentally if said hollow isn't filled on purpose.

And I don't want to "accidentally" end up with a project that isn't fun or worthwhile.

The same could be said of relationships, but I'll not dive into *that* analogy.

Time to figure it out. What major story do I want to dance with next? What other projects?

I signed up for an anthology project for later in the fall. That will be fun, but there are some things I need to do and learn and get out of the way before that writing begins in earnest—I know it will stretch me and kill brain cells at the same time.

So, short and sweet while I reset the gears. Turn the page. Explore the new chapter.

* * *

At this time, I'm power of attorney for three aging ladies. Three. Two are mine by blood, and being an only child (and an only niece—I have no cousins), their welfare now falls in my court. The other is my mother-in-law, where the hubs and I co-power-of-attorney her medical issues and wellbeing.

We've got a pacemaker, two bad bladders, diabetes issues, a fall off a ladder, a fall from the recliner onto a hoard of knick-knacks (urggg), three suspicious skin lesions, three eyeballs that need tending, two ear drum issues, a closed head injury, heart failure, kidney failure, stents and bypasses. And that's mostly in the last year or two since Grandma passed. We've been busy...

Enter the pandemic and things became vastly more complicated. I'll let you use your imagination there.

Lesson Learned: Caretaking takes its toll: Writing helps me recharge the batteries.

42. CONTENTEDLY EXHAUSTED

Several all-nighters (and at my age, that means awake 'til one a.m. Technically, since I made it to the next morning, that counts as an all-nighter. *Grin* Past that, there is no brain function no matter the milligrams of caffeine consumed).

Several up-waaaay-before-the-crack-of-dawn mornings.

Several up-in-the-middle-of-the-night stints. Thank you, stress-induced insomnia for helping me journey along in this ridiculous challenge I've given myself. I really did need your help.

However, no thanks to the stress-induced nightmares—border-line night *terrors*—for sucking away the ability to put one word in front of another until my hands stop shaking.

My nightmare thing has been interesting. When I'm deep in story creation—or deep in life stressors, which I've been swimming in of late—something happens in the creative part of my brain: Little Miss Muse refuses to go all the way to sleep, so she plays in whatever part of the brain creates dreams, and boy, does she get wild. Insanely wild.

Sometimes the nightmares involve people I love in perilous situations. Sometimes they make no sense at all, but I wake up sitting straight up (or I wake up and find myself standing—or halfway down the hall which is freaky). Cold, clammy, and shaking.

Disoriented. (Did I buy that wrinkled English bulldog puppy from the creepy guy at Smally's Lake last night? Did I remember to buy puppy chow?)

Why can't the Muse grace me with unicorns and glitter? Just once. Maybe twice. Instead of three times a week of, "Oh, crap, I'll never look at *that* person the same way again," why can't she put me in a log cabin, snow falling around it, fire lit in the fireplace, and me taking a nap. Why?

Short and sweet again this week while I continue with my gear reset.

I am thankful this challenge is over. (The challenge that I said would be done by March, but I extended it because of our family's circumstances and that ocean of stressors I mentioned. And since I'm the boss of my own writing, I can do that. Tweak goals and challenge dates to meet my needs.) I'm up to two finished shorts ready to go to editing. Finished and edited my entire novel. Ordered the cover. Got it ready to go to the first reader and ended up with over 50,000 words. Not too shabby considering.

Don't know if I ever want to do another YA/Middle-Grade thing, but I learned a gob by finishing this thing. This thing that popped into my head when both my kiddos were still in school and I was still a homeschool momma and dabbled at this magical idea flickering in the middle of a cornfield. It's finally finished.

Might do a couple more to make it into the ever-popular trifecta series once the love/hate relationship I've had with this project tips more toward the love side of things.

But in my opinion, I don't know of many trilogy runs where the second two are ever as good as the first. But I'm a sucker for firsts...

Watch for the announcement here on the blog or Facebook when the book goes live for purchase through Amazon.

Off to order my orange fountain pen.

* * *

I like my orange pen. That was fun.

I like my novel now, Switch, that was fun, too.

I'm nearly done with the sequel. Yes, I decided on the trifecta because I left Switch open to do so. And because standalone novels rarely stand on their own two feet for a newbie author.

Lesson Learned: Man, remembering how it felt to hand off that draft was amazing. Reminiscing puts fuel on the productivity fire...

43. BLAST FROM THE PAST

As I was digging through thousands of photos for my grandmother's memorial service, I came across these gems. Wow. That can't be me... that little girl in the photo. *My* kids were that small last week.

I chose these for the blog because I've rambled and meandered around some topics here that I found proof of in these pics. Proof that you, dear reader, may not have needed, but now I can say, "See, I really was a unicorn freak and nerd!" And evidently my family enabled me, their only child, in my pursuit of nerd/geek status.

(They evidently stuck with the mixing-bowl-on-top-of-the-head haircuts for quite some time as well...)

Let's unpack these shots bit by bit. This will be fun. At least for me.

Top photo, far left. By the lamp. A Smurf alarm clock. That sucker would wake up Rip Van Winkle from even his deepest dreams, wishing him a Smurfy Day. From the Smurfs I learned that if you wanted to cuss and get away with it, all you had to do was replace any offensive words with the appropriate form of "Smurf." Smurfing. Smurfy. Smurfed. Smurfedy-Smurf-Smurf-all-to-Smurf.

I had the cadence down pat for this—a talent modeled by my father, who Smurfed and Smurfed all the time.

I stopped doing this when I stopped talking out loud to my imaginary friends. Don't know that anyone ever caught me, but boy does it feel good to get *that* off my chest. Confession is good for the Smurfiest of souls.

Next, the pink-maned unicorn, a My Little Pony Moondancer. I only cared for that brand of toy if they sported horns in the middle of their heads. In my other arm is an unbranded (I believe) random plush unicorn. Not in the photo? Many other unbranded plush unicorns.

In my armpit is Rainbow Brite and her pony Starlite. Miss Brite succumbed to an awful fate. I'd stored her in a dresser drawer and found later that a mother mouse had used her hair and chewed off part of her face to make a nest for her babies. The mother, if you could call her that, must've absconded with some weasely rat. We found the stone-stiff babies, hairless and abandoned, still nestled in the yellow yarn strands and plastic nose bits. We tossed out Rainbow and Starlite along with everything else in the drawer because, well, Smurf it!

What you can't tell from the photo is that the paneling in my bedroom was bird-egg blue. And behind the clock were two bookcases, three shelves each painted pink and mounted to the wall. They housed my unicorn collection. Hundreds of figurines all neatly arranged. I'll leave this topic alone, since I've already bemoaned the selling off of this collection, and lest I start Smurfing all over again.

The bottom photo showcases my Strawberry Shortcake Baby. "Squeeze her tummy and she blows you a strawberry-scented kiss," is what the box said. I know because the geek in me looked it up on eBay. This must-have '80s item, new in box, would bring $140. And until I looked it up, I'd forgotten all about the kiss-blowing. Now that my memory's refreshed, I can smell that sweet, artificial berry breeze. Nothing like it in the world (unless you count the scratch-n-sniff stickers the teachers gave out for A+ papers in grade school. Grape was pretty good...).

I looked up the going rates for all the other items in these photos.

If I had left them untouched I could've traded them in for some spiffy fountain pens—ones with platinum nibs and golden ink.

Not in the photo? The Cabbage Patch Kid—homemade with black yarn hair and red apron and the strangest cloth face. I don't remember who made it for me. I do remember that my grandmother, may she rest in peace, told me that Cabbage Patch Kids were being possessed by satanic demons all over the United States and I'd better cover her face up before I went to bed. I never liked that doll... I did like the branded ones, a preemie with a yellow nightgown and a "regular" one in a white outfit with tiny blue flowers. And I remember visiting Babyland General Hospital on a vacation to Georgia. Babies growing right out of cabbage heads all over the place. It really was magnificent.

Next, we have Wicket the Ewok. I'd frequently remove his hood and dress up my Boston Terriers as Star Wars pooches. (I'd also put Strawberry's bloomers and bonnet on my girl dog. She seemed to enjoy it very much.) I think I had wanted Princess Kneesaa, but I didn't specify this and, turns out, Santa isn't a mind reader.

And last but not least, (and I almost missed this bit until I scanned the photo in...) An E.T. Extra Terrestrial T-shirt. I had several E.T. items, but my favorite was a ceramic statue. I remember it being a few inches taller than a water bottle, a full-body likeness of the little alien mounted on a wooden base. I don't remember what happened to it. I do remember crying during the movie when the government agents showed up in their hazmat suits.

I also remember dropping candy trails in the woods, hoping something exciting would happen.

Nothing exciting happened.

At least not that *anyone else* could see.

Lots of exciting things happened in my mind's eye, though, where Ewoks and unicorns trotted gleefully through the forest with me and my Boston pups.

And we'd all meet up with Wonder Woman down by the creekbed...

* * *

Check out the photos in the About the Author section. That little girl of yesteryear would be so proud to know her adult-ish version is still enamored by all things Ewok...

And Little Miss Muse sits in the corner taking credit for all my childhood idiosyncrasies. They were all her idea.

Lesson Learned: Cleaning the attic may afford a trip down memory lane and a nice steak dinner if you're willing to sell your childhood on eBay...

44. FISHING FOR WHALES

The other day, I was shopping for a few odds and ends and picked up something sweet for the hubs. He doesn't care for chocolate*, so I opted for some throw-back Bazooka Joe Bubblegum complete with comic strips. Though, in all fairness, I didn't know that's what I bought, I just saw classic pink bubblegum and grabbed a pack.

When I was a kid (I'm sensing a theme lately...nostalgia is setting in hard these days), I never asked for Bazooka Bubblegum because I enjoyed blowing bubbles or chewing the stuff. I only asked for it because of the comics. And, oh, the disappointment that would set in when I'd unwrap a piece of gum and carefully unfold the comic from around it only to discover I'd already collected that particular strip. They should be more careful when packing these things. Give a variety. How hard could it be?

Now, the new comic strips are not quite like the old ones. Vintage comics offered telescopes or gold-plated pearl rings or two-bladed pocket knives (try giving away one of *those* in a kids' consumable these days). And you had to snail-mail a few hundred comics or so many cents to an actual physical address. I never went through this process with Bazooka. I did mail off for some Cracker Jacks or cereal giveaways. And oh, the anticipation of receiving some fifty-cent item in the mail five (or twelve) weeks later was almost unbearable. It's amazing how one can elevate the importance of something so trivial when one is an eight-year-old.

Now, in our sterile, digital universe, the freebie is available via an online code. Instant access. Which unlocks TV activities and games on their website. No anticipation. Nothing to hold in your hand. But then again, kids these days don't know what they're missing.

I'll stick with the hold-it-in-your-hand mini comics for now. If they ever bring back that gold-plated pearl ring, I'm all in.

Thanks, Bazooka, for bringing back the memories, though.

Back to the comic:

Poor Pesty. Having fun, dreaming, wishing, and drowning some worms. Maybe thinking about being a pirate. Then along comes someone "supportive" to point out the error of his way.

I laughed way too hard at this 28-word story. I even taped it to my office wall.

Why?

It sums up this author/writer business. Brand new, I am. Newbie extreme here in 2019 and not afraid to admit that I know less about what I'm doing than an auditorium full of freshly graduated high school kids.

I'm fishing off the side of a bank. I have no idea what's in the pond. Or if there's anything in the pond. I might be in the wrong pond altogether and the body of water I need is fifty miles away, south by southwest, surrounded by rabid alligators. I don't know.

I'm just having fun. Dreaming, wishing, drowning some words.

Some have said, "You'll never get published" or "The market is flooded" or "Writing fiction is a fool's errand." "Some" defined as those contributing to the general popular opinion out there on the great wide web. "Some" is occasionally defined by the ones a little less "digital" who have this opinion but are afraid to tell me to my face. That's okay. I'm sure they're being supportive, like Bazooka Joe. They surely mean well...

All of them *surely* know what swims in all ponds everywhere because "They" have so much collective experience. Sometimes, I wish the "Somes" and the "Theys" would pack up their fun-smothering opinions and go jump in a pond. Then they would know what's in said pond. First hand, even.

Since I have no idea what I'm doing, I may as well be like Pesty and fish for whales. I don't have anything to lose.

You may as well be like Pesty, too, in whatever endeavor you should want to try.

Dream a little.

Wish a little.

Have fun a lot.

And drown a few worms, words or, as the fortune suggests, try your hand at being a pirate. You don't have anything to lose.

*How does one simply not care for chocolate? I care deeply for chocolate. I especially care about Lindor Truffles and Ghirardelli Dark Chocolate Sea Salt Caramel Squares. I also care that one takes care to place anything Reese's Cup in the freezer for a spell before consuming.

* * *

On the blog, I posted a photo of the little comic. I'll sum it up, as posting a photo here may land me in deep copyright infringement territory:

Pesty is fishing. Bazooka asks him what he's fishing for. Pesty replies "Whales."

Bazooka points out there are no whales in the pond.

Pesty suggests there are no fish in the pond either, so he may as well fish for whales.

Now, go buy some Bazooka Joe and support the nostalgia. And if you don't like it, save it (probably lasts longer than McDonald's fries or a Twinkie) and shove it into your kids' stockings at Christmas. Tell them 'bout the good ol' days!

Lesson Learned: Shut out the noise and dream big. Bigger even.

45. UNEXAMINED ASSUMPTIONS—#CHARACTERBUILDING

In another lifetime, I had a supervisor that told me a story. Where she got it, I don't know. It's one of those stories that's "out there" somewhere, but it's not mine and it wasn't hers. I found articles that reference the tale including *Snopes* and *Psychology Today*, but these sources don't seem to know where it originated, either.

I'll attribute it appropriately if I can find the original author. This line serves as my disclaimer: It's not mine and it's likely changed drastically from the original telling... whenever that might have been.

Here it is in a nutshell:

A young girl watches her mother bake a pot roast. The mother preps the meat with spices, and before she twines it, she cuts the ends off the roast and tosses them in the garbage. Now, these ends weren't full of fat and gristle. There is good, edible meat in the wasted portions.

"Why do you do that? Cut the ends off like that?"

The mom continues spicing and arranging the meat in the roasting pan and surrounds it with carrots and potatoes. "It's how you do it. My mom did it this way."

"But why?"

The mother pauses, wiping her hands on her apron. "I don't know. Go call your grandmother." She slides the roast into the oven and leaves the room.

The girl calls Grandma. "Why do you and Mom cut the ends off your pot roast before you put it in the oven? Isn't that wasteful?"

The grandmother pauses for a moment before answering. "Well, I don't know why your mother does it, but my roasting pan is small and the roast won't fit if I don't cut off the ends."

Or so the tale goes, and some versions have the too-small-pan spanning more than a couple of generations. It's a classic, "We've always done it this way" example. An act of necessity for one poor cook unable to afford an appropriately sized pan decades ago is passed down from mother to daughter until someone dares ask "But why?"

I've been thinking and studying a lot about characterization. How to make my imaginary friends come to life on the page. How to avoid cliched "paper people" and create a human that stays in your head for a while. I started brainstorming ways to make my characters come alive. Some of those ways lend themselves nicely to blog posts. Because if we really think about it, the methods of developing fictional characters aren't that different from developing our own character. (Except I haven't figured out how to give myself super powers yet.)

We connect with fictional characters when we see bits of ourselves in them (be they the protagonist, the misunderstood side-kick, or *gasp* the antagonist). We've experienced something similar. We believe something similar. We've felt what they feel. We rationalize and make excuses like they do... the list goes on.

(Whether we *like* those bits or not is altogether a different topic. See next week's post...)

The next character I create will go through this. Have his world turned upside down because what he's believed for generations—and what his family had believed—is challenged. It's not a new idea by any length, but it does open unique story opportunities. Even if the story isn't all about the "But why?", adding that bit in there deepens character's motives and makes him relatable.

Most of us have had our systems challenged. And I don't know anyone who enjoys this experience—it drives us out of our comfort zones.

And if you don't know what this feels like, spend the day with a four-year-old. Or a teenager. Your motives and methods for everything you say and do will come under scrutiny.

How many of our actions, intentional or habit/reflex, are based on unexamined assumptions?

Because someone taught us how to do something a certain way and now that action is engrained?

Because someone told us something and we believe it and adopt it as truth without question?

Because, well, maybe we don't even know why we do things until we stop and ask the words (or until a four/fourteen-year-old asks the words), "But why?"

And if you do stop and ask, or it's demanded of you to give an appropriate answer to a child, and your answer is "just because" or "that's the way I've always done it," maybe it's time to examine your assumptions—whether they be behaviors or beliefs.

What is at my character's foundation that makes him who he is? What's at your foundation that makes you who you are? Why do we do what we do?

What's my foundation?

And is that foundation built of sand? Stone?

Or are those "foundational assumptions" simply bubbles filled with the hot air of those "wise ones" who've gone before and "ain't never did it no differnt..."

* * *

This one is a lesson unto itself. I'm finding the older my kids get, the more my base of beliefs are questioned—by them and by myself.

Lesson Learned: Frequently visit your belief system. Don't be afraid to tweak or altogether change if you're found in the wrong—even though you won't like it.

46. LET THEM LIE — #CHARACTERBUILDING

Last week, I meandered through a concept to deepen character development, the one where the poor schmuck's always done something a certain way based on a faulty or misguided assumption (and aren't we all poor schmucks at one point or another in our lives?).

This week, after taking some time to write a few shorts while waiting on book edits, I came across the stock photo above and found it massively appropriate for the topic.

We all deal with lies and—delusions of grandeur—every single day.

We lie. To those we love. To those we don't. And we justify it. You know, even the little stuff, like when your significant other or friend asks if you like their new haircut. Or the dinner they cooked. Or their piece of art. Lie and make them smile, or tell the blatant truth and deal with the pouting for the rest of the day.

Or, if we're skilled, we can sidestep the direct question by offering an indirect response: "Do *you* like your haircut/dinner/art? Well, that's all that matters. Wanna go to the movies?"

Sometimes that diversion works. Sometimes not, if the person doing the asking is equally as skilled.

We are lied to. By those who love us (see the above paragraph) and by those who don't (mainstream media, anyone?).

We lie to ourselves—this one may fall into the 'delusion' category. We have this image in our heads of who/what we are and then we ask or expect others to aid us in that delusion instead of being honest and looking at cold hard facts—about how we could make forward, positive change if we'd get our heads out of our derrieres.

Some of the epic lies/delusions we allow to take root in our heads: "I'm okay, I got this." "He/she must really love me because they (fill in the blank here with some ridiculous act of selfishness on the part of the he/she)." "If I only had X, my life would be grand." And on and on.

All based on feelings, not facts.

And some of us have that little "helper"—be he real or imaginary —who is all too eager to hand us our king's scepter and keep us in la-la-land dancing a jig with our delusions and lies.

My grandmother, spunk she was, was once asked by a sweet young lady that age-old question with no good outcome—"Do these pants make me look fat?"

And Grandma prided herself on honesty—at least with others when she could one-up them; with herself, she was the Queen of Denial—so she told the girl the pants did, in fact, make her look fat.

I asked dearest grandmother if she thought her response was a little cruel. Grandma shrugged and said, "If she didn't want to know, she shouldn't have asked. And I think she needed to know."

Well, alright then.

So, if you're ever in the mood to fancy yourself an author (a delusion I've entertained a few times over the last few years) or you're forced by a wicked English teacher into some piece of creative writing, let your characters lie and be lied to.

And especially let them lie to themselves. That makes them ultimately relatable. Because even though we may read to escape our reality, we still connect with those imaginary people on the page when they act just like us. And think just like us. Even if we'd never admit it to anyone else.

Watching the characters realize the errors in their thought processes, watching their delusions be illuminated, and watching them overcome those hurdles gives the rest of us poor schmucks a little hope.

Hope from imaginary characters with imaginary problems.

Sometimes fictional characters will cause us to take a good look at ourselves in the mirror and ask what we could do to change our own belief system. To face reality. To stop lying...

But be careful who you ask. Don't ask yourself—you'll just feed your psyche another line of bull. And on the other end of the spectrum are those brutally honest octogenarians—so attempt that audience only if you're thick-skinned.

And if you're the one-in-a-billion who doesn't suffer from delusions of even the smallest grandeur, congratulations! Hold on a minute...

I'll be right back with your scepter.

* * *

The photo for this post was of a standard housecat looking in the mirror and seeing himself as crowned king, complete with robe and scepter.

I've told myself no fewer than three lies today:

Lie 1: I'll write when I get home from taking yet another near-octogenarian to the doctor.

Truth: I'll be brain damaged at the end of that doc appt. No writing will happen.

Lie 2: I'm eating healthy all day.

Truth: Let's not let those unhealthy leftovers go to waste.

Lie 3: I'll eat healthy tomorrow.

Truth: There are still more borderline unhealthy "pandemic stock-up foods" in the pantry.

We shouldn't let that go to waist... Wait a minute. Waste. Waste is what I meant.

But, truth be told, *waist* is what will happen.

Lesson Learned: I'm still lying to myself about stuff. I need to knock that crap off.

47. 21 SHORTS!

It's done! B. A. Paul's first anthology consisting of only my twisted imagination.

Check it out here for the paperback and here for the e-book. (As of today, the e-book and print versions haven't 'synced up' on Amazon's pages yet. When that happens, I'll post a single, updated link.)

If you have Kindle Unlimited, you can read the e-book for free—even if you don't own a Kindle. You can download the Kindle reading app for any device for free, as well.

Some of the shorts in 21 Stories have appeared here on the blog. Some haven't yet, and, with Amazon's exclusivity policies, may not appear here for quite some time.

These stories helped break loose my rusty creative gears and got me writing again. They were part of the challenge I did a couple summers back—thirty shorts in thirty days.

What a ride that was.

And what a ride this first physical book was! Talk about picky tech issues. Margins, gutters, and spines! Oh, My!

But I think I like the result. Something I made that can be held in my hands and cuddled. Yeah, I know. I had babies. But they needed lots of food and clothes and they'd throw up and cry and stuff along the way. And I loved my babies big. Still do.

But they grew up and stuff, so...

I got cats. But they need food and toys and they throw up and cry sometimes. And I like my cats. I do.

But they have sharp claws and stuff, so...

I created this. This nice, clean baby just needs to be read. No feeding required. No blood-drawing piggie toes.

Now I'm on a push to get my first middle-grade novel, *Switch*, into publication. Almost there [insert giddy little jump and squeal here], so watch the blog and Facebook for more on that.

And watch the blog for a sneak peek snippet of the novel coming soon...

* * *

Okaaaayyy...

So this book, a bundle of a hodge podge of shorts in multiple (read that as WAAAAAY tooo many) genres as my effort to do something with 21 shorts rattling around in my laptop with no third-party publication sales and no way for readers to see them.

Problems? Readers who enjoy my "sweet" stories don't necessarily care for my twisted horror ones.

Readers who prefer those twisted bits of grit, don't always connect with the stories that feel like the Hallmark Movie Channel writers took their coffee break in my office.

So, I erred. Newbie error, but an error nonetheless. And by the time *Life Along the Way* goes to publication, *21 Short Stories: Momentary Escapes from the Mundane* will have been taken down from Amazon and only exist on my personal bookshelf to remind me not to do that again.

I now have enough shorts in each genre to repackage them into appropriately themed/genre-specific collections that you can find them on the blog.

Lesson Learned: There are always more lessons to learn and relearn. Publishing indie requires trying, failing, and then trying again with those lessons. And more margins, gutters, and spines. Oh, My!

48. IN MEMORY (MEMORIAL DAY)

I've been a bit nostalgic of late. Caring for Grandma and going through her belongings and photos and listening to tales of family has a lot to do with it.

So does this date.

Memorial Day.

I came across many photos of my uncle and grandfather in their service uniforms. And I remember the map that Grandma hung on the wall to track my uncle's whereabouts while he was in the Air Force. And watching the news reports and them wondering where their son might be in the midst of the fighting.

It's a humbling memory when one considers that countless families across The States are doing the exact same thing as I write this.

I'm so incredibly grateful for my freedoms. Freedoms I spent nothing to gain, just having the divine providence or sheer dumb luck to be born on this side of the ocean and on this piece of land under a flag of red, white, and blue. I am well and truly blessed in these United States of America.

Here in Indiana where I have the freedom to worship how I choose, vote how I see fit, and dream.

Here in the Midwest where I can write fiction and blog posts and put them out for the world to read. Where, when the desire strikes me, I can abandon such activities and without fear for my life get in my vehicle, drive down the road, and watch a movie or go to a concert as a result of someone else taking advantage of *their* freedom to sit in an office or under an oak tree and make up dialogue lines and music scores and plots—holey or completely filled in—and put them out in some form for me to see.

I can visit a library and read others' views and experiences—real or made up—and not fear imprisonment.

Freedom of speech. Freedom to move about. Freedom of thought.

What a wonderful concept.

And thank you to all who've served and are serving. Thank you for being willing to put your lives on the line, your families on hold, and give up dreams of your own to serve our great country.

And a special prayer of gratitude goes out for those who've lost loved ones, sons, daughters, husbands, and friends to the fight for our freedoms.

You are remembered.

You are appreciated.

Thank you.

* * *

This one posted on the actual date of Memorial Day 2019. I titled it the same as the one in remembrance of Grandma, then, after it went live, realized what I'd done.

Lesson Learned: Make—and keep up with—an inventory of titles. And number the dumb things, so when projects like this come along, you'll know when you've hit another milestone to be thankful for.

49. TOP TEN TECHY PEEVES

This adventure of book publishing has my hair falling out, hives protruding from places I didn't know they could protrude from, and cats running scared from my office when sanctification is lost and the projectiles start flying.

Not the *writing* of the stuff. The writing is grand fun.

But the learning curve of picky margins, bleed edges, gutters, and drop caps that float five inches above first paragraphs, those are another matter—and all on a laptop that had wanted to give up the ghost back in September. I limped it along, but probably would have saved a large slice of sanity had I broken down and gotten a new one months ago.

10. Restart. Restarting the computer for it to recognize some installation.

9. Ghost installations. I didn't think I installed anything to "help" me do something better?!!???...

8. By the way, why didn't my antivirus software stop #9 to begin with?

7. Updates. Thanks Word, for requiring me to sign in to my account all of the sudden. To type a simple document. I don't

remember my password. And since you moved that one button two micro-centimeters to the left, now I miss-click.

6. "An account already exists with his email. Select Reset Password and we'll email you a link to reset your password."

5. Emailed link from #6 says I can't use an old password. The same @*$@$ password I just used to try to access the account to begin with. I guess I did remember.

4. Cat, recovered from her earlier fright, walked across the keyboard. Caps lock was on.

3. Laptop decides it needs to run a diagnostic on itself all by itself when I'm trying to upload a 258-page document to Amazon. Thanks. For slowing the process down even further because...

2. Glitchy internet.

1. Updating one tiny piece of tech to handle higher internet speeds, then every other piece of tech hooked to that one decides to punk out.

And AGAIN WITH THE PASSWORDS!!!!!!

On the upside, everything in the house has been replaced and — knock wood, throw salt, and say prayers—our internet is working fine. For now.

Until...Bonus Peeve!!

Power outage.

* * *

I remember this day. Very well.

And that day had a sister come to visit a few months ago. Very frustrating when your "day job" and your "dream hobby" rely on everything to work in synchronicity. Then enter husband who can't access Netflix and kid who can't do school or *gasp* game.

Poor cats.

Lesson Learned: Keep track of the passwords, for crying out loud. And no...
You WON'T remember what you changed it to.

50. PSYCH! JK, LOL

Warning: This blog contains spoilers for *Lost, The Sixth Sense, Star Wars, Poms*, and *Avengers Infinity War* and *End Game*. You've been told.

Last week I hit on tech peeves. This week, I'm still on a rant.

About one of the biggest cheats in fiction.

Because I've been reading lots of short stories. From all kinds of authors in all kinds of genres. Just to study the form and to prepare for an upcoming workshop I'll be doing in November. Some of them are amazing.

And some of them cheated.

In one story, a St. Bernard—never before mentioned or alluded to in the slightest—walks up and has just what the main character needs to survive hanging from his neck. Really?

Here's how it happens. At least I think this is how it happens: A writer (or group of writers) creates his way into a corner—which isn't bad, it makes for excellent conflict: How will the characters solve the dilemma? How will it all end?

The writer doesn't know how it all ends. Or the series is canceled and everyone gets in a hurry. Or it was time for dinner or a bathroom break and then...

Then he does the epic, "Oh, the previous story of which you've spent hours (reading/watching/listening to) was actually all in a character's head. It was all a dream!" Psych!

Or the writers drop in a coincidental piece of magic or weapon or friendly neighbor that we've not met to save the day.

Or *everyone* turns out special, even though we've been told only special people are special. (The Jedi? Anyone can be a Jedi? Come on.)

And then the piece is marketed to us as clever storytelling.

Don't cheat, folks. Just don't.

If your main character—or the entire cast of characters—is asleep, hallucinating, going to die, or going to be rescued by some cosmic power, SET IT UP IN THE OPENING! Don't try to psych us out. Your audience isn't that addle-brained.

I was (still am) a big *LOST* fan. I fell in love with the characters and their backstories. But twenty minutes into the pilot I remember thinking, "This better not be a they-were-all-dead-or-dreaming kind of thing."

Hurley, bless his heart, even called it when his imaginary friend takes him to the cliff's edge and tells him to jump. Turns out, if Hurley had jumped, nothing (else) bad would've happened, because, PSYCH! They were all already dead. But if this was the setup for the ending, it was too far into the series to be accepted (episode 43). Because no fan at that point wanted to believe the characters were all dead or dreaming. We're okay with Hurley being off, given his lottery curse, but he can't be dead.

By episode 43 (likely far before), fans were already invested. IN LIVING PEOPLE WITH A PLAUSIBLE OUTCOME.

I felt ripped off. Followed these people for 121 episodes and they were dead?

The Sixth Sense did it right with their already-dead main guy. Nicely set up, just enough clues that when you go back and watch the thing again, you see what you missed the first time through.

My mother wanted to see *Poms* for Mother's Day. Not my preferred movie genre, and, quite frankly, after her last pick (the title of which I'll keep to myself because I still can't believe I sat through *that* particular film), I was more than a little leery of the thing.

But right from the opening, you know, or at least are presented with the possibility, that Diane Keaton's character is in some sort of life-and-death battle. She's having an estate sale for herself, for crying out loud. And watching commercials for cremation options.

The writers did a good job of setting up the ending. And, even though it wasn't something I'd go see on my own, I'm glad I went. Not a bad story at all.

End Game also did it right. I'm not a comic book reader, so I've trusted the big screen script writers to navigate me through the world of all things superhero.

And Marvel is excellent at this. And we trust them even if we watched half of the characters we love disintegrate to ash before our eyes.

We already know Thanos wants to purify the universe. Dr. Strange already told us there's only one way it can end, and we believe him, honest sorcerer that he is. We already know about the magic of the stones and finger snaps and time travel. Because the Marvel writers did an excellent job of setting all of this up. They didn't pull the "Oh, here's a bit of power you didn't previously know about, and this is just how it goes. And by the way, this extra character is going to show up out of nowhere to save the day." We already know the extra character from the previous two movies (no matter what you think of Carol, the writers *did* tell us about her and established her into the Avengers' world).

So, help me out if you notice I've written something with a poor set-up and less-than-satisfying ending in the realm of hallucinations, dreams, and magical save-the-days. I'd rather write about a ghost-whispering superhero cheerleader than a St. Bernard that comes out of nowhere to save an already-dead character.

* * *

If any of you have a coincidental piece of magic or weaponry or friendly neighbor to save the day, send them my way. Real life needs a few of these "coincidences."

Lesson Learned: Think it through. If it can't be thought through, think differently. Just don't cheat.

51. BETA READERS

I'd written this a long while back as a journal entry (like four years ago) and came across it when I was cleaning out files and backing up laptops. I thought it was hilarious. Brought back memories. And that flash fiction piece? It really was a flop. It has major issues and needs reworked, but wow.

My dear sweet hubby has now read nearly everything I've written (minus the blogs, somehow that's not his thing), and I owe him my undying gratitude (and a lot less attitude) for his support and encouragement.

And did I learn a lesson since four years ago. Unfinished pieces stay in the office from start to finish. Only then do other eyes get to see...

The ALL CAPS bits are where I've reflected on that hot-tempered day.

I wrote my first flash fiction story. My heart pounded as I typed the words. Very carefully chosen words written under a time constraint (we were getting ready to be late for something) and adrenaline. It's a count-down type story, with tension building in each time increment, and a smoothly wicked villainess. (I STILL THINK SHE'S SMOOTHLY WICKED. I'LL USE HER SOMEWHERE...) I just didn't have the ending nailed down. I printed what I had so far, two pages, double spaced. I only needed one more "time increment" and then it would be done. I printed it to see where I could cut words and consolidate language to make it crisp and clean.

I let my hubby read it before I did anything to it. I sat in eager anticipation as he read through the first page. His face never changed. His pupils didn't dilate. His leg didn't bob up and down in anticipation. He just read it calmly.

"It's not finished."

"I told you it was rough and it wasn't finished. But what do you think so far?"

"I don't know because you didn't finish it."

"But *so far*, what do you think?"

I can usually read him like a book, but he gave me no clues whatsoever. "I think you should finish it." (HE WAS RIGHT.)

I snatched the copy away from him and sulked back to my computer. The flash fiction sits taunting me from on top of the novel I've printed out (THE *SWITCH* NOVEL THAT IS NOW FINISHED —YAY!!!) because I've stalled. Which is on top of a homeschool guide waiting for more lesson plan development (I CAN'T REMEMBER WHAT THIS EVEN IS. I'VE SLEPT A FEW NIGHTS SINCE THE HOMESCHOOLING DAYS). Which is on top of the notebook filled with ideas for publishing. Which is on top of the desk that needs to be cleaned. Which is on top of the floor that needs to be mopped, and well, you get the picture. (NO PROGRESS ON CLEANING DESKS OR MOPPING FLOORS. I NEED A MAID.)

And now the bubble of excitement I had about the countdown with the villain has now popped.

What I learned from this:

Never watch a beta reader read your material. It's too emotionally draining. And looking for micro expressions of approval is exhausting. (NOW I JUST PRINT THE STUFF OUT AND LEAVE IT ON THE BREAKFAST TABLE. SOMETIMES I EVEN FORGET WHAT I GAVE HIM TO READ.)

Never try to make a beta reader out of someone who *only* ever reads the Bible and the sports page. (HE'S MAKING GRAND PROGRESS)

Let the husband be a husband. Not an editor. At least my husband. If your husband is an actual editor, this may work well for you. (HE'S PRETTY GOOD AT NABBING TYPOS HERE AND THERE. I STILL NEED A COPY EDITOR—AND A MAID.)

Check the emotions at the door before handing over a manuscript to be test-read. Deal in the facts and just the facts.

Finish the story first. No one has time to read something twice.

It may be a very good idea to have someone you don't know well (or at least doesn't share a roof with you) be the beta reader.

I love my dear hubby and he will always be my first beta reader. But he doesn't get to read any more of my stuff. Ever. I won't even write anything in his next birthday card.

I'll let Hallmark handle it.

(I WAS *VERY* ANGRY AT HIM, AND THIS WAS MY TEMPER TANTRUM. I'M NOT ANGRY ANYMORE, HE WAS RIGHT, AFTER ALL.

AND I DO LET HIM READ MY STUFF.

I ALSO WRITE A LITTLE IN HIS BIRTHDAY CARDS...)

* * *

So this was fun. An annotated blurb on an already-annotated post. Ditto the lessons learned.

Lesson Learned: Ditto, again.

52. THE LAW OF UNINTENDED CONSEQUENCES

Sometimes, even with the best of intentions, things don't go as planned.

Macquarie Island is a tiny bit of land off the coast of New Zealand. Here's its story in a nutshell:

Macquarie Island's untouched breeding grounds for penguins and seals draws the attention of sailors.

The sailors drool and set their greedy "wanters" into high gear and hunt the creatures for blubber and fur to near extinction.

During these hunts, rats from their ships invaded the island.

Rats and mice flourish due to lack of predators, endangering human food sources.

Humans introduce cats to take care of the rats and bring rapidly breeding rabbits to the island for a food source for humans. And the cats and bunnies breed like, well, rabbits.

The cats eat rats and rabbits, but then the hungry felines turn to the sea birds, consuming the fine feathered foul at a rate of 60,000 per year, disrupting the ecosystem even further.

Humans try to reduce the number of cats to save the birds.

The bunnies, left to their happy ways without predators to keep them in check, gobble up nearly half of the island's vegetation—

which is a bigger problem than if everyone would've left the original stowaway rats to do their thing to begin with.

So, from the early 1800s until now, man caused one huge mess. And we can't figure out how to clean it up without causing further unintended consequences.

A plus B equals C.

Sometimes.

Every solution to the island's problem seemed logical at the time. But "C" can't always be predicted or found. (Neither can the values for X and Y in most high school classrooms...)

All of this makes for great fiction writing. This is where the twists and turns come into play. This is where we see our characters reveal themselves—when things don't go their way, how will they respond? And then the author/writer sends that character through another equation.

Will A plus B equal C this time, or will there be another elephant up a tree somewhere?

The thing about consequences? They fan out and drift like aerosol from a spray can. You never know how far the consequences of one simple choice will spread.

People are unpredictable. Our planet is unpredictable (even though we think we've got Mother Nature all figured out). Fiction worlds can be erratically unpredictable (as long as the author doesn't cheat—see the post Psych! in the drop-down menu).

How much worse can it possibly get?

The answer in fiction? A lot worse. Think of "The Old Lady Who Swallowed a Fly." She died, of course.

The answer in real life? Even worse than that... Think Hurricane Katrina. One solution led to a thousand other problems.

In fiction? Consequences are fun to play around with and brainstorm outcomes. Authors love all those "elephants up a tree" scenes. Picking one of a dozen things that could happen and turning it into a twist or turn.

In real life? Well, real life doesn't need *our* help making stuff up—it's got the market cornered.

* * *

Note: The photo for this blog was an illustration of an elephant up a tree staring across a vast desert, thus the reference. I now have this image as my laptop background.

In epic fashion, the year 2020 and all of its issues is another firm example of this law. All of our fixing, tweaking, halting, regulating, etc. has had a massive amount of unintended consequences—the totality of them won't be known for decades to come.

Lesson Learned: Try to keep the elephants up trees in the fiction and out of the real-world scenarios. If you can...

53. TIME WARPS

There's a funny thing about calendars and time blocks and schedules and deadlines.

I like deadlines. They're black-and-white numbers that don't lie. Something due in three days? I have 72 hours. Easy.

Something due in five minutes?

I have one minute to breathe and four to get it done.

Easy.

Now, I've never been a procrastinator where work is concerned, far from it—unless it's housework. In fact, I usually have the opposite problem. Deadline for a project three months out? Start it as soon as the idea strikes (which usually means I'm starting without all the needed facts and then proceed to get hours into something only to find out that I'm on the wrong track).

But lately, because of life and such. You know, life? Tires and fires and drama and trauma. Deadlines that linger further out are whispering evil notions to me. Something due in a week? Wait five days. Or six. Or six-and-a-half. No worries. You'll get it done.

Still easy math.

I took an afternoon not too long ago and inked in (not pencil, ink) writing time on my calendar, AKA my brain on paper. It's a spiral-bound book with plenty of room for long to-do lists, because I like those, too. Black-and-white, get-it-done-and-move-on boxes to check. It makes me feel productive. And this paper calendar is often my only tether to reality and the passing of time. What square am I in today? What's the number of the square? Do I put on dress clothes or my work uniform of T-shirt and jeans?

When Grandma passed away, I had an odd sensation of missing time altogether amid grief and her end-of-life tasks. I remember seeing Valentine's Day supplies in the front of Walmart on clearance and thinking, "Wait, we haven't done Valentine's Day yet." The same sensation happened again with St. Patrick's Day and then again with Easter, but not quite so intense.

But anyway, I don't know what I was thinking—spending an afternoon scheduling writing. It seemed like a good idea at the time. It also seemed a good idea to use red ink to delineate writing tasks from household duties and my "real job" tasks. But then, well, life. Good life and bad life and crazy life. And then all those little red writing reminders and lists in my calendar became laughable suggestions and now I'm scrambling to even get the very basics of creativity under control.

A couple of years ago I did one short story a day. Midnight deadline. Daily. For thirty days. Didn't miss one deadline.

Now, I'm shooting for one short a week, a blog a week and several thousand words on my work-in-progress. Which is overall much less writing than that intense daily challenge was.

And funny how something that only took a few hours every day now takes seven times more hours of thought and fiddling. Because I have seven days to think and fiddle with it.

The activity is stretching to fill the amount of time in the deadline.

Or maybe it's that life has poked a hole in my clock and the seconds are leaking out like coffee from a micro-crack in a Styrofoam cup.

I tried to psych myself out, too. Give the tasks a daily deadline.

Try to get ahead. Nope. Not working.

Especially with the housework.

So, because I evidently love punishing myself with self-inflicted time constraints, I'm about to schedule a time to schedule more time to get more writing done—on schedule.

After I white out the previous red marks.

Break the tasks up into bite-sized chunks. Draw little boxes next to each item to check off when complete. Seven days in a week. Seven opportunities to do something I love, if only for a few small ticks of time per day.

Easy.

But this time I'll schedule it all in pencil...

* * *

One of the early "pandemic" memes that circulated on Facebook was about how the most useless purchase of 2020 was a 2020 calendar. I was quite disappointed. I bought a nice purple calendar, spiral bound with those big beautiful boxes and vowed 2020 to be the year of schedules and rhythm and "control." Hahahahaha.

Lesson Learned: I ain't in control of anything that can be put on a calendar and then marked off. There's no such thing as control.

54. THE NAME GAME

I can't keep names straight to save my life. Those belonging to real people nor the imaginary folks running around in my rough drafts.

Someone comes up to me and introduces themselves or a friend. I've lost their name in 3.2 seconds. And it's not that I don't care. I just can't seem to hold onto that bit of information until I'm exposed to it more than once. Until I experience a memory or an event with that person.

But after a brief encounter? Man, don't quiz me on it.

And writing short stories and secondary characters in larger works is even more of a challenge. Because I've never shaken these folks' hands or had lunch with them (although I do have conversations with them in my head while having lunch with real people when the topic drifts to weather or mowing grass).

I can't tell you how many times I've had to scroll backward through the draft for a name of a character so I could complete a scene or a bit of dialogue.

I've taken to writing down every name and a little reminder of who they are in the story on a legal pad next to my laptop.

But it doesn't end there.

I also do a "Search and Replace" on my word processor. Because as sure as I've said Angie is the waitress, that waitress is called Angela, Angelique, Annie or Angel. So I search for "An" and see where Little Miss Muse left name bombs for me to clean up.

Evidently, she's not too interested in names, either. She's only interested in the creativity of what this body did or where that body went. No names. Names aren't all that important to the story, or so she believes. And she's poisoning my real-life name-remembering ability.

Or maybe this comes from years of working at home and my clients are named with company numbers for anonymity. And because there are no faces to put with these clients. I've never met them in person, either, to my knowledge. It's the nature of my work.

On really stressful days, sometimes I call my husband "Spencer." That's the dog. *Was* the dog. Spencer has been gone a while now. So that's always awkward.

Sometimes I try looking around my office to grab a first name quickly off the spine of a book or a printout laying around. And in those moments, everyone's name is James or Nora. And I've used those already.

I'm trying to avoid using the same name over and over, because if those short stories ever become a series, there'd be massive confusion for the readers.

And I'm massively confused enough already for all of us.

When I name a batch of characters for a new story, I tend to lean toward a few standards. Matt, Maranda, Marie. Not sure why. I know a Maranda, Matt and several Maries. But my characters are not based on these real-life people.

My cat's middle name is Marie. And the three little rescue kittens I had to name so we could stop saying "This one and that one and the other." So out came Minnie, Moose, and Mable. All "Ms".

Don't know what the "M" thing is about.

And dear hubs is concerned that I named the cats. I called him Spencer and said it would be okay.

I digress...

To try to remedy this, I bought a baby name book, boasting over

25,000 names with the plan to cross off the names as I use them. Problem is, 24,598 of the names are foreign, and my characters aren't. Mataniah. Mudiwa. Mehtar.

See what I mean?

Sometimes I hear a name out in public or scrolling on the credits of something I watch. I think, "Wow, that'd be a great first name if paired with that other person's last name. And it's so cool I know I won't forget it, so I don't need to write it down."

Then I forget it.

I'm also horrible at actor names, musicians, and street names. That last one causes some problems. Especially when the road name is a number. Or a direction word.

So if you see me wandering in the middle of nowhere because my GPS is out, I won't know what road I'm on, and I probably won't know which road I need.

I'll gladly accept your help.

I'll remember your kindness. My gratefulness will be genuine.

But I'll likely struggle to remember your name.

And if I do remember it and it doesn't start with "M," it'll be the name of my next character.

* * *

I had a list of names that I did remember to write down. And now I've used all of them and need more. The baby name book still helps, but man, sorting out the nationalities is a bit of a chore—if I can't pronounce it in my head, my readers will likely stumble too.

Lesson Learned: Baby name books, name generators, and more movie credit scrolling is in my future.

55. HAPPY LITTLE ACCIDENTS

So...going to Vegas in seven months!

Not because it's Vegas. Vegas as a stopping point to pick up a rental car and drive to the Big Dam and down to the Canyon seems like a good fit. Vegas the town seems loud and large and with a few too many humans. And for this introvert, that in and of itself will be a comfort zone thing.

I'm going there because it's where the training and the networking will take place for a short story anthology workshop. Details on that to come later.

But, to shake loose some of the short-story-form cobwebs since writing Switch and learning the new techy stuff of software and platforms, I decided to write some short fiction pieces to writing prompts. Because that's what the Anthology Workshop will require: writing fiction pieces that hopefully fit an editor/curator's idea for inclusion in a unified book. Like Future Visions: This anthology is all futuristic Sci-Fi shorts. The only difference is, I didn't write my story for FV to a prompt. It was already written. I submitted it because the theme fit, not because I was told to write a certain thing.

Writing to prompts is a whole 'nother critter. And these are simply prompts with a wide word count range 2K-10K, no genre limitations, no character limitations. Just write it.

Some of the prompts have been awfully vague: May Day. Mission Critical. Pink Hat.

Oh, my.

But, from those prompts came stories I would've never explored.

May Day I turned into Mae Dae, a story about a young girl about to age out of the foster system and her views on the world in the midst of bullying. A one-and-done type of story.

The other two became happy little accidents.

Like a Bob Ross thing: Oh, you meant for that story to go that realistic direction? That's okay. Throw an alien in it and no one will ever know how far it drifted from the original plan. Conrad and Coral, other-worldly beings on a mission, are born.

Or hey, now that you *want* the story to be sci-fi or magical, let's set the thing in a real-life scenario and make it a cozy little mystery. Zane, the ex-Denver homicide detective turned zoo security guard, materializes.

And Conrad and Zane will become short serials. I have three such short story series now. Three! Happy little oopsies. I'll release the singles, then compile them into a full-length book when I have enough material to warrant that:

The Recruitment Saga: Future fantasy dystopia. For when I need to let out the darker magical and mystical urges.

Detective Zane: Broken-hearted guy helping broken-hearted critters. For when I feel like throwing someone in jail. Real jail.

Conrad and Coral: Intergalactic crime-solving aliens stationed on Earth. For when I want to have just plain fun and anything goes. Because, well, aliens in sub-par bioidentical suits!

And the sequel to Switch is moving along just fine. Sketched the loose outline (loose enough for Little Miss Muse to wriggle around and still have fun, but for my left brain not to go into cardiac arrest over plot holes—no throwing aliens into this one!) And the first ten chapters are in rough draft form! Yay!

I'm off to write to another prompt. I want this one to be dark and creepy, so Little Miss Muse will most probably turn her nose up at my left-brained plans and create a sweet little love story with a happily ever after.

Who knows? Maybe she's got another happy little accident up her sleeve.

* * *

I missed announcing this, but those "prompts" are from another short story challenge put out by Dean Wesley Smith (links in the back of the book to his web page and WMG publishing. Unsure how long he'll offer this unique opportunity). For this, it's one short a week for a whole year. If you hit with no misses, you get gobs and gobs of training in one form or another. I completed this challenge in April of 2020. Thirty in thirty days was intense. 52 in 52 was equally so, but for a whole different set of reasons.

Lesson Learned: It's hard to split focus between that many shorts and the longer novel. Other authors may have been able to do it. I need to focus on one or the other. Little Miss Muse is ADHD and may like to think she can get me to skip around, buuuut, not so much.

56. PAIN POINTS

You know those claims on products? Those ear-ticklers that promise to ease our pain points?

Easy to use! Simply...

A breeze to install! Just...

Quick and painless! First...

Never (fill in the blank here with some hated feeling/task/expenditure) again!

And on and on the sales language goes. And I'm a sucker for sales language.

In fact, I think I may have come about this flaw through genetics. Four generations strong, actually. Buying into absurd advertising promises because we like a quick fix to whatever ails us at the moment.

QVC, HSN, and those "Order now and we'll double your offer" television commercial ads love my gang.

Well, at least others in my family. I have a slightly different addiction.

For one lady, it was anything colon cleansing. Sorry for all my visual readers out there, but once you hit 80 years old, bathroom habits evidently become of critical importance.

Or anything that would help her sleep. Pillows. Some essential oil concoction. White noise machines.

For another lady, it's spinning mops and cleaning supplies.

Another goes for ageless-ness products and clothing.

For another guy it's any gadget or gizmo promising to make life comfortable—whatever comfortable is defined as in the moment. Ergonomic mouse. Back support brace. Compression socks.

But do they really work? Really, really?

Some things do—a little bit. Some things not at all because we "didn't give it long enough." Or didn't follow it up with "super colon cleanse step 45."

My hang-up?

Online courses.

Learn THIS and you can do THAT with ease.

Follow this method and you can construct that product in your sleep.

What (some big name) did to successfully (some dream of mine) in just (an unrealistically small number) days.

But does this advice really pan out?

Some does. Some doesn't.

I've learned to hone my e-learning spending. And I do much, much research on the so-called "experts." If they haven't been in the indie publishing industry at least as long as the first Kindle screen lit up, and if they have no proven record of sales success continually since then, I move on.

Lately, I'm studying all things publishing platforms. And it really does help having someone screenshot what the next step is. It can be a lot to navigate.

And I gladly hand over a few dollars for the pro to show me rather than spend countless priceless hours struggling with rejection emails:

Sorry, your content didn't post because...

Install the latest version of (fill in the blank with software I didn't know existed) to continue.

Unfortunately, you missed step number 2,349 and need to go back to start.

Your gutter isn't formatted properly.

Reboot your computer, we've given you a virus.

I still feel like the schmuck in the photo. Poor guy. I know his pain.

So now off to tackle another platform task and get in some more chapters on Switch's sequel.

Before the internet bots and trolls dig through my online footprint and send me ads for another magical e-learning course to ease what ails me.

* * *

Admitting your hang-ups is the first step in recovery, right?

I'm no where near recovered. Far from it. During the pandemic, I hit the e-learning hard—partly because I had no creative spark with all the caretaking issues and decisions-I-never-knew-I'd-have-to-make-in-2020, and partly because I earned my courses for completing 52 in 52. Online writing course fodder! Plenty to keep me busy... and learning.

Lesson Learned: Lots of them. Every day. Keep learning...

57. THE TEMPER TANTRUM

I should simply be happy that she showed up for work today. At the same time as I did. She's made only the rare appearance over the chaotic summer. Chaos has a way of sending her pouting into a corner.

My "Little Miss Muse."

Not an angel, by any stretch of the imagination, so don't let the graphic fool you.

More like a mischievous winged imp. Coming and going as she pleases. Concocting self-proclaimed brilliance and dumping it on me —usually at two o'clock in the morning when I'm nowhere able to process what she's doing.

Rarely when I sit down to begin a project.

And especially not when I'm trying to finish one.

She's that part in all of us—especially alive and well in younger children—that generates ideas (brilliant, genius, dastardly, danger-ous) that seem to "come from nowhere." Those sparks of thought that raise our eyebrows and sprout goofy grins.

Those what-were-you-thinking moments.

Sure, on our own, we're relatively intelligent, logical humans.

And many of the humans I know are way beyond relatively

intelligent.

But that creative part comes from somewhere deeper. Darker. Dreamier. Sometimes deadlier...

And though my Little Miss has made an appearance today, she's is in some sort of a mood. And according to her, all my ideas—the ones I've worked so hard on without her grand assistance—suck.

She might be right, but a sucky-and-done job trumps brilliantly incomplete. At least in my logical left brain thinking.

I'm in the middle of a writing project. I want it off my mind. I want it done. So I can take Little Miss out for a grand adventure. And I promised her I would. Later.

But not right now.

Right now, I'd like her to supply a couple strokes of genius to the current work in progress. I'm not asking for much. Just one or two tiny little sparks. Whatever color she prefers. Red? Pink? White? Doesn't matter. Come on, Little Miss.

Buuuuut... Nope. She's currently having none of it. "That's a sucky plan." She's got me in chains.

She's a toddler.

With a massive IQ, much higher than mine or anyone I know. She's the most brilliant, able-minded, fantastical being that ever existed. At least that's what I tell her to make her feel good. Prime the pump, so to speak.

Bribery with this particular creature requires more than chocolate chip cookies or a shiny new toy from Walmart.

Nope. A massive ego dangles from her massive I.Q.

And she's got a temper to match.

Today she's locking up my process. I have a small, simple outline. She has plenty of room to play. Like putting a child in a playpen.

Not even a playpen.

More like putting a child in an acre's worth of beautiful backyard where towering oaks guard a babbling brook. A simple fence surrounds the serenity and allows ample room for exploration and ideas and...

But she wants to see what's over the fence.

Stick her fingers through the wire.

Kick the fence post until the earth that holds it gives up.

Jump the gate and take me with her into the great unknown.

Away from my outline. Away from my plan.

And run naked through the field toward the pond.

So I tell her that her ideas (sans the nudity) are awesome, I jot them down on the legal pad next to my computer, and I promise her we'll revisit those marvelous works of imagination.

Later.

But right now, we need to focus on our work in progress. Which, by the way, Little Miss Muse, *you* helped me come up with to begin with. Wouldn't you like to finish this?

Nope. The chains stay on.

Other authors have described their "muses" as blue-winged birds, gently floating on the breeze, bringing them morsels of goodies to put into their stories. Or cats. There are lots of cats, purring and chortling out helpful bits of advice.

Stephen King has "boys in the basement" that send up ideas. But in his analogy, at least they're somewhat contained, not running amok with cigars hanging from drooling mouths dripping ashes and slobber onto unfinished manuscript pages.

But he's also been at this writing gig for decades. I wonder how long it took him to build that basement? How fortified is it—steel, concrete with rebar, kryptonite? Do any of his boys ever attempt a coup? Would he sell me the blueprints? Things to ask should I ever meet the man.

My muse? She's a toddler.

Half-naked.

Jumping the fence and spinning on the other side in the wide openness with firecrackers in one hand and a lighter in the other. "Chase me, chase me. Before I set your soul aflame and render you useless, you meager human slave."

Fine. I give up.

What would *you* like to do today, Little Miss?

And off I go, after the firecrackers and lighter have been secured

217

and the clothing zipped and buttoned. I take her by her tiny hand and let her lead me off track. Just for now.

She smiles. Takes a few steps. And holds out her other hand.

So I give her back her firecrackers. She tucks them under her armpit.

The lock turns slowly. She smiles again. A sinister grin with a cocky little tilt of the head. She holds out her hand.

I give her back the lighter.

The chains fall off.

And a new story line starts as sparks—not red or pink or white, but a dark purple of her own choosing—fly from the keyboard.

I sigh and settle in for the ride, simply happy we're both still clothed.

And that she showed up for work today.

* * *

The graphic was that of a vintage typewriter bound with a heavy chain, and an as-close-as-I-could-find likeness of a winged cherub (imp, purple) with hands outstretched, keeping those chains locked with some magical, unseen force.

Little Miss says she remembers this day. It's the day she "trained" me.

Or so she believes.

She's rolling her eyes at me though, picking at the orchid nail polish on one of her chunky toes. "Like you'll ever be fully trained. I'll be dead five times over before you JUST LISTEN TO ME." A glitter puff explodes over her head.

Excuse me a moment while I deal with the attitude dripping from the corner of the room, lest she light Stella Marie's tail on fire...

Okay. I'm back. The cats are hunkering under the bed, but I'm back...

Lesson Learned: Caution in naming and spoiling muses—it puts them on a power trip.

58. SOMETHIN'S GONNA GET YA

A very long, weary summer is winding down. Long because, well, life happened this summer on several fronts. Good things and bad things and all manner of emotions from elation to devastation.

Weary because life happened on several fronts and it seems the heat and humidity will hang around forever.

And weary because our furry rescue babies have decided three a.m. on multiple random days per week is a good time to beg for wet food.

And if we ignore their cries of "I'm dying right this very second" and kick them out to the bonus room—with water, dry food, and litter box—they go on a hunting spree. Killing things dead and hiding them in said room.

Now that part of the house smells like roadkill.

Proving that these fur babies aren't hungry at all—or they'd have eaten whatever carcass they'd come across.

Nope. They just want us tired and addlebrained so we become a little more liberal with the Fancy Feast Florentine with garden veggies and white salmon.

And as I write this, I'm enduring yet another hospital waiting room hoping the guy sitting across from me wearing that blue-and-white face mask is doing so because he's afraid of what *I* may be carrying. Hoping that he's not wearing that blue-and-white face mask, flimsy and gaping around the right side of his mouth, because of what *he's* carrying.

I sit here while a family member endures the pokes and prods and anxiety of some pretty serious tests. Tests that will determine major medical decisions in the season to come.

My job is easier. Waiting out here with Face-Mask Guy and complaining about how bad my house smells. Even though being here makes me want to don the hardhat and safety vest and snort hand sanitizer.

Oh, wait. Maybe not the hand sanitizer, because—

I just scrolled through social feeds and my email a moment ago.

I get those emergency alert emails. The ones with the heads-up regarding SUV-eating fog or house-twirling tornado threats.

But lately that emergency network's been emailing lots of product recalls. Lots and lots. Dozens of foods and drugs and hand sanitizers. A couple are pumpkin-spiced products—lotions, cookies, soap. Yeah, Fall!

The culprits spawning these recalls? Salmonella (don't eat any salad—ever), botulism (in the salmon—watch out kitties), Listeria monocytogenes (wouldn't that be fun?), E.coli, blue plastic bits. Glass particulates.

Blue plastic bits? Glass particulates? Really?

The wording on a recalled piece of medical equipment: *The connector could disconnect from the endotracheal tube, resulting in insufficient oxygenation of the patient.*

Great. The very thing designed to aide my breathing in the event that I swallow too many blue plastic bits and glass particulates may very well smother me.

Sweet.

The door swings open and a nurse calls a man's first name. Face-Mask Guy rises on shaky legs and follows her dutifully into the labyrinth of back-room X-ray suits and CT scan arenas.

Poor thing. I wonder what sent him here.

I wonder how my family member will fare. I wonder if the results will send us down another sterile labyrinth in a different part of the hospital.

I wonder if they stuck me in a head-to-toe machine, would they find a half dozen ailments that I didn't know about? Likely.

We're every one all full up on dormant problems. All of us ticking time bombs. Isn't that fun to think about?

Pumpkin spice, blue plastic bits, and ticking tumors?

It unsettles me. Somethin's gonna get ya. I'd better write fast.

Better finish this dream of mine before the arsenic-laced pumpkin spice hand sanitizer soaks into my skin.

Better finish this next short story and blog post before the radiation seeping through the should've-been-replaced-long-ago lead barrier reaches my feet here in the waiting room.

Better call the loved ones and tell them what they mean to me.

Better...

Better...

Better just chill out. 'Cause somethin's gonna get me. Maybe not today or tomorrow or even this decade.

But something will. Sometime.

Worrying about it will most certainly cause one's demise sooner rather than later.

Enjoy the season. The dream. The loved ones. Take the precautions you can take.

And stay off the recall sites. No number of hardhats, goggles, or safety vests can shield you from the gazillion dangers that lurk around every corner.

I'm looking forward to crisp, humidity-free air and the bursts of colors from the trees before they go dormant for the winter. Facebook and Pinterest are ablaze with mum decor, baggy sweaters, and flavoring all things with pumpkin spice aromas.

I'll take the sweaters and the mums.

You can keep the pumpkin spice hand sanitizer.

Update: Five minutes after I ran this blog post through my spell check, I got another email ding. Check your chicken, people. Check your chicken!! Especially if it's extra chewy...

Also your trampolines, post-tattoo itch creams, and snowmobiles. Apparently, you could break your neck and overdose on lidocaine all while setting yourself on fire in the snow.

* * *

The facemask thing though. If I only knew what was coming to all of our futures. This was posted in August of 2019. Who knew in September of 2020 those masks are mandatory and to see someone without one is more alarming than seeing someone with one.

And, as timing and the cycles of life and illness would dictate, I was just in a waiting room (no, make that two medical waiting rooms) yesterday, and await a phone call today on lab results for the same loved one that was mentioned above. The battle continues on many fronts—

Including deciding which brand of hand sanitizer snorts the best...

Lesson Learned: More than one somethin's tryin' to get all of us... Stay off the recall sites. Stay off the news. Enjoy the moment. You don't know how many more you've got left...

59. DEAR FOOD BLOGGERS

So, Little Miss Muse is off pouting in the corner, a purple tizzy haze hovers over her curly hair. She's ticked because I'm not taking her on that grand adventure I promised.

Because, for heaven's sake, I need to get some meals prepped. So I can free up the writing time to do the adventure. And not have to think about menus. And prepping.

If you don't know who my Little Miss is, check out Blog 57. She's quite a character.

If you don't understand what I'm about to say, check out Blog 20 where l explain my hate/hate relationship with all things culinary.

And now I shall relate another irritating cooking irk for the record:

Dear Food Bloggers, for the sake of us who are just trying to survive, please stop cluttering your pages. And for the love of all things food and nutrition, please post the blasted recipe at the TOP of your blog.

I'm talking to those wonderful people who can look inside a fridge with three ingredients and come up with a five-course meal. My Gma was like that. I am not. I can see a *full* fridge and think we need groceries.

And I'm grateful these experts and kitchen-dwellers post their recipes for dummies like me online. But here's my exacerbating process:

Search Pinterest for something easy to prep, cook, and do in bulk so I can get out of the kitchen.

Click through to a foodie/cook/chef/mom-gone-rogue blog page and try to find a recipe.

I'm greeted with a gorgeous professional photo of, let's say, beef stroganoff.

And then another photo. Of the ingredients. Okay.

Then of two ingredients in a bowl. And on and on. And verbiage and perfectly delicious paragraphs about the funny thing their partner did while they were cooking, or that their dog ran through with muddy paws at step 24 and the cook needed to stop and clean the floor.

Then, step by step by step she goes on, and by the time I've declined signing up for the newsletter on four different pop-up screens, I've forgotten step one.

Okay, where's the list? The instructions? The printable, concise recipe?

So I scroll three miles further, and accidentally click on an affiliate link. It takes me to Amazon to buy this person's favorite $692 blender. I did not know one needed such a fine piece of machinery to cook beef stroganoff. But, I'm no expert.

Click the back arrow.

The page reloads the hi-res photos. AGAIN.

Finally find the bottom. The final photo. Then I click on the *print recipe* button but apparently not ALL the photos had loaded yet, and in that latent period, my mouse, instead of hovering over the printer icon, now hovers over the... Labor Day Paint Sale at the local hardware store link and I'm off the page. Again.

Now, I know good and well one does not need paint to cook beef stroganoff. However, I also know, from experience, that I may need to repaint after *I* cook beef stroganoff. IF I CAN EVER FIND THE RECIPE!!!

Try one more time, because now I've invested too much time to give up without one more round in the ring…

I find the printer icon and pause, making sure the entire 234,084-megabyte blog page has loaded.

Watch the little load icon twirl and twirl.

And while we wait for that process, I know what you're thinking. I'm some eco terrorist. Wasting ink and killing trees to print out my foolish recipes when I could just use the screen it's displayed on now.

I'll direct you to the link above again. I am not a safe person in the kitchen. Sure, I could display the recipe on my laptop or iPad and put it on the counter. Where I'll splash/slop/set fire to my expensive electronic gadget rather than a simple sheet of paper. Paper which I'll keep forever if the recipe works out for me. (You should see my paper the breakfast bubble-up casserole is printed on. Bits from twelve eggs, cheese-something and a brown, ruffled corner from being too close to the stove.) Now imagine If I'd used my laptop…

The printer icon is still twirling.

I look over to the corner. At Little Miss. She's still twirling, purple sparks dancing from her eyes. She's about to leave and take her creative juice boxes with her. Straws and all.

I look back to the screen: Cannot connect to the content at this time. That's the message I get for all the hard work and time spent on Miss Cook's beloved recipe blog.

I unplug the laptop and toss it into my carry-all. In goes a highlighter, my favorite fine-tipped ink pen, and my yellow legal pad. I nod for Little Miss. She grins big, more sparks and glitter fly. "Save some of that for later. We're gonna need it," I say. She hops in the bag.

I drive to the library where I and Little Miss string some words together. And when I need to stretch, I start a pile. Of cookbooks.

Pages with stains and ruffles and waves from other kindred spirits who've slopped and dropped and burnt their attempts. But with no affiliate links or sign-up pages. Good-old-fashioned, tree-killing cookbooks that I likely won't read, but I check them out, nonetheless.

We string some more words together. Satisfied and off for her nap, I pack up Little Miss and my toys and tomes and head for the

Mexican restaurant. Where my good friend there doesn't judge me and hands me a hot meal I didn't have to cook (saving me thousands of dollars in blenders and paint supplies) in a bad-for-us-all Styrofoam take-out box.

"See you tomorrow," he says with a smile.

He probably will.

* * *

Mexican Restaurant Guy knows our family. Knows us. Loves us. We may invite him for Christmas dinner—if he brings the food, we'll supply the table to put it on...

Lesson Learned: Be kind to the readers—don't clutter the pages!!

60. SUIT UP, STUPID

Do you have "that thing" where, from experience, you know if you just did the dumb thing, the day falls into place and becomes more productive?

For some, it's morning quiet time or devotions. For others, it's exercise or a healthy breakfast. Sometimes it's phone-free time or making to-do lists.

I do some of these all of the time, and others sometimes. But I've discovered something, a "thing," about writing, in particular, that I'd not realized until this past month. When I "suit up," I'm more productive.

The words come faster.

Miss Muse shows up and is ever so slightly more cooperative. Though she thinks high heels are fun. Not happening.

Even the cats give me my space. As I type this, they're all passed out. One on the back of the couch. One at my feet. And one in the cat tree in the other room, thank goodness, because I think she ate too many crickets last night, and there's an aroma about her if you know what I mean...

They've settled because Mom's got shoes on. Tails and toes out of the way, gang.

Not barefoot. Not fuzzy socks (which is sad because the weather will turn cooler soon and fuzzy socks are just wonderful). Not flip-flops, (which is also sad, because if frostbite wasn't a thing, I'd likely wear flops all year round).

Nope. Good, supportive, lace-up tennis shoes.

Now, lest you think I'm one of those freelancing sluggards who lays around all day in my pajamas, let me enlighten you. If it's much past seven a.m., and I'm still in my pajamas, somethin's goin' on.

I'm ill. Very ill. Like flu, pneumonia, or mad cow disease.

I'm injured. Likely sciatica and I physically can't get dressed without a great many tears.

Or, klutz that I am, I'm due to be somewhere in attire that I lovingly call my monkey suit: Slacks or a skirt (good grief shoot me now), blouse, dress shoes (another bullet?), hair done, jewelry, etc. On such occasions, I'll remain in my PJs to avoid slopping breakfast or dirty dishwater or cat litter on said monkey suit.

My standard work uniform (seeing as how I'm hidden from my clients' views by the thick cloud of cyberspace and I tend to care not what others think of my attire) consists of denim on the bottom and a Goodwill T-shirt on the top. Pretty simple. No monkeys involved. Nice and easy. No thinking required. Grab it from the top of the clean pile and go.

Versatile enough to go from computer screen to litter box to mailbox back to screen and then—oh, shoot me again—the kitchen, where I'll eventually have to tackle dinner. And if I slop and trash said Goodwill shirt, well, half-price Saturdays are always around the corner.

Shoes? Those I try to do without. I feel confined. Maybe that's why I don't don jewelry of any kind during the week, either. Confinement. Breezes over bare feet is more my speed, especially in the house.

And I'm not a runner or jogger. That'd end more treacherously than my very worst attempt at making a meal, klutz that I am.

But lately, when I've got the lace-ups on, something in my brain goes, "Time to work." My focus is improved. My productivity is on point for much longer.

And Little Miss is over in the corner—pouting because I took a break from our WIP to whip off this blog— chides me, "See? If you had suited up every day this summer, we'd have ten more novels done."

Well, maybe not ten. She likes to exaggerate. Definitely two. Two's a good estimate.

A few days ago, I slipped my flip-flops on after I got dressed in my denim capris and a red Star Wars-themed T-shirt. (I tend to keep the laundry done. This red shirt is always the clean one on the top these days. Maybe I should rotate it out to the blue *Y'all Need Jesus* tee I got on clearance at Walmart.)

I lasted long enough to clear my queue from my "real job" deadlines. Then, I slipped those puppies off my feet, curled my legs underneath me on the couch, and went down the rabbit trail of nonsense for way too long on the iPad.

I was researching. I needed a break from the desk chair and the laptop screen.

Oh, the lies we tell ourselves...

And repeat the next day. I was getting stuff done, but only the bare minimum.

Little Miss in her purple tizzy said, "Suit up, stupid. Let's go play." Genteel and dainty she ain't.

I listened to her. I really shouldn't let her boss me around so much, but she brings the magic occasionally, so I allowed it.

I tied up my purple tennis shoes (purple, huh. That little imp was probably with me in the shoe store when I picked this pair out), and I logged a few thousand words in short order. I'm clearly better with shoes on.

So why don't I, and why don't you, *always* do those things that make us more productive, more positive, more "with it"?

I have no clue. You probably don't either.

I'm just glad that when I slack, I've got my little imp to remind that I'm daft and to go suit up.

So, when these kicks wear out, Little Miss and I will find another pair worthy of grand writing marathons.

"Purple," she says. "With sparkles. High heels this time? With straps."

I veto the heels, 'cause my claustrophobic feet ain't going into those torture chambers. And I prefer my neck bones remain aligned and unbroken. But who am I to argue with her about the color?

Purple it is. Maybe with a hint of sparkle.

* * *

Shoes on. Black with purple trim. Laced up all secure.

Little Miss clumps along in her high heels to the rhythm of Cash's "I've Been Everywhere, Man" that somehow jumped into my Pandora lineup.

You've not lived until your Muse dances half-naked save for violet stilettos and halter top, wings a flutter to Johnny Cash, bottle rocket in one hand, flickering lighter in the other. I'm tellin' you...

I had to turn that off and put on white noise. Raindrops on the car roof. She's miffed, but I'm back to concentrating...

Retie the laces.

And productivity happens. Go figure.

Lesson Learned: Just do the things that move the day forward... And maybe tighten up the choice algorithm on Pandora a bit.

61. THE BIG BIRD MAN

My son and I recently attended a local comic-con. We enjoy walking the aisles, scoping out the cosplay costumes and meeting artists.

I met one local artist that really stood out—unique style, down to earth personality, and super talented. We made a connection and I may hire him for some commission covers down the road.

Always at these events are a lineup of celebrities. Now, I'm not one to go all weak in the knees because So-And-So is in the building. Or Guess Who is taking selfies and signing autographs. As I sit here typing this, I can't think of one mainstream actor, actress, or other Big Name that I'd stand in line for.

But this year's comic-con was different.

Because the Big Bird Man was on the docket. Caroll Spinney. The guy in the great yellow-feathered puppet for nearly fifty years. He also worked Oscar The Grouch.

I saw his bio on the website before we went and informed my son that I didn't care what he busied himself with while I waited in line, but, by golly gee, I was gonna hug this man and tell him what Big Bird did for me.

Really, sounds corny, right?

Picture this: An only child back in the early eighties. A tube television—one of those monsters that occupied an entire third of a living room's corner and had to be worked manually—no remotes. Sculpted brown carpet. Brown paneled walls.

Dad's at work. Mom's cooking or cleaning or studying.

Only a couple of Boston Terriers and my own imagination to keep me company. Now, I can't remember what came on first, Mister Rogers or Sesame Street, but I do remember at one time PBS ran them back to back. But when the show went off the television screen, little Beth kept it going in the living room. No time for boredom when my imagination could carry on the episodes, mashing and mixing the characters and adventures.

Big Bird's giant nest occupied one corner (completely invisible to the rest of the universe, mind you, as was Mister Roger's Trolley). Oscar's can occasionally showed up. Sometimes the Fix-It Guy set up shop if need be. And I'd yack and chat and pretend for hours. Who knows what my mother thought. I know this went on for quite some time before I realized talking out loud to invisible beings was generally frowned upon.

That imaginary place, where anything can happen and anything did, and where I, a scared little girl, could control outcomes and interactions and other's reactions, was of vast importance to me, even if I didn't know it then.

It remains of vast importance to me, evidently, because, all grown up now, that imagination muscle—having been dully worked for far longer than most people willingly admit to exercising it—serves as an escape. A place to control and vent and fly away on yellow feathered wings—with the help of Little Miss Muse, of course.

And I was going to stand in line and tell Caroll Spinney these things. Hug him tight. High-five. Something.

Then the day came to meet him.

And I was smacked head-on with numbers. He did his Big Bird gig for 50 years. The man is 85 years old now. And he'd just had cataract surgery. He couldn't stand. He could barely see to do autographs.

My number, that double-digit weight that starts with a four and ends with a none-of-your-business, also hit me.

No spring chicken am I.

I looked around. Most of the people in the line were my age or a little younger. All waxing nostalgic over yellow feathers.

As the line snaked down the chute, an overwhelming sadness enveloped me. I wondered if he wanted to be at the signing, fans lining up, taking selfies, demanding that he sign this bobble or that stuffed creature. His wife helped. The staff at the comic-con helped and directed. By the time I reached the table where he sat, I told the staff not to make him sign anything for me. He was already tired, and the line had just started.

He wore heavy glasses to cut down on the glare from the fluorescent lights. He didn't stand. We were directed to sit in a chair next to him. We could put an arm around him. He wasn't sure where the cameras were.

I almost left the line.

I didn't post the photos from that meet-and-greet because by the time I sat next to him, I was trying not to bawl and didn't trust myself to speak. I just whispered in his ear, "Thanks for the memories, Mr. Spinney." He nodded. I'm not sure he heard or understood what I said.

His wife assured us as we waited to see him that he loved being out and meeting fans. Loved the autographing and the photo ops. I hope so. I hope he enjoyed himself despite the struggles he was having.

His work gave this timid little girl a place to work out imagination's mechanics. A place to dream and to feel competent and safe.

He'll never know that. Not really. And that's okay.

I can only hope that when I'm 85, someone, somewhere might think, "Wow, she's *that* old? And she's still writing? I remember when I read..." and that person might go on to tell about how a line in a book or a connection with some fictional character that I made up opened up a pathway of imagination for them.

A place to feel safe.

A place to escape.
A place to dream...

* * *

Rest in Peace, Mr. Spinney (1933-2019).

Lesson Learned: Remember your art reaches further than you think...

62. PLATEFULS OF FROGS

By the time this content posts, the calendar will indicate the last Monday any of us get in the great month of September. Summer's slipping away, even if recent temperatures in our area don't quite have that crispy nip of fall. Pumpkin spice EVERYTHING!

(Not a pumpkin spice fan. Actually had to stifle the gag reflex when the kids were small and we'd carve pumpkins. The textures of the snotty guts didn't bother me. The smell, though. And, thank you very much, I'd prefer not to spice all desserts and comfort beverages with it for the next three months. More for you all...)

But right now, it's the Monday before that last Monday. I have self-imposed deadlines looming (finish Switch's sequel), a challenge I'm trying not to fade out on (23 new shorts done since April, 29 more to go), and all my ducks have scattered to various ponds. Said ducks are staging protests, laying eggs (more ducks to come) and generally goose-pooping on my well-though-out-plans (why do I bother??).

So today is a clean-up day. Catching up from a long month of unexpected life flops.

Along with the relocation of my flock, the events of this last week have created bombshells and messes and frogs.

Platefuls of frogs that must be eaten. One ugly frog at a time.

The frog analogy isn't my concept. A guy named Brian Tracy literally wrote the book on it. You can check it out here. And since I've read the thing, he's made a workbook and flash cards. His simple concept came top-of-mind often in the last few months.

If you have lots of frogs (tasks, to-do's, activities), eat the ugliest one first.

Ah, but at the moment, Dear Mr. Tracy, all of my frogs are of equal grotesqueness.

So I shall flip a coin, close my eyes tight, pinch my nose...chew and swallow that first ugly task on the plate.

Then repeat.

All day long.

So short post today. Off to grab one of those warty amphibians before he takes a cue from the ducks and finds himself a mate.

May your winged ones line up obediently in October and may all your frogs be pumpkin-spiced—if you're into that sort of thing...

* * *

I was tempted to pull out 2019's calendar to remind myself what was happening around this time—but I've got a good guess or three, and quite frankly, I don't need the influx of memories of medical issues, family drama, and general life junk. I currently have enough of the same—flavored with the essence of 2020—to do me, thank you very much.

I'd rather eat pumpkin-spice flavored frogs than to look back on those months.

Lesson Learned: Memory Lanes are good for the soul. Warty Frog Freeways, not so much.
Forward...

63. THIS LOVELY LARD…

…Just sat on my plateful of frogs (see the last post in the archive).

Cars blowing up. Plural.

Cardiac muscles misbehaving. Also plural on that.

Fevers flaring, requiring comfort food.

And you know it's bad when *I've* been called on to provide comfort food. I nearly cooked the darn CAT in the process, so I had to let Walmart handle the majority of the heavy lifting. True Story. More on that next week.

And someone sent us a fire pit. Also true.

We didn't order a fire pit, either on purpose or by accident so far as I can tell.

We've not been in the market for one.

But there it lurks in its giant cardboard shipping box in my garage. Begging for kindling and a lighter so we can roast our dogs and toast our mallows. Yeah, right. Like I've got time this week—or next—to kick back around a firepit that someone sent us. Either on purpose or by accident.

Yup. Still had several frogs of my own making to eat. One by one. Was getting a handle on them, too.

Then this guy shows up and just squashes them.

Oh yeah. Those flat amphibians *still* need tackled. Ugliest first. I guess they won't be as juicy since he's flattened them. So there's that.

I also think Little Miss Muse is trapped under his giant derriere. If I look closely enough, I can see bits of purple glitter oozing from under his tail. Either that or those stress sparkles are back and I need to go see my Eye Guy and get a refill of my blood pressure medicine. Add my heart to the naughty list.

Man, will Little Miss be wholly honked when she gets untangled from piles of elephant flab.

Who knows what stories will topple out of her once she's free and breathing. She'll likely keep me up for days. Horror will be the genre of the week.

So, I'm headed to the garage to dig out the roasting forks from the fire pit we didn't order.

Hopefully they're large enough to eat this fellow.

One bite at a time...

* * *

The graphic for this post was a giant, yoga-posed elephant.

And, since I'm doing these follow-up blurbs in order, no need to wonder what happened during this time. It all came back in crystal-clear, hi-def.

Along with a SECOND fire pit. Both pits, over a year later, still in their boxes and still from unknown senders, lurk in the garage.

And, if my crystal ball isn't on the blitz, we're likely to have a repeat of it soon. Aging parents don't "un-age" and some medical issues go dormant, only to rear up. And all three of my ladies are on the calendar for no fewer than ten different doctor appointments in the next few months. And that's on the low side of things.

Lesson Learned: Frogs and elephants can't be helped. Toast a S'more and move on.

64. HALFWAY THERE

Two years ago, I did a short story challenge: Thirty Shorts in Thirty Days. Nailed it. Well, sort of. A couple of the stories won't see the light of day. Ever.

A couple winners sold. A couple had ideas too big for the short form and are decent novel starts. The rest have been bundled into collections and some have been posted on this blog as Free Fiction.

And thank you to all who've commented and encouraged me along the way. Your words mean more than you know.

So...since I had so much fun with that one, back in April of this year, I entered another one. One story a week for a whole year.

I just turned in my 26th. Halfway there.

Halfway to more consistent writing habits. (Well, as consistent as one can be with the unforeseen health issues, unplanned car breakdowns, and unordered firepits—plural on the pits).

Halfway to lots of learning (if I hit the mark, I get free training from my mentor, not to mention a gob of shorts to sell and market).

Halfway there.

This one is by far the harder of the two challenges. You wouldn't think so, but any task seems to grow to fit the time allotted, so it's taking me "longer" to get one done per week than one per day. I've more time to "fiddle" with ideas and tweak paragraph order, etc. I have 168 hours instead of 24. That's not necessarily a good thing.

Of the 26 so far, two are slotted for publication. So that's fun. Some are waiting to be read by editors of mainstream publications. Some are waiting for me to edit them. Some will be used here on the blog for Free Fiction and some will be bundled into a second anthology. It's been fun.

Covers are all done and ready, too, should the need arise. I've found the covers help me remember what the story is about. Titles alone don't ring a bell. With 56 shorts and counting, I'm bound to forget a plot or two...

A couple of the stories have born worlds to revisit and explore in greater detail. A couple are novel starts (seems the Sci-Fi/Fantasy genre takes me over and I can't quite get the word count down under 10K).

My Learning Takeaways:

I can use *anything* as an excuse to not write (Weaning the pen collection, rearrange furniture, meal-prep on paper—cause you know I'll just order takeout in the end, kitty cats, and my favorite: Tomorrow, tomorrow, I love ya, tomorrow).

I feel better when I've written. Endorphins? Sense of accomplishment? A little checkmark in the calendar that today's word count's been reached? Whatever the root, that feeling is starting to trump the above "I can't write because..." list.

Little Miss Muse can use *anything* to springboard into Storyville. (Be careful what you say/do around me. She's always listening).

Shorts give Little Miss Muse time to play in a different sandbox and allow my brain and her magic to refresh from the larger work in progress.

Publishing (traditional markets) is a slow-moving vehicle and needs a reflective red-and-orange triangle plastered to its rear end.

I can be forgiving of myself. That larger work, Switch's sequel with a rough-draft-done deadline of 10/22, came to a screeching halt over the last couple of weeks—and not as a result of any of my typical procrastination techniques. Life was such that frogs and elephants that could not be contained blossomed and grew, and my mental capacity just wasn't there to do five things at once.

So I hit the reset button, focused on the shorts for those weeks, and moved forward. Little Miss was stuck under a rump (see last week's post), and that allowed me some good sleep.

Now she's back.

Dreams. Ideas. Bossiness. Even down to the image for today's blog. I'd picked out a 26 in gold with gold leafing. She saw the purple petals and well, purple it is.

Cool thing about goals. If you make any progress at all, and then things stop, you've failed forward.

Hoping not to stop. Hoping to post a large, purple/gold 52 in April.

Hoping to get Switch-The-Second's draft done by Thanksgiving. I've got a solid start.

Off to write #27. But first, I'll head to Amazon for frog repellant.

* * *

The frog repellant didn't work. May as well have sprayed Acme's All-in-One Frog, Duck and Elephant bait. Not repellant.

Oh, well. Switch's sequel was a real pain in the brain... I sense a theme of that since I kept mentioning it over and over.

Lesson Learned: I can't write shorts and a major WIP at the same time with Frogs, Elephants and wayward ducks. I forgive me.

65. COUNTING ON IT

Overwhelmed and oblivious to the date or season or time of day. That's where I've been staying. I know when it's Sunday because the hubs is off work and we don the monkey suits and go to church. After that, time-tracking is all downhill. Multiple times this year. When I think back to January 1, and all that's happened since, my brain whirls. Days and weeks blur into months and seasons, and, in my mind, we've gone from snow to blood-boiling heat to rain-soaked autumn leaves within the span of seventy-two hours.

We were discussing Christmas the other day, and my pathetic internal time tracker wasn't, well, tracking. Christmas? Did I miss Halloween and Thanksgiving and, wait, did I miss the vote? Don't we need to vote before Christmas?

And then hubs asked about trees. What are we going to do this year? We put up two trees last year—one for us and one for my grandmother in her little apartment. The last tree she'd enjoy as last Christmas was her last.

I'm counting on this Christmas to be weird. Bittersweet. Different. Glad we got that family group photo on the previous 25th . Glad we put up two trees.

Last Christmas was Cosmo the Cat's last one, too. He also enjoyed our tree as much as Grandma enjoyed hers, but I don't think Grandma chewed on her tree's branches. Nor do I believe she laid underneath it to take naps, but I didn't watch her 24/7, so it's possible… (And before I get nasty emails, I'm not being disrespectful. Gma, may she rest in peace, would find that comment funny—or she'd tell on herself that she'd accidentally stumbled and really did lay under the tree for a bit to gather her strength. That wouldn't surprise me one bit).

As my slow-to-process brain pulled itself from the past back to the current conversation on trees and décor and whose-house-we-gonna-land-at-this-year, I looked around the room.

We have three new family members since January.

Stella Marie. You met her in Blog 38.

Amara Mino. My son's cat.

And Malachi Maxwell. Our summer (was it summer, really?) rescue. A malnourished little boy who, along with his two sisters, had needed milk replacement and who'd nearly met demise when demon children tried to kick the kittens into oncoming traffic. My daughter witnessed this, scooped up the trio, and, poof! Our shed became a nursery.

And I truly thought each time I went out to feed them that I'd find one or more of them dead. They were that scrawny.

The little girls did well, grew, hunted, climbed, and generally did all things cat with relative ease. They graduated to barn life, happy and free to mouse and hunt on a friend's farm for the rest of their days.

Malachi? Weeellll, he wasn't cut out for barn life. He nearly died in our shed when he tangled himself in an old hammock net that I didn't even remember we had—or it wouldn't have been there in the first place. Passed out right in front of me. I'm blowing in his face as I untangle his neck, glad he breathed before I had to attempt mouth-to-mouth. I think I knew then, even before his oxygen-deprived lids opened slowly and he purred through his pain, that he'd be ours.

I knew before I noticed he was always about five steps behind his sisters. He'd try the kitty-see-kitty-do thing and fail miserably. Falling out of trees. Running into things. No clue how to play or hunt or pounce without mimicking, and simply being still if his sisters weren't in sight.

We kept him. Farm life would eat him alive.

He's well, we think, other than that dimwit quality. He's attempted a ride in the clothes dryer. He's tried—more than once—to jump into a 350-degree oven. It takes him thirty seconds to fall from a three-foot desk. I'm not sure how he manages to be such a dork. That early malnutrition? Oxygen deprivation? Uuuhmmm...being a boy? (Okay. *That* was a little disrespectful but compared to the sisters and our two rescue girls, this boy is just, well, not right. I've got nothing else personally to go on with this. Cosmo was raised by dogs, and not as cat-like. Not a good comparison. And I've had many girl dogs and only a couple of boys. The boy dogs were, well, dimwits.)

He really likes watching TV. He prefers crime shows and legal dramas with lots of back-and-forth dialog. He also enjoys watching publishing videos and writing tutorials with me, especially when the instructors talk with their hands.

He loves his ball track. He pretends he's a lion on a gazelle hunt by chasing a little white ball around a closed plastic circle. For an hour at a time.

He bats fuzzy felt mice in his paws, and when they disappear under the couch, he still bats with his paws, his poor little mind not processing the mouse is gone. He's batting a ghost.

He tags along after his adopted adult sisters. Stella, a mother in another life, patient and playful with him. Amara, the boss of the space, cleans his ears, then beats him thoroughly about the head (and he allows this!!!). He still mimics, watching how the big girls do things, then attempting (and usually failing) to do it on his own.

He cried after me the first few days in the house. I couldn't get two hands free to get writing or work done, so I stuffed him in a cross-body bag and papoosed his butt into naptime against my ribcage. I'd wash dishes and type and do housework like this to keep him out of danger and away from Amara's claws. (Reminded me of keeping my infant son away from my daughter when she was a terrifically curi-

245

ous/terrible-two-year old intent in experimenting with the new baby boy. Those days were much more stressful and, likewise, I never knew what day it was. Cats are easier than humans, if you're wondering. And the cats are not the reason why I don't know what day it is. I think that fault lies squarely with the humans.)

Back to the Christmas conversation. Hubs wants a tree and lots of décor on display. I'm counting three cats, none of whom have seen an indoor Christmas tree.

I'm counting the number of times the tree will hit the floor. At two a.m.

I'm counting the number of times the vintage Clothtique Santas will be drug from the fireplace and hidden in the bathtub, the cat tower, or behind a litter box. At three a.m.

I'm counting the number of times Malachi tries to hang himself with garland or lights or with whatever rope/fishing line/twine we rig to keep the tree upright. At four, five, six, and seven a.m. as well as every p.m. counterpart.

And I'm counting on the fact that we'll try a tree and a few Santas. I'm counting on losing it when we pull out the decorations and Cosmo's old stocking is still tucked away with ours. That emotion will remind me of Grandma's lasts and on and on it will go.

I'm counting on heading to the Dollar Store, drowning my sorrows in three new red stockings for the new fur babies. Along with all the goodies that Santa Cat will tuck inside.

And I'm counting on the fact that I'll lose lots of sleep once the décor goes up.

It's okay. It doesn't matter. It won't make much difference.

I'm counting on not knowing what day of the week it is until March of next year anyway.

* * *

I'm laughing my head off. "March of next year?"

That would mean March 2020 with an equally loose grip on reality and the passage of time.

And then church closed down, and no monkey suits were worn, and so I really had no anchor during the week to remind me of the day. For months on end.

Uggg.

And, as luck or karma or the good Lord would have it, Malachi—big boy now, bigger than his sisters—wiggled his way into my lap for his 38.9 seconds of cuddle time just now. Where did my little papoose buddy go?

He's all grown up, just as daft, and still requires my intervention every two weeks to untangle him from some oxygen-depriving mess.

And Christmas 2020? I can't even imagine what that will look like. I asked Little Miss. She's got nothing, and she's always got SOME-THING to dream up. It's a black hole on the calendar this year.

We shall see.

Lesson Learned: Stock up on sanity when you can. You're gonna need it.

66. THANKS

America has its fair share of problems.

America has its fair share of mistakes.

America has its pouty days of political upheaval, and the he-saids, she-saids, and they-saids can certainly bog us down. I know I've been steering clear of all things news-related recently.

But it's still the best country on the planet. I'd not want to live anywhere else.

To freely stroll leaf-caked sidewalks, the crispy footsteps frightening undecisive squirrels from their hidey holes.

To freely gather with family and friends for meals and movies and fun and worship.

To read what I want. Watch what I want. Go where I want. Think what I want.

Or to sit alone in my office and make up stories for fun and profit.

There's no better place than these Great States.

Thank you to all our Veterans. I'm humbled by your service and sacrifices.

Our country may have its fair share of issues, but this American will always be grateful America had you...

* * *

"To freely gather with family and friends for meals and movies and fun and worship."

This was painful. "Freely" has a different ring to it less than a year later. I write this in September 2020. The virus continues to do its thing and "free" is now a hot-button topic. Political upheaval doesn't begin to describe the news cycles. The he-saids, she-saids, and they-saids are front-and-center on everyone's minds.

I still wouldn't want to live anywhere else. America is my home. I'm still thankful for the servicemen and women. And to their families.

Lesson Learned: Appreciate what you have today. It could be gone tomorrow.

67. PLASTIC WRAP AND THE GREAT UNKNOWN

Almost lost it today. Sunday. The Sunday that the Geniuses-That-Be decided long ago that we should tamper with time.

Set those clocks back. (Some of us Indiana folks remember days when we didn't participate in this hoo-ha).

Manually in days gone by, but now, the digital overlords do that while we sleep. Give an hour. Take an hour.

Soon they'll want two. Then three. One day we'll wake up and our phones will tell us the government needed all of November and two-thirds of March.

My cats don't understand this. Their stomachs are on a biological hunger timer set five months ago.

It'll take two weeks for me to stop thinking, "If this were last month, it'd be (INSERT PREVIOUS TIME HERE)."

Mothers of small children hate these times of year. I know I did. Tried all manner of things to save sleep. Get sleep. Push mealtimes.

Ridiculous.

So I almost lost it. Right there in the kitchen. (You know, my favorite room of the house). Trying to wrap up the leftovers from lunch. Plastic wrap. And I'd sprung for the brand name, too.

But alas, as soon as the see-through cling was free of the razor strip, it jumped onto my arm in static glory. And I wadded it into a mess trying to get it straightened out.

Attempt two resulted in the same.

Attempt three—with me holding the box feet away from my torso, closer to the plate of roast and potatoes—not much better. Took five times the amount of wrap to get that cow secured and into the fridge. (Hubs better eat it, too, after all that effort).

So even when I make a semi-edible meal, something in the kitchen's gonna get me. That room hates me.

Coupled with the sleep issue from the time change issue, I nearly lost it.

My sanctification.

My temper.

My rapidly thinning desire to do anything domesticated.

And my equally thinning sanity.

Because I really need those leftovers to be saved. And eaten at least another time.

Because next week...the week after Daylight Savings Time...is an unknown. Too many variables from too many directions to accurately gauge any meal planning, work schedules, mental capacity levels, or kitty cat craziness.

Therefore, in my sleep-deprived state, and facing the fear of the great unknown, I'm plowing off several of these blog posts ahead of time. My Web Guy will feed them into cyberspace. Week by week. Bless his heart for putting up with my issues...

So for those who know me personally, if it seems blog content doesn't match current life content, it doesn't.

It was planned that way.

At least for a few unknown, pre-holiday, lots-of-plastic-wrap-wars-coming weeks.

Here's a quote. Because I almost lost it today. No idea who to attribute this quote to, but I agree with it wholeheartedly. If you know the original source, message me and I'll credit it. Right after I've untangled me and possibly two cats from a suffocating mess of Saran wrap.

Re: Daylight Savings Time: *"Only the government would believe that you could cut a foot off the top of a blanket, sew it to the bottom, and have a longer blanket."*

* * *

At the time of this writing, we are about a month-and-a-half away from another Fall time change. Already the memes are swirling about dreading an extra hour of 2020.

And, to be fair, I do believe the government actually did tell us it needed all of last March and possibly all of this coming November. Little Miss sits in the corner all sassy, nodding. "Uh-huh. I should run for congress. I could do just as well."

Scary thing is, she probably could.

Lesson Learned: Vote Little Miss Muse for President this fall. What other options are there?*

*Man, did I score some major brownie points with this one. She's twirling, spinning, sewing her violet victory sash... and I sense a few more chapters to spill onto the current work in progress!

68. AND SO IT BEGINS

The writing.

Well, the writing began quite some time ago, decades really if you count that space epic written in pencil on lined notebook paper when I was ten.

But the official writing for the grand Anthology Workshop in Vegas starts now! This week marks the first anthology prompt, and it's due next. I'll be half-crazed, carpal-tunneled, and nearly blind by the time this thing's done.

Six paying editors. Six shorts.

Then read all six shorts written by the 49 or so other authors.

Then Vegas in February to see how our stories stack up to the editors' opinions and tastes.

Great fun. Completely terrifying.

Way more work and time than was required of me in any of my college classes—some college classes put together.

Way out of my comfort zone—The city thing. The crowd thing. The "meet new people even though I'm a social dork" thing.

And way, way out of my league. The ladies and gentlemen at this workshop have established careers. I'm just getting started. They have millions of words under their belts (or quills or pens or keyboards).

I'm pushing 200k. Measly compared to the collective writing genius of this group. Some, no doubt, will likely be award-winning story-tellers.

I'm super excited to learn from this group, read their work, and hopefully come back with a boatload of craft techniques and business ideas and maybe a new contact or three.

I've been doing a short story a week since April. Up to 32 tales now, so I've got a good rhythm down.

But, because these six upcoming ones are, well, going to be read for sure, they *feel* more important. And because this trip is a major bucket-list thing for me, these tales *feel* heavier.

They're not. That's just fear talking.

And feelings lie.

Assigning importance to ideas or events. Putting pressure where there should be just fun.

It'll be okay. (Sometimes I lie to myself—a lie disguised as assurance and tied with a big ol' bow for effect.)

I've had lots of practice. 32 shorts this year so far. 30 in a previous one. Several sales. No big deal, I say (as Little Miss Muse does jump-and-squeals, spreading purple glitter in her wake).

I've got some ideas, but what good are those when you've no idea the prompts coming down the line?

I have an idea for a heart-felt western. The prompt will be sci-fi dystopian in Kentucky.

I have an idea for a sci-fi horror tale. The prompt will be Hall-mark-Christmas-ish—with llamas.

I have an idea for a creepy mystery. The prompt will be feel-good fantasy set on Jupiter.

Me and my bright ideas won't win the plan-ahead game. No plan-ning ahead on this one. (The triple-A control freak in me is curling into the fetal position. Little Miss is doing a jig...)

I'll just wait and watch, I tell myself. Sketch out some loose thoughts. Leave the rest of the board blank for the prompts. And pray Miss Muse doesn't decide to go on holiday with her amethyst-bejew-eled cell phone on silent.

I feel so sorry for my hubs. He's super supportive of my writing, but for the next few weeks, things may be a little tense around here. Read: Dirtier-than-normal house, less-than-normal food prep (he may benefit from that one), and three attention-deprived cats.

If any of you see him between now and mid-January, please check on him. He likely won't be okay.

It's bound to be lots of hand-wringing, gut-wrenching fun.

Sprinkled in purple glitter.

* * *

Writing for those weeks was all great fun until people started landing in the hospital. No, not from writing or starvation. But due to no faults of their own, aged ones do the aged things and sometimes stuff happens. And stuff always happens while other stuff is happening. I bet you've experienced this phenomenon.

Still, those long weeks of waiting for and writing to the prompts was the best learning experience ever. And reading 40+ stories to each of those six prompts, great fun. Best trip ever, too, and so glad it got squeezed into the calendar before 2020 kicked our collective rumps.

Lesson Learned: Go for the bucket list things. Then make a new list.

69. VOICE REST

After a long week of caretaking the universe, my body cried uncle, played host to the community crud bug, and sent me to the couch for several nights. And to the clinic.

Where, thankfully, we found the virus hadn't wormed its way into my lungs (bronchitis likes me, and I wanted to kill it before it had a chance to move in for six weeks. And pneumonia? I wouldn't wish that on anyone...). No huge deal, just a bad cold that zapped energy and seared vocal cords more than anything else.

And the nice nurse practitioner says complete voice rest. No talking. No whispering. Twenty-four hours.

Ha.

Though the thought of not speaking about anything to anyone for a stretch appeals to my introverted nature, my control freak and bigger-than-they-should-be opinions didn't quite take to that.

Neither did the three critters and two boys I live with. The cats didn't like me clapping, snapping, and stomping at them when their curious/mischievous/animal natures emerged. Which happened every thirty minutes while I was ill. Not so much when all is smooth. (I don't think they liked me on the couch.)

My boys didn't much care to read from a screen or text message when I'm sitting four feet from them and could just tell them where the butter is.

Or what time such and such is.

Or how hot the iron should be for that type of fabric.

Or whatever else they couldn't find or didn't know.

This would have been impossible with young children—or very old folks—but I did okay. I caught myself scolding the bitty boy cat once—then reverted to clapping at him. Something like "Don't lick that—" That was three words.

And then one very squeaky, strained, and exasperated "*really?*" escaped my throat during the hubby's football game. Before the game started, actually. Aimed at the commentators on the surface, but maybe aimed at all fans of those pre-game, post-game, mid-game, post-post game conversations.

Really?

Now, I understand commentary explaining plays as the action happens. Who has the ball? Where on the field? Flags? Rulings? All that I can see as necessary.

But that other stuff? That they get paid for? To fill time???

Here's a rundown of the lines that drew out that painful squawk.

Big Dude Commentator #1: So, my very famous colleague who gets paid a million per season to commentate, what does the home team need to do to win this game?

Big Dude Commentator #2: Well, they need to move the football down the field and score touchdowns.

Big Dude Commentator #1: Exactly, #2. I couldn't agree more...

Score touchdowns to win the game.

Wow. I don't know much about football, but...

Really?

It just came out. Word number four on voice rest.

Really?

It went on and on. The over-stating of the massively obvious. *And they were serious.*

Hubs was enthralled, hanging on every word. I imagined the fans of both teams sitting on the edges of their recliners or couches or bean bag chairs equally enthralled. Nodding in agreement as they chomped their pretzels and swigged their beverages.

I imagined how the players, watching the replay of the game, would sit and nod in agreement. The losing team going, "Man, we should've listed to Big Dude Commentator #2 before the game. Maybe we'd have won..."

I took my hands—both of them—and covered my mouth tight lest I set ablaze anew my poor vocal cords with a massive rant.

Had I the breath, dear hubs would've gotten quite the earful on how the airwaves would be better served with documentary pieces on the history of the stadium or the host city. Or a spotlight of a player that did some good in their community.

Or how regulation footballs are manufactured.

Or blooper reels (though the live commentators were covering that, unbeknownst to them).

Or kittens on parade.

Almost anything else.

If I hadn't already germed up the couch, I'd have found a new place to be. But, the couch was my spot for a few days and so football it was.

Big Dudes stating the obvious. Cats licking things they shouldn't. Hubs hot under the collar because his boys didn't do well. (How is that fun? A constant fog of frustration over something you can't control?)

And I couldn't yell about any of it.

Four small words in 24 hours, five syllables. Not too bad. The line may end up in a story one day:

Really? Don't lick that...

* * *

The virus in question was not COVID, unless some of the "theys" are correct and it was here in early December of 2019. Still, though. No lung symptoms, so its doubtful. Mine was a nasty bug, but not that nasty, I don't think.

I've moved the "Really? Don't lick that" to the top of my idea-fodder page. It'll be game time for that one soon. Very soon.

Lesson Learned: Next time a bug hits, make up the "germ nest" in some other room of the house so as not to have to watch commentators state the obvious...

70. BRAIN FOG

I missed the signs.

With the caretaking and managing calendars for other house-holds and the holidays and caretaking and illness with the voice rest and hacking my fool head off and the caretaking...

I missed the signs.

Subtle signs at first. Always blamed on stress and running and too much of this activity and not enough of another.

Signs of thyroid brain fog.

I knew I needed lab work. I put it off because, well, life.

And when the fatigue from the cold virus seemed to be dispro-portionate to the symptoms (since there was no pneumonia or bron-chitis), I vaguely started piecing together the reason for *some* of my issues.

Lack of concentration.

Tired to the bone.

Just give me a cat and my couch and my fuzzy blanket please.

And don't talk too fast because I can't follow your train of thought. I can't even follow my own train of thought. I'm not even sure I have a train. Or tracks.

And the conductor is out on stroke.

Strike. He's on strike.

I finally got to the lab. The lab got back with me. Unhappy.

Get to the doctor, they said. You're about to go nuclear.

Well, maybe that's not quite how they put it, but that's how my under-hormonal thyroid brain fog perceived it. My doc called in a new strength.

It'll take weeks to even out from a swing this far off normal. Not that I hover around the normal level often, but this is waaay off. Like I know what I want to say, but I can't find the correct nouns. Weird.

Like I know I should switch around laundry and do something to the floors, but the thought of it sends waves of weakness through my bones, so I just sit and think about it. Now what's that thing called? That sucks up the kitty hair and dust? The swee, vee, vacuum! It's a vacuum.

Worst was driving in the big city and coming upon unfamiliar roundabouts looking for the hospital where my loved one will be poked and prodded once again. In the big scheme of things, she's got it far worse than me.

I've lost nouns. And energy. That's all. They'll come back. Some day. Hopefully with a well-rested conceiver.

Conduit.

Conductor. That's him!

Roundabouts. May as well strap me into Elon Musk's rocket to the moon as the first test subject. As the pilot. I'd have about as much of a clue.

May as well. Roundabouts. Our good neighbors across the pond can keep them. Us rebel colonists could do without. Especially when the colonists crave sleep and clarity of thought. And certainly us rebels who put off blood work and drive foggy headed from our simple right-angle intersection towns. Urgg.

Who thought those round road mazes were a good idea?

Someone in the middle of a thyrodic brain-fog flare.

And I'm still trying to tag along on the story challenge. Number thirty-something this week. Scary close to not being able to string cohesive thoughts together. (Bless your hearts if you're still reading this post. Wow...) But short stories are more forgiving than longer works.

So are blog posts. Five hundred words at a time. Little by little. Small sessions. Then a nap.

Well, not a nap right this very second. In the hospital foyer. At least I don't think so. Maybe...

At any rate, I'll not attempt any work on the novel. I'd like that one to be written clearly.

Little Miss Muse still wants to play, so the needles and test tubes and dose changes haven't scared her off. Even bought us some new tennis shoes. Purple. She likes them. But I'm too tired to lace them up and get to work.

Later, Little Miss. Later.

I need a fuzzy blanket and a cat. And my couch.

I hear her stomp off in a purple tizzy. Pouting. Or maybe that stomping is the sound of my heart palpating in my chest, a symptom of the thyroid dance.

I hear her huff and hiss, leaving a trail of lavender attitude behind —or maybe that's the ringing in my ears, my thyroid gland sending a fleet of Salvation Army soldiers to park their red buckets and brass bells in my ear canals. That's fun, too.

Fleet? Isn't that ships? Or planes? No, that's a squadron.

Hoard? No.

Salvation Army Troops? Brigade?

I'm gonna give up on that nuisance.

Network.

Nuance. Ha. The word is nuance. Maybe.

(Boy, won't the edits on the short story manuscripts from this era be fun?!??)

Hopefully by the time this posts, a couple weeks from me writing it, I'll be in the clear. Literally. Little Miss is sure rooting for that day.

So's the vocabulary checker on my word processor.

* * *

Thyroid problems suck. That is all.

Lesson Learned: Schedule routine lab work every six months, symptoms or not.

71 . CHRISTMAS LISTS PAST

Got nostalgic again during my thyroid-induced "downtime." Started thinking back on past Christmases—waaay past ones where I was the scrawny tow-headed youngster with big eyes and high hopes on Christmas morning.

I requested—and never received, mind you—a magical wand that worked. So I made myself one out of rolled-up black construction paper, Scotch tape, and a foil-tipped end. Couldn't fire the thing up though...

However, aside from this, I was pretty much spoiled rotten. Here are some of the requests from little Beth's past Christmas lists:

Go to the Head of the Class— As an only child, I had no one around to compete with. But I do think I asked for this specifically— geek/nerd that I was. I don't even think we popped the carboard pieces apart.

Solar Quest—Monopoly in space! But better. My BFF and I would play this until we ran out of money, then we'd stop for a crafting hour, make more money, and continue the game. And looking at that price tag on eBay, I wish I'd kept it. No idea what became of it.

Cabbage Patch Kids—Yup. Barbie, not so much (though I know I had a Peaches 'N Cream). Grandma freaked me out a little bit though.

Told me Cabbage Patch dolls could become demon possessed. Then I worried that the handmade-one was staring at me while I slept. That fine gift was a bit creepy with her scrunched face and black yarn hair, and I began to fear Grandma was right. I stuffed her (the doll, not Grandma) down deep inside my toybox and played with the ones that came sealed in the box from the factory—a kid and a preemie. Mom even took me to Georgia to visit the Babyland Hospital. I kid you not...

Unicorns—of all shapes, sizes, and materials. Though, I'm glad I experienced the unicorn renderings of yesteryear. I'm always more than a little disappointed at the big-eyed ones in the stores today. They look completely ridiculous. Now? Every creature in the little girls' toy section has a horn on it. Llamas. Owls. Monkeys. Come on. Let them be unicorns. Let them be magical with proportionate eyeballs, please.

I remember lots of office supplies, even at a young age. Notebooks, folders, pens. Stickers were always a big deal. Books. Lots of books in whatever series I was sucked into. I specifically remember boxed sets of Little House on the Prairie and Chronicles of Narnia.

The surprises were the best, though. I remember quite fondly my dad gifting me a remote-controlled dog much like a dachshund. He'd had me convinced that he'd bought a real pup (I was disappointed, but only for a minute). The living-breathing-opinionated Boston Terriers we had at the time didn't appreciate this piece's mechanical wriggle and shrill bark.

I came across that epic post of a little girl's $4k Christmas list during research for one of my short stories. Wow. The specifics. And the price tags! My folks would've boiled me dead had I gone to these extremes, I do believe.

And the spelling! What she needs is a visit from Merriam-Webster. Not so much Santa.

Today, if I had to make a Christmas wish list, no money could buy what my wanter desires: Peace. Quiet. A nap worthy of a broken thyroid.

And for cranium horns to belong exclusively to magical unicorns with right-sized eyeballs.

And for my magic wand to start working. Any day now...

At any rate, I wish you all a Merry Christmas filled with memories that will one day be cherished as those nostalgic "good ol' days."

* * *

Little Miss pulls out her bottle rocket as I read this, tap, tap tapping the end of the thing (unlit, thank goodness) all over the items on my desk. "Who needs a wand when you've got one of these babies?"

Aaaand she lit it.

She's off.

So are the cats.

She's squealing at me. "You gotta dream bigger, Beth. Gotta dream bigger!"

BOOM.

Lesson Learned: Dream bigger. And buy fireproof furnishings.

72. CHEESE AND RATS!

Funny thing. I'm looking at one of my seven (yes, seven—not a typo) calendars and trying to figure out this blog's topic. Of course, it's the last one of 2019, so a look-ahead-type thing.

Like everyone else is doing. Because I'm a still a bit thyrodic and the snark isn't coming in its typical free-flowing state.

So I hopped over to my stock photo site.

Typed in 2020.

And so many images of these numerals are in...cheese? Well, that reminded me of *Who Moved My Cheese?* by Spencer Johnson. Liked that book. Have a copy or two around here. Had the children's picture book that went with it as well. Thought I'd do a blog about that. May as well. The stock photos are abundantly, well, cheesy.

Who Moved My Cheese? is about adapting to change. Relinquishing control of outcomes. To find better "cheese" when your own supply of "cheese" runs out. Or gets moldy.

Or has thyroid implosions.

Whatever.

Adapting. Clearly haven't mastered that yet, as hinted (read: screamed) by the half-dozen calendars.

Calendars = control.

Calendars (the way I like to use them) do not necessarily equal organization.

Now before I get all kinds of "advice," let me clarify the number of calendars: Half are from the year about to expire. One is a dry-erase wall calendar where I attempt to control my writing life. One is my standard "brain"—all things life and work and family go into that one. One is for the next five years. A little goal setting/dreaming tool.

So half of them will be trashed come tomorrow. One wiped clean. One only written in pencil. And one real-life "brain" calendar that I'll lug and tug to church functions, doctors' offices, vacations, and house-sitting gigs to keep me on track and let me know that I'm actually sitting in church, a doctor's office, a hotel room, and that someone's pooch needs to poo.

If Little Miss Muse had her way, all the calendars would be purple with purple ink and a discombobulated mess of "We can write fifteen novels and fifty shorts and take twelve new writing courses in 2020. Won't that be fun?" When I remind her that while she may not need sleep, food, or to do laundry, I'm not so lucky... well, the pouting ensues afresh.

So I take my pencil and try to *realistically* schedule publishing plans for the next year.

As she sits in the corner and belly laughs at me. Because *that* plan worked so well last year. Multiple times. When every three weeks someone stole/moved/melted/molded/sold/shipped/ate my cheese.

Every. Last. Morsel.

And I'd have to get my palm-sized eraser out and rub holes in the months redoing the goals. Learning to write in pencil and not purple ink...

I'm a bit bitter. I'll get over it. It's a new year, right?

And a brand-new decade, even!

(Cue the massive pressure and the "I've got no clue where I'll be in ten years" anxiety.)

But, seriously, what's with all the cheese? And mice?

Help me out, Google.

Oohhh... Those aren't mice.

2020 is The Year of the Rat in the Chinese zodiac calendar.

I now possess a fifty-second Wikipedia knowledge of this Year of the Rat. I'm not sure what "standard" zodiac sign my birthday lands in. (Morbid curiosity, and Google comes to the rescue—I'm the tail end of a scorpion, or something. Had the two-paragraph description of that sign matched my demeanor–or mentioned my office supply fetish—I may have converted to a believer.)

And the Chinese stuff looks vastly more complicated. Evidently, your rat could be metal, earth, fire, or wooden.

And sometimes rats need monkeys, and dragons can need rats... 2019 was a pig. Throw in a rooster and an ox, and you've got the makings of a dysfunctional barnyard family reunion. I believe we had this event in 2019 with my own family. Maybe more than once.

Morbid curiosity strikes again, and Google tells me I'm a dragon. Too bad. Was hoping to be a unicorn. I do get to be a fire dragon though...so that's cool. However, I'm most compatible with a rat? Maybe *that's* where my cheese went...

Or it melted. With all of my dragon fire.

It'd take me a tenth of a decade or more to learn the intricacies of the Chinese zodiac. If stars and planetary alignments are your thing, great. Whatever finds your cheese or floats your goat (the Chinese have one of those, too, if you need one).

It'll take a tenth of a decade or more for me and Little Miss to jive on a publishing plan.

May take two-tenths of the next decade and twenty more calendars for my brain to accept that teens are gone. Long live (at least for ten years) the twenties!

Here's wishing you all a joyous 2020, regardless of your zodiac critter.

Or whether your cheese is missing...

* * *

What came after this Happy New Year wasn't altogether overall happy—and was downright devastating—for most of the world in some form or fashion.

All of our collective cheeses relocated in the glorious Year of the Rat.

And, as I write this, it's September 2020, so I'm about to "catch up with myself." So the lessons learned for B. A. Paul circa Fall of 2020 won't be as insightful—or maybe they will be.

I don't know what month you're in, or what year. I'll let you, dear Readers, learn what you want. Assign meaning if you want. Because, at this point, hindsight is 2020.

Lesson Learned: Streamline those freaking calendars! And always use pencil.

73. WHAT I NEED

Dove into a Netflix binge session in between short-story writing stints and my "real" job. I was craving some downtime after the holidays and I wanted to steer clear of my typical crime show/sci-fi stuff. Had my fill for the moment. (But if Disney saw fit to release another Star Wars episode, I'd have to pull myself up by my bootstraps and partake of the Force.)

Overall, though, space flights, detectives, and crime scenes aren't what I needed.

I wanted something...warmer. Which is out of character for me, but alas. It was how it was.

But I needed warmth with a similitude of depth not found in Hallmark movies or Lifetime dramas.

Enter "Call the Midwife." My Netflix feed kept bringing it front-and-center. And I figured if BBC (And Mr. Cumberbatch, *ahem*) did such a bang-up job with Sherlock, surely they've done other atten-tion-worthy pieces. And this one is based on the memoirs of Jennifer Worth, a midwife in England during the 1950s, working out of Nonnatus House, a nun-ran medical mission.

Think Downton Abby meets ER—with Nuns! And lots and lots of babies.

Per reviews, this show sparred some viewers into longing for another child. The magic of motherhood. The wonder of pregnancy. The miracle of birth. And those are all true and well... but...

That's definitely not what *I* need.

The countless deliveries on the show didn't tickle me that way. What I did realize, however, after another epic disaster in my kitchen, was what I *do* need.

I need a nun.

No disrespect intended by this at all, religiously speaking. I really do desire one of those wimple-clad women to come and, well, take care of me.

I'd even settle for Sister Monica Joan with her tick of dementia. She'd keep me cared for and provide endless fascinating conversations. Though she is quite fond of cake, and I'd likely suffer untoward gut issues from her insistent indulgences.

During more than one episode, even my pouting, tired Little Miss Muse stuck her head around the corner and winked at me.

That scene with the little boy on the staircase.

That dialogue between a grieving husband and the doctor.

That tiny snippet of post-war history that hung over those folks' heads—or lurked beneath their feet.

Those bits sparked something in Little Miss. A whole new host of short tale ideas sprung. Ones that I (well, Little Miss) wouldn't have tapped had I (well, Little Miss and I) not watched the show.

And now I, and Little Miss, have firmly declared that we must source one of these service-minded women to come and rescue us from our current state of unkemptness.

That's what I need.

Or, maybe—and this is a real possibility—I'm still suffering the effects of a busted thyroid gland and what I really need is a nap.

* * *

I've threatened to spend the very first of writing profits on a maid. I don't care what kind of maid. She/he can even be a poorly qualified one. At this point, even a clogged Roomba with a dying battery would be better at housekeeping than I am.

Lesson Learned: Take a nap when you need it. Recharge the batteries. Don't be a dying Roomba.

74. ELLERY QUEEN, Y'ALL

They came last Tuesday! My contributor copies for my first professional magazine sale!

I must admit I did one of those little jump-and-squeal things when I saw them, three of them, all bound in clear plastic waiting for me on the kitchen table (because my son got the mail, depriving me of the joy of pulling them out of the mailbox myself. Come to think of it, since he did that, he may have saved me from getting run over by a car. If I'd have done my jump-and-squeal at the box, I'd have likely landed in the road. So, thanks, Son!)

The story is available in the January/February 2020 edition of Ellery Queen Mystery Magazine in their Department of First Stories section.

I'm too excited. And I'm drooling to read the stories tucked between the glossy pages, but I'm still in the middle of the Vegas workshop assignments, and soon I'll be reading hundreds of thousands of words' worth of short stories for that workshop.

So, Ellery must wait.

It may go with me on the plane, though.

EEEK!

The only thing better that could've been sent to my house was that nun I ordered last week. The company tells me they're out of stock, though, and likely won't be replenishing their nun supply for quite some time. Bummer.

If you'd like to read "The Dragonfly," you can get a sneak peek of it on the magazine's website. To see what happens to Jory, you'll have to go here. They've got print and digital options.

If you'd like more information on this long-running, award-winning publication, see their website.

A great big thanks to the editors over there. I greatly appreciate working with you. It's a true honor!

* * *

I'm still in awe "Dragonfly" made it into their publication. The original links in this post have been disabled (for those reading on their screens), because they update their website with the current issue's sneak peeks. The main website link still works.

Otherwise, for those folks reading this in paperback, you can visit elleryqueenmysterymagazine.com and search their back issues.

"The Dragonfly" in its entirety will be working its way into a collection soon. So be sure to watch bapaul.com for updates.

Lesson Learned: Revisiting blog posts with outdated links and missing images is a bit of a chore...

75. BANANA STICKERS!

It all started with The Mouse.

I swear I didn't intend to develop a disorder. It just happened.

My already-too-soft spot for office supplies/stationery grew a little weaker while I stood in the produce section that day...

Mickey Mouse greeted me in Steamboat-Willie fashion. A retro-style memento of times gone by. I got the bananas home, freed them from their wispy plastic, and hung them on their little rack. I opened the cabinet above them to put away something else and noticed a nick in the wood on the inside of the door. I took the Mickey sticker and covered the spot.

The next trip, I found another bunch of bananas and a new style of Mickey. And it all went downhill from there.

For a while, it made shopping a little less mundane, at least in the produce section. Search the bunches for an image not yet on my cabi-net. And (please don't turn me into the police) sometimes I'd switch the stickers from a too-green bunch or too-dark-spotted bunch to the bunch that interested me.

I've been known to snap a photo of the inside of the door so when I buy bananas the next time, I don't end up with a duplicate sticker.

It's a sickness. A dirty little pleasure. Little Miss gets a kick out of it. Wishes they'd do a unicorn series or purple fashion accessory series. I told her I didn't think the powers that be had that in the works...

Dole puts out themed (read Disney) stickers on their fruit. And I just, sort of, well, collected them. I was super stoked when Mickey gave way to the Avengers. But, as I'm not a huge banana fan, and at that time my guys were also swearing off the yellow ovals, I wasn't able to collect the whole gang.

Chiquita puts stickers on their bananas, too, but they're more artsy-fartsy and less poppy-culturey. I tried, as you can see, to embrace the artsy-fartsy, but it just wasn't doing it for me.

I'm not too worried about running out of space. If the banana stickers fill the inside of all my kitchen cabinets, I can always start new lines in the bathroom...

However, I have wondered what I'll do with this collection if we ever sell our home. Those stickers are really, really stuck. Maybe I'll leave them for the next occupants. Bump up the selling price of the house by five percent or so... Who knows? Maybe someday they'll be worth their weight in bananas!

Addendum: Before y'all shun me because I'm hopelessly flawed, here's a bit of an update: THERE ARE PEOPLE SELLING DOLE BANANA STICKERS ON EBAY!

AND OTHER PEOPLE ARE BUYING THEM!

I am, however, truly bummed that I missed out on the Star Wars series. That was a tough one to swallow. I can sleep tonight, though. There *are* others like me.

But I won't be buying my banana stickers on eBay. If I did, how would I occupy myself in the produce section?

* * *

Aaaand, we're back to both brands putting their branded stickers on the bananas. But I wait. Surely the movies will return and Dole can help Disney advertise something. Anything. Anything at all to make buying produce interesting...

Lesson Learned: I'm not sure there is one. I guess it's okay to be silly stupid sometimes.

76. LOVIN' IT

It's the LOVE MONTH!

Good grief.

A year ago this month, by grandma passed away. I remember seeing Valentine's Day items on the clearance shelves and having a hard time remembering if our family had even acknowledged that it happened. When life goes upside down, holidays are not so front-and-center.

This year, I'm prepping for the Anthology Workshop, and with general life stuff, the LOVE MONTH crept onto the grid that is February once again. Without my permission.

And I realized it snuck up on me after I'd already chosen *Shortages* for February's free fiction. Shortages isn't a love story... it's more of a drama, and if love did come, it was a "came too late" deal.

At any rate, as I looked through my choices for the blog, I realized I haven't written any feel-good LOVE MONTH stories. I have dad-kills-the-boyfriend stories. I have retired-detective-loves-his-zoo-job stories. I have a light alien "romance," but those two other-worldly dorks haven't figured out how to live among the humans yet, and so *Conrad and Coral* will stay locked in my "someday" vault until I clean them up a bit.

And I have a woman-meets-stray-cat story, but that could go south fast if I were to tag it with a Valentine theme.

In the truest sense of the romance genre boy-meets-girl stuff, I got pretty much zip.

And I've no desire to write one.

Maybe because I'm perfectly contented and in love with my man. He's cute, he's corny. He's been mine for nearly 25 years. The meet-cutes in romances and love story "catch me if you cans" just don't do it for me. Can't seem to make them feel real. I got the real deal. And I'm perfectly happy with him.

Got two kids I love dearly.

Got the mothers and the aunts and uncles. Love them too.

Got great friends that keep me centered. Love them.

Got three rescue fur babies that I love. (And don't tell the humans, but given the day and the drama, sometimes I *like* the furries better. Don't get all condescending on me—you know that person that popped into your head—the one where you'd rather bathe your skunk-sprayed dog in a galvanized tub of ice water stripped to your skivvies on a snowy day than meet the human for dinner. You *love* them bunches, but *like* is in another ballpark.)

Got a job I don't hate.

Got a hobby that I love that could very well take over the job I don't hate.

I'm blessed and contented. God is good. And isn't that at the base of all true love?

I digress from the sappiness (and my INTJ-ness doesn't do sappy-ness well, so that may be another reason I'm short on the LOVE MONTH tales. CREEPY MONTH tales? I could conjure those up all day long).

Look around at what you love. If you're cynical enough to believe you don't love anything, look around at what you don't hate.

If you have the eyes and capacity to read this rambling sap of a post, you are, at the very least, blessed.

* * *

Poor February. It's always under so much pressure. No wonder it can't decide how many days it has.

Lesson Learned: Keep lookin' for the good stuff. There's always a bit of good stuff.

77. FLYING LESSONS

I started this writing thing about six years ago (as an adult, anyway. I'd always loved writing as a kid and, looking back, I should've let that little girl go free. Oh well... At least we're up the right tree now.).

I remember exactly which office chair (now long gone) I sat in. A small Walmart-put-it-together-yourself computer desk (also long gone) held a desktop computer that, with any given keystroke, threatened to ignite a series of combustible reactions and send the tower into outer space. I seriously worried about the safety of that thing. That device long ago went to the electronics graveyard.

We still had Cosmo Quasimodo the Cat and Spencer Doodles the Schnauzer/Welsh mix terrier. Cosmo was in the window, and the breeze took his white hair and floated it all over the room. But I didn't care. Spencer was staked outside on his lead, sunning himself and barking his fool head off at anyone brave enough to walk the road leading behind our home.

But I didn't care.

Creativity (or so I thought) had struck and I was gonna do it, by gosh, by golly. I was gonna sit down and write the dumb book.

The blinking cursor teased and taunted me as I plugged away one word at a time about a red balloon bobbing and hovering above a lazy river. A child had let the oval orb go from a nearby carnival, and...

Nothing.

About five hundred words in before the great block. And the cursor laughed at me. One horizontal wink after another.

At that time, I worked nearly full time as a medical transcriptionist and homeschooled our kids. My world was medical records, school reports, and all things factual.

So I gave up the creative for the concrete (read this as: FEAR, though I didn't know it then). Stuck with the familiar grind and medicated that ridiculous notion of fiction writing with a hefty dose of "pull-it-together, Beth. You've no time."

I don't know that I'd even had time to read a novel for pleasure, let alone think about how to put one together. One word at a time.

When the urge hit again—and it hit really hard about three years ago—I knew I'd need a mentor or a teacher or an online class of sorts to see if I could shake loose the cobwebs that had ensnared those creative sparks (sparks I've now named "Little Miss Muse"). I needed someone to kick me out of the tree, parachute-free.

I took a creative writing course from Holly Lisle. Great fun. That's where the idea for *Switch* came from with Oliver and Hedge and Earl.

But I didn't finish the book. Wrote half of it and stopped. Blocked again. I'd lost my way. No one would read the dumb thing anyway, so why bother. (Read this whole paragraph as FEAR.)

Then I found Dean Wesley Smith's blog through one of Holly's blogs (down the rabbit hole of procrastination, but boy did that trip pay off in spades!) and his point of view on the indie author realm opened up a whole new world for me.

Dean wrote about Heinlein's Rules, and they just made sense.

Robert Heinlein was a sci-fi author who started back in the '40s. He's credited with 32 novels, nearly 60 short stories and other essays. I don't know that I've ready any of his fiction, but Heinlein gave sage advice to anyone wanting a career in writing. I'll paraphrase, but you can read the summary/reference info here.

Write it.

Finish it.

Don't touch it (except for typos and such).

Put it on the market.

Keep it on the market.

Super simple. Super difficult. I've been through the stages with a couple of shorts, mostly ending at #4, but never consistently with all of my written pieces. Let me break it down further because ranting here on the blog helps me plan.

Sometimes writing takes a backseat to life, which is fine, but I like to think I'm writing things in my head. That doesn't count. That "head work." Gotta get to the computer. Butt-in-chair time. (An upgraded chair of the bouncy bungee variety. I like it so well I just know when it's time for a new one, the company won't make them anymore, such is my luck. Tempted to go purchase four more just in case...)

Finishing (stopping and starting and procrastination) is hard. Hardest part for me on this one now is the middles. I can see the end of a thing and Little Miss Muse scampers off to another idea because she and I both know where the story will go. Why bother coding it out in black-and-white letters? Butt leaves chair and finds other activities to do—even cooking, for crying out loud—leaving characters stuck in proverbial trees swinging naked from all the loose ends.

I was a re-writer. Now I have so many ideas I don't have time to change plot lines and character motivations, and, and, and... The story stands as is. I'll fix the errors, but that's it. Little Miss will stand for nothing more in this vein anyway—she's running through the backyard right now scaring squirrels, playing chicken with the passing cars, and generally pitching a purple fit...

Finding a "home" for my "darlings" is daunting. I don't even know what genre my stuff lands in half the time. I take about an afternoon a month and try to send out a few, but boy have I failed at this one. I could self-publish all the shorts, but getting a "yes" from a magazine or anthology sure is wind under the wings.

Keep it on the market? Failed here, too. I got the rights back to my first short story sale, "The Removal of Blue Sky." I sent it to a couple of other places for reprint, but no luck, so it stagnates in my laptop along with the poor creatures that I've not bothered to do the first thing with after typing "the end."

As of this writing I've finished one novel and self-published it to market, one collection of 21 shorts is done and on the market, and 51 other short stories are loose and flapping in the wind with their britches hanging down around their knees. Some shorts have sold, some are on the market, and two shorts are in #5.

My goal for 2020: Take at least twenty of those loose stories through all five steps out to live markets. Self-publish the rest or use them here on the blog. Keep plugging new content through Heinlein's System.

Generally, despite Little Miss's ADHD, 2020 is the year to follow the rules—with no parachute!

I did hunker down and get a gob of my shorts into self-published collections. Some are still out to market. So that's better. Still bobbing like a drunken yo-yo through all five steps, though.

Lesson Learned: Bobbing through the steps is better than a full stop.

78. VEGAS, BABY!

As I sit here, the calendar just flipped over to February. February 2nd to be exact. I'm writing ahead to prep for travel, family obligations, and generally buffering in time to allow for the inevitable chaos that always creeps up before a trip—especially a much-looked-forward-to trip.

You know how it goes... Best laid plans and carefully calculated calendar pages are uprooted by illness, unexpected visitors, acts of God, blown tires, and the coronavirus (big news as I write this—hopefully it won't be bigger news in a couple of weeks...)

So, by the time this blog goes live, I should be in the middle of my Vegas trip. Three hours behind, so don't call me—I'm likely asleep. Or, if insomnia has hit, or my jetlag hasn't resolved, I'm prepping my notes and over-stimulated brain cells to get to the Anthology Workshop on time and ready to learn.

Note on jetlag: Daylight savings time (of either the spring or fall variety, doesn't matter) throws me off for two weeks. For fourteen days I walk around thinking "This time XX days ago, it was XX o'clock. Now, it's one hour wrong. It's just WRONG!). Stomach, brain, sleep. Always off. So it is very likely that I've not adjusted. Probably won't adjust until the day I fly home, and then I'll have another adjustment.

(Not a huge fan of change, in case you've not picked up on that particular character flaw of mine...)

There are folks coming from all over the globe for this workshop, and I shouldn't complain. They've got it much worse than I. Three hours should be no big deal, but as I sit here on 02/02/2020, I'm thinking my persnickety internal clock probably won't cooperate.

Next week is Free Fiction.

Then, after I return and my internal clock stops spasming, I'll update the blog with news and learning and anecdotes. Hopefully a few photos on the Facebook feed, too.

Unless something awfully amazing happens, then, well. What happens in Vegas...

* * *

Such a fan of that Anthology Workshop. Great networking with other writers. Great learning. Great laughing. And not one person's eyes glazed over with talk of craft and publishing and covers, and and and...

I enjoyed it so much so that I signed up to do it again in 2021 within days of landing back in Indiana. But, due to the nature of things, it will be 2022. So off a year, but still. My seat's reserved. Something amazing to look forward to.

Lesson Learned: Grab those lookin'-forward-to-it moments. Those don't come by often, either.

79. ANTHOLOGY WORKSHOP 2020: A NEWBIE'S TAKEAWAY

A few weeks ago, Little Miss Muse and I left for Vegas to attend an anthology workshop. I (along with forty-plus other writers) crafted six short fiction pieces to submit to various anthologies or magazines.

Excuse me. I knew this would happen... Little Miss just nudged me hard and rolled those impish eyes at me.

Yes, yes, Little Miss. You supplied all the genius for those pieces. Now be a good little muse and go play with your bottle rockets. Gotta get the blog in, dear.

Okay. I'm back. She's been high maintenance since we landed in Indy. Itching to death to start 29 new shorts and 19 novels all in the next week. If I don't toss her an ego stroke every now and then, she's simply impossible to live with...

The tales were written and turned in over the course of November and December last year. Then everyone's stories (nearly 300 of them) were read by all of the attending writers and the seven editors that sat on the panel—the same editors that would decide whether any of those manuscripts would make it into their respective projects (different anthologies or magazines).

But the most important thing (aside from networking with some jaw-dropping amazing writers), and the thing worth the hassle and the work and the travel, was the learning gleaned from listening to seven professional editors critique the manuscripts in front of the whole group. That panel has forgotten more about publishing than I could ever hope to learn.

It was a glorious five-day glimpse behind the curtain of the submission universe as to how editors think and their differing processes when scouring massive amounts of reading to build a magazine issue or short story collection.

Seven opinions, sometimes they agreed, sometimes they didn't. In all cases (whether the manuscript up for discussion was mine or the guy's sitting behind me or the gal's in the front row), I picked up on bits of craft or business or form. And in all cases, the only opinion that ultimately mattered out of the seven belonged to the single editor (or in one case father/daughter editor team) who was in charge of the project at hand.

I knew it would be brutal, having my stories critiqued like that. I imagined it would be like standing naked in front a room full of strangers, and as soon as I (uh, we—Little Miss and I) stepped off the plane in Vegas, I'd wondered what in the world I'd gotten myself into. I wondered that multiple times over the course of that day before class started—I'd felt like I'd crashed into someone else's family reunion. No one made me feel that way, it was all internal on my part, but it seemed that, aside from a few other newbies, most everyone knew each other.

Hugs and happy catch-ups abounded at lunch and dinner. Everyone was kind and full of wisdom curated over years of attending this workshop and hours and hours and hours to infinity of butts-in-chairs writing time.

And anytime anyone mentioned a cat, no fewer than a dozen phones would whip out from pockets and purses creating a collective breeze that could be felt all the way to The Big Dam.

I. Kid. You. Not. Cats everywhere. And no one thought it was odd. Not in this group.

And as that first day went on (and definitely after the first day of class), I had to wonder why anyone would want to stand naked in front of a room full of people not once, but five or eight or even twelve years. What was I missing?

I'd come to Vegas with the firm belief that this was a bucket-list thing for me. A once-in-a-lifetime experience to learn and grow as an author. But the more I listened that day before class started, the more I realized that this event had the strong possibility of sending Little Miss Muse packing up her gear to live with another newbie writer in another part of the world if I didn't find her something to do.

Little Miss, free spirit she is, caught sight of the shark tank swimming pool, and I decided before class started each morning that I'd drop her off at the pool (though I confiscated her firecrackers and made her promise to keep her bathing suit on and her wings tucked in). She's got such an ego and can be so moody, I just couldn't concentrate on the learning at hand and deal with her sprinkling and spitting purple glitter all over the conference room.

Wee into the night hours after a long day in class and wonderful lunches with the editors, some of us newbies piled like cordwood on our couch and licked our wounds and concocted generalized analogies regarding our experiences that don't translate so well in the light of day and when one isn't so slap-happy and stupid tired. I'll spare you those and give another that may help.

I had a pile of six blankets that I carefully knitted. I chose the colors and patterns and textures. I finished some off with fringe, others with satin ribbon. Some were chunky and thick. Some were dainty and tightly woven. Some smooth, fit for a newborn's swaddle. Some rough and itchy more fit for a saddle blanket.

For five days, the editors unfurled each blanket in front of the room and spoke their thoughts out loud. They looked through the blankets. Some liked the patterns. Some liked the colors. Some were too big for what they wanted. Some were too small. Or the wrong color. Or not fit for their couch. Or the editor was looking for a blanket for a king-sized bed and I'd provided more of a table runner thingy. (I've no idea, Little Miss had the knitting needles and EVERYTHING would have been purple had she gotten her way, so a little left-brained sensibility balanced out her obsession a few times).

Some editors would tug at a stitch and I feared the whole story would come unraveled right there in the room. And for some editors, that stitch was a deal breaker. Others liked the overall blanket enough to overlook the wayward threads.

Once, I got the feeling that the editors thought my blanket had come from the pile the Spanish brought over laced with the pox. Burn it. Burn it and never look back.

But that was, again, internal on my part. Fear reigned supreme at times. Nothing was personal. It was all about the blanket/manuscript. No one told me to burn any of my stories, but on that particular critique, I was eternally grateful Little Miss was swimming with the sharks. No telling what she'd have done.

My takeaway: Valuable networking. I'm not alone anymore. There are others like me. Those with desires to create a career out of sitting alone in a room and making things up. I met those with office supply fetishes and cat stories and the ability to talk writing and publishing and all things books for hours on end with not blink toward boredom. And I met those who never once judged me despite the fact that not once did I successfully find my way to my hotel room without incident.

I've made writer friends!

My tally? Out of six, three of my blankets were good fits for the editors' projects and counted as sales. (Giddy little jump-and-squeal moments, I'm tellin' ya...) I'm waiting to hear back on a fourth one—a strong maybe.

Would I go back? Well, let's put it this way: Even if I never made another sale to the panel, the answer would be heck yeah. Because it's not about the sales; it's about the learning and networking. Learning and networking are priceless.

Annnddd... I've secured my seat for 2021. The good Lord and the universe willing, I'll go back to stand naked in front of a room full of people with six more of my blankets. Let them pull and tug at the threads. Let them stomp on them and wad them up and set them on fire. I'll even let them drag a blankie or two off to The Analog Couch (more on that another time).

Let them help me be a better writer.

I get it now. Why people do it more than once.

It might very well classify as a sickness.

I've already contacted the Golden Nugget's lifeguard. I figure I'd give him a good heads up about the Little Miss Muse in the purple bathing suit. Better check her bikini for pop rocks and firecrackers and match sticks.

Hers are waterproof...

* * *

If you're curious about or interested in any of the in-person workshops by this group, here's the link: https://www.wmgworkshops.com/

Hopefully things will be up and running soon out west...

By the way: That shark tank swimming pool really was cool. I wonder if she spooked any of them into spitting out a few rows of teeth. Sharks are no match for my Little Miss.

Lesson Learned: Keep weaving the blankets.

80. PUBLICATION UPDATES

Keepin' it short this week and cleaning up loose ends.

Several have asked about where to find the stories I wrote for the Anthology 2020 Workshop.

You can't find them. Not yet. I'll let you know here (hopefully) when they come out and where you can get them when the anthologies are done.

As far as short story publications, here's what's available so far:

"The Removal of Blue Sky" is in Future Visions Volume 3, edited by Brian J. Walton.

"The Dragonfly" is in Ellery Queen Mystery Magazine January/February 2020 edition. The links in my original announcement post go to Ellery's current issue. So, you'll have to contact them, scour their back issues, or *gasp* eBay to find it, as it's currently off newsstands.

And, in the process of surviving the holidays and life in general, I failed to mention this one: "Leftovers" is in Pulphouse Fiction Magazine Issue #8, Fall 2019, edited by Dean Wesley Smith. It's available through WMG Publishing as paper, e-book or subscription. It's also on Amazon.

I have well and truly caught the short story submission bug. Lots are "out in the mail" waiting on answers. A few others have a tentative "sold," but until the contracts are signed and the fat lady sings (or at least has her giddy little jump-and-squeal moment) I can't count them as published.

Anything can happen to disrupt this industry. Crazy elections. Crazy coronavirus. Crazy technical issues. Life in general. Name it. So no counting chickens before they hatch, no notchings of the belt, no happy jigs, and no twisting the tops of the celebratory diet ginger ale bottles. Not until contract time...

I'll just write and mail the next one.

And the next.

And the next...

This industry moves slowly, and there's not much in the way of instant gratification. But when those successes do come, it's like getting hooked up to an adrenaline drip and, at least for a few moments, I'm on top of the world.

Hope you have a productive week of successes and forward momentum despite the crazy times we've got going on. Find what primes your adrenaline pump and go for it!

* * *

I'm not a fan of shameless self-promotion, but alas, here it is. A list of the works is in the back of the book...

Lesson Learned: Self-promotion feels much like walking outside with no clothes on.

81. A NOD TO MR. BOB

The last round of thyroid-itis hit just before Vegas when I found myself too tired to move or think, so I plinked and plugged away at "real job" work and fiction word count while cuddled up on the couch, laptop balanced atop my fuzzy unicorn blanket. An occasional passerby cat provided companionship (though lately my furry rescues are fairly ungrateful—fabulous little traitors who prefer my son or husband to me...fickle felines).

When the brain cells fizzled after a work session and the fatigue overtook, the ringing in my ears would start and prevent real rest. So background noise was a must. But what to put on that wouldn't require me to pay real attention and would be a bit relaxing?

Netflix has Bob Ross!

Yes. I'm that person who binge-watched (and often thyroid-napped through) Bob Ross with his fuzzy locks and happy little brushes and double-primed pre-stretched 18x24 inch canvases (but I could choose whichever size canvas works best for me, he said so...). There's something about his soft demeanor and the tisking and whisking of the brushes against the canvas that is utterly calming.

And the man never—and I mean never, ever—got paint on his shirt. Hand me a palette with that much gooey goop smeared all over it, and I'm covered in thirty seconds. Ask my husband what it's like around our house when I try to paint something simple with one brush and one color. Let alone a rainbow and tons of brushes to choose from. Hats off to those neat painters out there, but I digress...

I remember watching Bob Ross's "The Joy of Painting" with my grandpa. Grandpa had his chair—you know that one piece of furniture that no one else sits in? He had *that* chair. Where he'd sit with a coffee cup balanced on one of the wooden arms (it still has those mug-worn spots in the finish) and where he'd hear Grandma yellin' some to-do list at him. He'd sit there with his long legs crossed and he'd grin at me, ignore her, turn down his hearing aid and turn on PBS.

I remember Grandpa grinning when Bob showed clips of Peapod the Squirrel or other wildlife. Or when Mr. Ross would use the term "happy little accident."

And then there's those Bob Ross-isms like "Cabin-ectomy" when you paint a cabin and need to clean up the edges or the "Bravery Test" when you're about to plant an enormous evergreen right over the top of a mountain.

I remembered the names of his oil paints: Midnight Black. Prussian Blue. Alizarin Crimson (when I was a kid I thought he was saying "Lizard" crimson). The bits of advice like a thin paint will always stick to a thick paint, and if you try to work on a dry canvas, you'll be in "agony city."

But Grandpa grinned the widest when Bob Ross cleaned the two-inch brush. And Bob loved cleaning those two-inch brushes. He'd dip it in odorless paint thinner, "shake off the excess" into a trash can, then "beat the devil out of it" as he slapped the bristles ferociously against the leg of the easel. Then Bob would grin as big as Grandpa and say, "I just love cleaning the brush."

This week, I've been doing some self-editing of the shorts I've written for the one-a-week-for-a-year. And, thank you Mr. Bob Ross. Your "isms" have made my "agony city" go much smoother. And I think I'll take your advice with the devil thing...

Wow. Little Miss Muse sure did run off with a brush or two in more than one story. Happy little accidents everywhere. But I'm not re-writing them, just fixing errors.

Like where I put in the wrong character name, abruptly changed the weather or vehicle type/color (I can't even remember what I drive, let alone what my characters are scooting around in), or where I allowed a character to meander about making toast or talking to herself for way too long...

That's when you've gotta shake off the excess and then beat the devil out of it.

And grin.

So to speak.

Now, I don't know that I'll ever be so happy proofreading my own stuff as Bob was when cleaning his brushes. But it sure makes me smile to think of taking a manuscript of white paper with little black marks on it and shaking the snot out of it against a red ink pen.

Or maybe this whole analogy is still a residual effect of thyroid brain, Daylight Savings time, and the pandemic chaos that grips the world. I don't know. I don't think I much care.

And thanks, Mr. Bob Ross, for the lessons, for the -isms, and for bringing back those glorious moments I spent with Grandpa in front of the television set on Saturday mornings.

We have that chair. It sits in our sunroom and has become Amara Mino's favorite place to bathe when the weather allows us to be in that room. It matches nothing, style wise. It's old, but I don't think I'd bring myself to get rid of it. I can still see Grandpa sitting there. Reading the paper, watching the evening news, laughing at Hee-Haw, and turning down his hearing aids to avoid Grandma's incessant nagging.

Lesson Learned: If my dear hubs ever needs hearing aids, I shall get him the new-fangled kind that pair with my phone. No tuning me out, Bucko!

82. THE ANALOG COUCH

One of the myriad of tidbits learned from the Vegas workshop was a concept called "The Analog Couch."

Now, I'm not sure if this term is common among fiction editors or if it was just the editors on that particular panel (I'm a newbie to this whole publishing thing, remember). I'm not even sure if it needs to be capitalized. So when the phrase crept into the manuscript critiques, I picked up on it, made note and kept listening.

Then it happened to my manuscripts. Twice.

I started asking questions. What is this couch they speak of? Is it a real thing? Is it editor lingo? Am I supposed to know about this piece of furniture? Everyone around me seemed to understand and go with it, nodding heads in understanding, and I'm sitting in the back of the room going, "What did I miss? Help me out. Clueless Newbie Alert!"

Of course, I'm the clueless newbie who was too stymied by terror to raise her stupid hand for fear of asking the stupid question, "What is this magical, mysterious sofa?"

Is it like that couch in "Friends" where they all gathered at the Central Perk coffee shop?

The one the Golden Girls fought and bickered on with the wicker base and floral cushions?

Or is this thing more like a therapist's couch? A "lie back and let me dig around in your head" deal.

Turns out, it's like all three.

It's where readers go sit and think after they get kicked out of a story. The story's logic is broken. The scientific premises may be flawed. There's information flow issues.

They sit and they think, and they dig around in the mud of it, and sometimes bicker and sometimes laugh.

The analog couch is the place readers go when your fiction world causes them to pause or stop reading and say, "Now wait a minute. I don't think that works. What about..." and they start analyzing the crap out of a story element. They sit on this couch (figuratively speaking) and think.

And they may never go back to the story. And that's the problem.

Writers should write in a way that readers never ever want to put down the story and go sit on a couch of any fabric or pattern and think.

But I did that. Or Little Miss Muse did that. We did that. Several times.

She and I. Well, we broke science and forgot about logical information flow. And we didn't even know there was a couch.

I guess as a movie-watcher/television-show consumer I do that thing where I stop watching, or I pretend to watch, but my brain gets hung up on something that seemed off. Sometimes I've hit the pause button and yelled at my husband about how utterly ridiculous the story was...

I *know* I do that when I watch the news. Hopefully, in the case of current events, you do too. The information flow seems off. No one can spell logic. And, usually, somewhere someone has broken science or at the very least, broken all sense of common sense. *Insert enormous eye-roll here with a long, drawn-out sigh*

So I was familiar with the feeling, if not the actual couch.

As far as manuscripts go, now we know. Little Miss and I. And I care. I care a great deal and will try to write and proofread in such a way that the readers' needs come first. Do things make logical sense? If they don't, is there a purpose to it that serves the story?

Little Miss? She doesn't care. She thinks its fun to break things and hide information and blow this up and tip that thing on its head. She'd break science all day long and do so illogically and with great glittery glee.

I Googled "Analog Couch" in various forms before writing this blog.

I Googled it real good.

And found nothing about this concept.

I discovered answers to how far should I place my couch from my television. I was offered deals from major retailers on all kinds of sofas, sectionals, and recliners if I ordered within the next four hours. I was even presented with a plethora of textbooks on digital and analog communication systems. Written by someone named "Couch."

But this concept? Nope.

So I'm still not sure where the term originated. Maybe someone could comment on the Facebook feed and give a link to a source.

And as I continue my proofreading of the stories from this one-a-week challenge, I'm now acutely aware of this Analog Couch. And I'll try to keep the readers off of it.

* * *

I've done about twenty of these blurbs today. Reading, reminiscing, making notes of things I really want to pay attention to and those "lessons learned" that really hit home over the last few days.

"I think I need a break, girl."

Little Miss is jumping on my couch, twirling her sparklers. "Let's break something."

"No. It's time for a break. Not breaking things."

"Let's send them all to the couch!" She pumps her chubby fist in the air.

"Given the state of things, many of them have been on their

respective couches long enough." I know I have. Time to move forward.

"Lets break all the science!" She lights the sparklers, not with her bedazzled Zippo, but with her breath. Show off.

"I think breaking science has already been done enough this week." I grab a diet Ginger Ale and hand her a can of grape soda. She slurps it, it runs down her front and onto Malachi Maxwell's tired toe beans. She giggles. He runs, spooked. He can't see her. He only knows something's wrong with his toe beans.

Definitely time for a brain break. I've broken my last neuron for the evening.

Lesson Learned: Time to set a timer while working on this project. I've been sitting way too long...

83. THE GREAT CHALLENGE...CHECK!

I signed up for this amazing ridiculousness last April. In 2019.

Before 2020.

Before thinking about holidays and family chaos and health issues and travel plans and computer glitches.

Definitely pre-pandemic.

Before.

52 weeks ago.

Man, a lot can happen in 52 weeks.

And this last season has taught us all that a lot can happen in 52 minutes, but I digress.

The challenge was simple: Write one short story (at least 2,000 words long) per week for one year. The reward? A lifetime subscription to one of WMG Publishing's offerings of incredible—and sometimes intense—learning opportunities. (As far as I know, as of this writing, the challenge is still open, if you dare...)

Quite the carrot. Kept me in the race when I felt like quitting.

And boy, did I want to throw in the towel on more than one occasion—especially during last summer's life tsunami. And another life-stopping event post-holidays.

The third massive urge to drop it all hit hard a few weeks ago when Little Miss Muse watched some stupid news broadcast over my shoulder and declared, "Nope. Not up for quarantine with you and three cats and the menfolk." And she packed her firecrackers and all her lighter fluid into her perfectly purple suitcase and left. I don't know where she went—likely got a cheap flight and is relaxing on an empty beach, seagulls gliding in the breeze above her head, waves crashing gently on the shore. More on her next week. That impossible little imp...

Despite it all, I learned a gob, had a gob of fun, and now I have a not-so-small pile of manuscripts to spit-shine and publish. It should keep me busy for a while, or at least until Little Miss Muse drags her sun-burned rump back to Indiana and we kick back into novel mode. (Little Miss and I abandoned an entire cast of characters on the side of a road in rural Illinois. They've been waiting there for months in suspended animation, twiddling their thumbs, waiting for the go-ahead to re-enter the sedan and head to Chicago. Soon, gang. I promise. Soon.)

A few of the stories have found homes in various publications. Some are out to market, waiting for an answer. A few are novel starts. Several have already shown up on the blog as free fiction. Most will be bundled into collections, and I'll throw them up on Amazon in the next few weeks.

Thanks to all who encouraged me along the way and listened while I vented about the process. Thanks to Little Miss for those sparks of creativity when she did manage to show up for work (maybe if I stroke her ego, she'll come home sooner rather than later...).

Congrats to all my fellow writers who likewise made it through, and gobs of encouragement go out to those just starting or nearing the end of this massive challenge. It can be done!

And may *your* muses remain steady on the payroll!

* * *

The link to see if these challenges are still active is www.wmgpublishinginc.com/workshops-and-lectures/.

Lesson Learned: Carrots are so worth it.

84. JURASSIC PARK TRUISMS

This movie is one of my all-time favorite adventure flicks—and the one I tend to pause on when channel surfing. Sick, tired, or in need of background noise, Jurassic Park hits all my happy buttons. If you've not seen it (the very first one, 1993), this blog has tons of spoilers. Stop reading, go watch it, and then come back.

If it's been a tick, watch it again. And pay close attention to the dialogue.

I still laugh at some of the lines, even as they topple out of my mouth. (I know, I know...I scold my dear hubs for watching The Andy Griffith show as he pretends he doesn't know that Barney's about to shoot his foot off with that one bullet, but this is about me now. And I'm allowed to know every line in this particular Spielberg flick.)

A few days ago, I found it airing for free, and I listened with a whole new set of ears—ears of a head-spinning writer in the middle of a pandemic. Some lines fit the world-wide scenario we find ourselves in. Some exchanges fit what's going on in my own house. Many fit my current writing predicaments. I'll share a few. You listen for yourself. See what sticks.

Here we go:

"I hate computers," says Dr. Alan Grant when he's at the dig in the

opening scene and everyone's using tech instead of good, old-fashioned digging and education to unearth fossils. I, too, have a certain hatred of the things. But they're a necessary evil (I can't imagine the wrist strength required to chug out manuscripts longer than a page without one). However, my laptop reminds me every other day that it's about to give up the ghost and turn into a digital dinosaur soon. The screen jiggles and wiggles just like the one in the movie. Soon... Very soon.

"That doesn't look very scary, " says the unnamed idiot kid at dig site regarding a velociraptor. I can hear government leaders all over the world say the same as they look at the puffy coronavirus sphere. Ahem. Then Dr. Grant schools the kid in all things vicious raptor, right down to the gutting.

Well then...

"The kind of control you're attempting is not possible." Dr. Ian Malcomb (my favorite guy in the movie), warns the scientists they're out of their collective minds. I thought I had a plan and a fuzzy sense of control over my life as I flew home from the Vegas writers' workshop in February. Yeah. That's what I get for trying to make all of my dinosaurs female. Or putting my ducks in a row, heaven forbid.

"Hold on to your butts." Ray Arnold (Samuel L Jackson's character) when the scientists, lawyer, and two children start their tour of the dino-themed amusement park. Yeah. This quote is multifunctional no matter what industry or crisis you're in. He also said this as he tried to reboot the park's massive IT system. How appropriate. Rebooting a system.

"Life finds a way." I fear Dr. Malcomb will be correct once again as we get further into the pandemic. A virus has a way of finding a way, too. So do goats, pigeons, monkeys, bears, and reindeer as these creatures overtake the now human-less landscapes. Very interesting what nature's doing at the moment.

Or, you could be more optimistic than I and say humans will find a way (to overcome, to come together, to make a difference). And we will. For a bit. But I'm a realist. And we'll likely find a way to royally screw up the next crisis, too.

"How can we possibly have the slightest idea what to expect?" Dr. Grant explaining the ridiculousness of the park. We can also put this quote directly into the mouths of every doctor, politician, statistician, business owner, and author.

"He left us. He left us!" Lex screams this as the lawyer abandons the kids to save his own rear only to be eaten by the T-rex. She says this again to Dr. Grant as he tucks her into a drainpipe for safe-keeping until he can get her brother out of a tree. She's completely and thoroughly freaked. Her voice is high. Her eyes are bulging. She's shaking with fear.

And this is the moment that hit me the hardest given my internal struggles during this global wildness.

This is me to a T.

Not because I'm spooked of the virus, as serious as it is. Not because I'm petrified to be around people (though that wasn't my introverted self's favorite thing in the first place). Not because I've lost a chunk of my "day job" (because I have, but it'll come back. Maybe). Not because my husband has days off work all willy-nilly and I never know how to cope in the kitchen.

But this is me in my writing office.

Because...

Little Miss Muse. The one that keeps me company as I create. The one that whispers those glorious gems of dialogue and sprinkles glittery ideas from her purple bag of tricks as I plod away at the keyboard. The one that holds my hand through plots thick and thin. The one that reminds me she dropped a "Little Miss Muse bomb" five chapters ago on purpose and slaps me upside the back of the head to remind me to use it. Weave it in. Don't waste the magic.

Her. Little Miss. That creative purple winged imp disappeared when the pandemic showed up.

She left me.

She left me.

Don't have a clue where she's run off to, or what she's doing. Even this blog post, which should bring her out of hiding to have a tiny tidbit of fun, isn't cutting it.

I've left my office window open. Baited her with firecrackers that I've caked in purple glitter—her favorite shades of lavender to be exact. I've stocked her favorite purple soda, grape bubblegum, and Chunky Monkey (gag me, but that's a muse's pantry for you). Even bought her a brand-new pair of high heels (purple, of course). The ones that go clickety-clack when she dances as my keyboard makes the same sounds.

In the meantime, I've switched gears. The 52 story challenge is done, and I've got proofreading and publishing to work on. I've got classes to take.

And I'll wait. But not for long. Because that novel is itching at the back of my brain. And if she wants any credit for that endeavor at all, she'd better show up. Soon. Or I'm going on without her.

Maybe I'll post a job listing for creative muses. See if there's a black-and-white polka-dotted dinosaur or an overweight cigar-smoking basement-dweller that'd be up for the task. They'd likely be less maintenance, but the training they'd require? Oh my. Please, Little Miss. Pretty purple pleases all day long...

Okay. Now that I've vented and gone all snarky, here's a little encouragement...

"Hold on to your butts."

When things reboot in a few weeks. Hold on.

If things don't reboot. Hold on.

If your muse or mind or money has gone missing in the coronavirus muck. Hold on.

At some point, the world will spin or jump or jiggle or jive. Whatever "it" looks like next...

Just. Hold. On.

And leave your window open a bit. Maybe allow a little ray of hope to wiggle through the crack and snuggle up next to you while you sleep...

Hold on.

* * *

Five months later and we're still holding onto our butts.

But I digress... I just looked up Jurassic World: Dominion. Production was halted due to the pandemic, but it's still slated for next summer.

Hold on.

Lesson Learned: Look for the rays of hope. Even if it means sitting in a crowded theater trying to enjoy yourself a year from now...

85. DRUNK DUCKS IN DAFFODILS

Yeah. You read that correctly.

I recently sent a friend a cheer-up card with a duckling on the front. She and I have joked for years about how I like my ducks in a row.

Nice, neat, orderly rows. On a single, peaceful pond.

The duckling on the card was nearly on its back, webbed feet in the air and looked a little confused. I teased her that all my ducks but one had left me and the lone survivor appeared to be an alcoholic.

I don't drink. But that one duck... he sure does. He's deluded enough to believe he still has a job. That presumption is, at this time, fabulously inaccurate. You can't get in a line if there's just one of you. Or in a row.

He seems to think I still have other ducks somewhere. In a line. Or in a row. And that I'll let him join the pack.

At this point, I don't even know if I've got a pond to put a duck on.

To make matters worse, I only recently started catching glimpses of Little Miss Muse loitering at the edges of the yard. She's been MIA for so long, I'd almost forgotten what she looks like. So I could care less about ducks right now. I'm trying to bait-and-switch a misbehaving purple-winged imp.

And now that yellow fluffball has taken to staggering around in daffodils, defying any wish or outright command of mine to find another home—because he's unaware he's been laid off due to COVID-19.

But there he dawdles and dilly-dallies.

In the daffodils.

To which I'm crazy allergic.

Those radiant flowers that signal the landing of spring like a ground crew guiding airplanes from the sky. They pop up in yards and landscaping—and in shiny pink and purple foil-wrapped pots in the entryways of grocery stores—just in time to coincide with my already-active allergy season.

What joy.

Those gorgeous yellow demon petals cast off microscopic invaders that sear tear ducts and inflame nostril linings.

And now, heaven forbid, if I walk past one of those displays—even with my pretty homemade Darth Vader-print mask—and sneeze? Into my elbow? Behind my mask?

Sneeze!!?? In public?

Ouch. That gets people's attention. Their already scared eyeballs widen even further over their homemade masks and bandanas and tied-around-the-face bedsheet shreds at that sound.

What a world this has become. People suspicious and scared of everyone.

So maybe that one last duck isn't as drunk as I think he looks. Maybe he's got a clue that I can't come near him, given his current location, lest I slip into anaphylactic shock. Hiding among the daffodils he can pretend he's got a job.

That he's still on the payroll.

Like I'm not gonna fire his fine-feathered tail when this is all over.

On further consideration, however, I think the straw hat he's sporting gives it away. He's definitely three or more sheets to all the winds.

At least by summer the daffodils will be dead and the roses will blossom. I've got no problem with roses of any hue. Little Miss Muse is partial to purple ones. I promised her a multi-dozen bouquet tied with a glittery lavender bow if she comes back.

To work.

In the office.

At the same time as me.

While I'm writing.

(Man, these days you've gotta spell out ALL the details, or the muses and ducks and politicians will find even the most microscopic of loopholes...)

If I can get Little Miss wrangled, *then* I'll deal with the lack of a pond.

And my flock of missing ducks.

But I'm still gonna pink-slip the drunk one, bless his yellow pollen-covered butt.

* * *

My flock (well, a flock, maybe not my original flock...) came back onto the calendar into those nice, neat rows of days of the week. But the flock I have now looks suspiciously like a herd of rabid rhinos instead of anything feathered.

Lesson Learned: Nothing wants to get in line. Muses. Ducks. Rhinos. Learn to work around the chaos.

86. MAYBEE, MAYBEE NOT

I'm writing this on a Thursday, I think. It could be Tuesday. I'm not entirely certain where in the week I am. I know I need a blog for next Monday. Probably.

Maybe.

The days have morphed into each other like dozens of drunk amoebas. Okay, okay. Pre-Pandemic Beth had trouble remembering what day it was, but *that* Beth had a routine with a job, caretaking errands, church, and... Oh. Yeah. Not nearly so many bombarding reminders of these "unprecedented, uncertain, challenging, trying times."

Try to watch a movie on regular TV? Every commercial boasts a "We're in this together" or "Stay safe at home" message.

So I switch over to commercial-free Amazon Prime and Roku reminds me. Gently, though. Thanks. I'd forgotten I was safe at home.

Facebook? Forget it.

Check the business email in hopes a *paying* client has emerged from the ashes? Uh... another round of unprecedented and untimely triggers.

Okay. So no screens at all. I'll venture outside.

The guy walking his dog past my house for the tenth time today?

Both master and beast donning masks. A grocery run to Walmart where mobs swarm the place as if they've won the lottery the day before Black Friday...

Nope. Not enough masks or hand sanitizer in all the world to deal with that. Didn't like crowds six months ago. Don't like them now.

Oh these unprecedented, uncertain, challenging, trying times.

Seriously, writers, get some new adjectives for 2020.

I have a thesaurus. Let's see.

Absurd. Preposterous. Fetid. Muddled. Rancid. Onerous.

Enter the UFOs, we can add "otherworldly" and "alien" times.

Cue the murder hornets and we add "venomous" and "searing hot poker rod" times.

Wait. Stop. This post wasn't meant to be a rant, but a more forward-thinking outlook for May. Shake off the negativity. Think, Beth. What next. Do some goal-setting.

Maybe... Pull out the planner I bought in NOVEMBER OF LAST YEAR. (hahahahahahahaha)

Writing something in it.

Tomorrow I will... dust! Yup. That's a good place to start. Saturday I will... vacuum.

Oh, good grief. Cross those out, I know I won't do them. I want to sink brain and energy into something with a tick more meaning than cobwebs and dust bunnies (though those "bunnies" are more akin to "moose" and pudgy orangutans could swing from one or two of those cobwebs).

How can one forward-think through this? I've still got that lone inebriated duck waddling around that I've got no idea what to do with.

Came across this YouTube short while reading Kristine Kathryn Rusch's blog. (Really, it's like the woman crawled inside my head and wrote her blog just for me. Thanks, Kris! And even if you're not a writer, you can gain some "reframing" through her insights.)

The video is hilarious. If only Pandemic Beth could travel eight months back. Explain, even vaguely, what was to come to clueless

Pre-Pandemic Beth. How would I have reacted with the knowing? Hard to tell, but the clip is sure fun...

It's not at all as dire as my rant-that's-not-a-rant paints it. We're safe. We're well. We've got amazing friends and family. We've got food and toilet paper and three rescue fur babies and roofs over all the heads. We're blessed.

Years ago I decorated one of my classrooms with bumblebees. The rules for the kiddos went something like: Bee kind. Bee on time. Bee prepared... You get the idea. Simple. Doable. Memorable.

If you're overwhelmed, go back to basics. And some days, accomplishing the basics of decent humanity is goal enough. What am I thankful for? How can I bless someone else? Smile. Wave.

Breathe in, breathe out.

Patience, young grasshopper.

Write down the dreams. Write down the goals, even if those goals look much like drunk morphing amoebas because of a foggy view of the future.

Maybe May will be better than April.

Economic collapse. Korea. UFOs?

Maybe not.

Shake it off. Focus.

Bee the bulldog. He looks fairly Zen, right?

Nothing at all like a murder hornet.

Inhale.

Exhale.

And now that I'm thoroughly grounded with a fresh attitude adjustment, I'm finally off to hunt the elusive dust moose.

* * *

The photo for this blog was a bulldog dressed in a bumblebee costume. Pudgy, cute. He looked as though it was his purpose in life to dress like a bee.

The video as of September 2020 has over 15 million views (and by the time I got around to the edits for this manuscript in December

2020, the search indicated Julie Nolke has posted Parts Two through Four).

And I'd totally forgotten about the UFO stuff. We quickly devolved into fires and floods and dust storms.

Again, we're blessed. We had some major wind that did a couple thousand in damage to the backyard, but no structural damage. Just another headache.

Maybe. Maybe. 2021 can be brighter.

Lesson Learned: Write right now. Stop procrastinating. It can always get worse, and there is no time machine to go back and warn myself of impending world nastiness.

87. BAIT AND SWITCH

A few posts back I explained how my Little Miss Muse went missing in action. The pandemic freaked her out. I know this now.

Because she told me.

Little Miss showed up earlier this week, peeking through the office window spooking the cats, especially Malachi. On Tuesday, the sight of her knocked him from his perch on my desk and sent him flying out the door and down the hallway, tail bushed, eyes bulging, and toenails deployed in a desperate attempt for traction on the wooden floors.

So Wednesday I increased the bait.

More grape bubblegum hanging from the tree limbs. Additional Chunky Monkey left outside the porch door in a Styrofoam cooler. Grape sodas at each corner of the house. If anyone had actually seen these attempts, they'd have thought me insane and called the authorities. Or at least gotten ahold of my mother. See if she could talk some sense into me.

From inside the house, I dangled a new pair of purple Stilettos from the curtain rod in the kitchen. That really got her attention. After a few hours of pouting and pacing and floating back and forth with great grape bubbles of gum popping from her mouth, she begged me for the shoes.

"Only if you come inside. Have a rational discussion. Talk terms."

She turned her chubby self around and vaporized from view. (Sometimes she does that, vaporizes in and out, leaving twirling tendrils of purple haze in her wake. Other times she just appears. Sometimes she slams doors and scatters cats. She's fickle and proud of it.)

I was determined, though. The uber high heels would burn a hole in her brain and she'd be back. She's got feet the size of a three-year-old's, but she loves stomping around in adult shoes. The racket she'll make in them will be awful, but anything, ANYTHING, to get her back to work was on the table.

I restrung more bubblegum. Hid leftover lavender Easter eggs along the foundation of the house, each stuffed with costume jewelry (you know, the kind that'll turn your fingers green and will lose the stones in a day, but kids love them). Adjustable rings with amethyst-wanna-be stones. Sparkly lilac beaded bracelets. Plum pendants. And teeny tiny bottles of nail polish. Purple, of course.

It worked. On Thursday, I heard a tapping at the kitchen window. She was gripping a bottle of nail polish in each hand and pouted out her bottom lip as she hovered in place, her little wings beating as fast as they could, sparkle flying off in all directions. Her eyes pleaded with me. A tiny line of grape-stained drool started at the corner of her mouth as she gawked at the shoes still hanging in the window.

"Are you ready to be reasonable?" And as soon as the words were out of my mouth I realized I'm never going to rationally reason with a muse, Little Miss or any other muse species. But something had to be done.

She buzzed backward, and I thought for a moment she was going to game the system, leave yet again and wait for more gum. More eggs. More high heels.

More half-melted Chunky Monkey.

But she was scared. Looking over her shoulder. Ready to bolt. Again.

So I brought out the big guns. From under the kitchen sink I dug out the firecracker, bottle rocket and rose bouquet. And a brand new purpled jeweled Zippo lighter.

I took down the shoes, and she floated closer, clearly concerned I'd not give them to her. Ever.

Then I held up the bouquet for her to see, turning it around and around so she could appreciate the entire piece. She shivered with excitement, glitter poofing around her. Then I showed her the lighter.

And into the house she came. Quietly, though. Timid and very much unlike her usual entrances. All three napping felines continued their slumbers as if I were the only other being in the house.

Finally.

She watched me tuck the lighter inside my back pocket as she settled on the countertop.

Now, something you must know about muses, at least the ones I've had limited experience with: They don't speak out loud. You've got to be still and somewhat quiet before they'll communicate. And my Little Miss goes from a college-degreed language grasp to two-year-old speak in the space of a sentence or less. Our exchange went something like this:

I have lighter. Part question, part statement, she pointed at my pocket.

"No. We talk first."

Huff and shrug. She belched. She reeked of grape soda and ice cream.

"You need to come back to work. I don't treat you badly, do I? Where have you been? What have you been doing?"

Scared. Overwhelmed. Too hard to play.

"Well, I was about to go on without you."

You need me.

"You're nice to have. But I could manage on my own." I turned to the sink to start the dishwater. She sat cross-legged on the counter next to me, toying with the straps on the shoes, sniffing the bouquet (not the rose part, the bottle rocket part).

Unlikely, given the whining you've done on the blog about my absence.

She had me there, but I wasn't about to give in. "What can we do to fix this?" I washed a few plates and forks, careful not to splash her. Trying to be indifferent. Pleading silently that she won't dematerialize and take the expensive gifts with her.

These are a nice start. She nodded toward the goodies. *Give me the lighter.*

"Terms first."

Terms first. Then lighter?

"Yes."

You'll cancel the want ad?

"Want ad?" I nearly dropped the dirty lasagna pan.

Oh. No. I'd threatened a few weeks ago to hire a new muse. She must've read it. She took me seriously. Good grief. She must realize no other author on the planet would spoil her like I do, thus the stalling.

I dried my hands and helped stuff her chubby feet deep inside the shiny stilettos because she was still clutching the bottles of nail polish. "Yes. I'll cancel the want ad."

Three cats scattered bush-tailed and wide eyed as she dropped from the countertop and clanked and scuffed across the hardwood toward the office, her little wings shimmering, her chubby body humming with excitement.

You really can't function without me, can you? She didn't bother to look back as she uttered the rhetorical question.

It was my turn to huff and shrug. I grabbed the bouquet from the countertop and followed her to the negotiation table.

We'll see how this goes.

Discussions have begun in earnest. Hopefully next week I'll be able report a reasonable, rational set of Little-Miss-Muse-approved terms—all bejeweled in amethyst and smelling of grape bubble gum.

* * *

She laughs at me from the corner. "You really do hear me though, don't you. You used italics. Now you're just flat out quoting me."

Great. Point it out.

I hear voices.

I glare at her.

She smiles.

She hovers over the keyboard, my fingers not mine anymore. The words, her existence and my awareness of it, tumble onto the screen.

"It's okay. I won't tell anyone."

Gee, thanks, Little Miss. I think you just did...

Lesson Learned: Be careful how much power you give your muse. They can be quite dastardly.

88. STICKS AND CARROTS

Short post this week as the negotiations with Little Miss Muse continue.

Give and take.

Pout and huff.

Carrots and sticks.

Mostly carrots for her (promises of purple pretties and lavender lovelies. She's one expensive muse...).

Sticks for me (deadlines, completed projects, and some resemblance of rhythm and routine).

But we are making headway.

I'm thrilled she's sticking around, even though the cats have not yet adjusted to her reentry to the home. She'll spook them, and we'll hear them scoot down the hallway so fast that their paws squeak like sneakers on a gym floor followed by an inevitable screech, howl, or thud of a body into a wall.

She thinks this torment a fun pastime.

The cats think not.

What we both agree on is that we need external deadlines. We're working on a system for that which doesn't require me to shell out tons of dough on competitions or challenges. I'm an adult, daggonit, and I should be able to set in place some method to produce consistent volumes of work.

Should be.

Perhaps.

But maybe I'm the one that needs the carrots.

A new fountain pen.

Notebooks, crisp and clean.

Reese cups. Little Miss agrees here, though she feels the orange wrapper to be ostentatious and that a lovely shade of amethyst would complement the sweet just fine. But she'd also add edible plum glitter to the peanut butter filling, so maybe we shouldn't take her word on this.

We also agree that even though nothing catastrophic has happened in our home, and we're blessed beyond measure, we're both grieving the loss of "what used to be."

A world where she and I understood the ins and outs and rhythms of my "real job" and writing was a welcome respite from that.

To solve this "stalled-out pandemic brain" problem, Little Miss has hired (out of her own pocket!!) the purple-clad sultan to get our donkey butts in gear. He came highly recommended by a couple of other muses she met while she was on hiatus from the office, though she refused to tell me who these other muses work for or their credentials.

We shall see where he leads us and if he lives up to his glorious reputation.

* * *

The image for this blog was in cartoon form, a donkey pulling a massive wagonful of carrots. On top of the carrot pile, sits a sultan-like man clad in purple and wearing a yellow turban. He's placed a carrot on a long stick and is dangling it in front of the poor donkey's snout.

I'm so glad we sorted things out. The Sultan didn't stay for long.

And he never broke his nondisclosure agreement with his primary author—I still have no idea what writer he works for.

"He's a consultant. I keep telling you." Little Miss rolls her eyes. She's adjusting the straps on her stilettos, getting ready to tap dance her way down the hall. The cats have been quiet. Time to stir things up, I guess.

"You guys stay in touch?"

She hops off the desk. Clickety clacking around the room.

"Sure." She smiles. A dreamy, far-away smile that reaches her eyes and makes them twinkle like the north star. I don't like that smile. I don't like that twinkle.

"Wait. Wait. You guys aren't a *thing*, are you?"

"I can't tell you that. It'd break my agreement with him."

"Is that who you're hanging with now when you go MIA from work days? The Sultan???"

She scoots out of the room before I can grab her, her purple haze exhaust nearly choking me out.

Well. My Little Miss Muse is having a fling. Go figure.

It could be worse, I guess. She could be dating a politician.

Lesson Learned: Don't let your Muse go missing and bring home a Sultan.
Or a politician.

89. JUMP!

"I write to entertain. In a world that encompasses so much pain and fear and cruelty, it is noble to provide a few hours of escape, moments of delight and forgetfulness."
Dean Koontz, Writers Digest Books 1981

A quote from the '80s, but nicely sums up the need for a temporary disconnect in today's charged climate—whether that climate houses actual climate issues, murder hornets, riots, viruses, rogue monkeys, or missing Little Miss Muses.

I've been enjoying a few hours of escape here and there, provided by the masters of fiction. Thank you, Mr. Grisham, for allowing me to jump into a conspiracy with Malcolm Bannister as he gives the government what they have coming (*The Racketeer*). And thank you, Mr. Koontz, for not only providing the intro quote but also allowing me to befriend Einstein and cheer on the retriever as he guides the humans in his life against the evils (*Watchers*).

And from Mr. Gardner Fox and Harry Lampert, thanks for creating "The Flash", my current binging go-to when I'm too overwhelmed for brain work. What a fun ride! Andrew Ross Breckman deserves a shout-out for "Monk", a series the hubs and I have laughed our way through in the evenings. Poor Mr. Monk. On the struggle bus more often than not... a relatable escape.

I'm grateful for distractions from the awful. I'm grateful for the creative minds that bring us "diveable" content in whatever form we prefer—be that music, movies, books, comics. And memes. I've had great fun with something so simple as a well-timed meme, the snarkier the better.

A shout out to the creatives. Without them, we'd be stuck with the news. Oh. My. Word.

No more of that, please.

And as far as the act of writing, I'm grateful for time spent in the chair, fingers plodding away at the keyboard and mind disconnected from this reality and hurled into a different one. Where anything is possible and the seconds disappear without worry, time dancing hand in hand with characters of the Muse's making.

(By the way, the purple-clad sultan has snapped Little Miss Muse and I back into alignment after our negotiations and the writing is coming along, slowly but forward! Big huge sigh of relief.)

Stephen King was interviewed by NPR at the beginning of the virus mess. I've taped this quote from that interview onto my laptop:

Twenty hours a day, I live in the same reality that everybody else lives in. But for four hours a day, things change.

That's my goal. To provide an escape for those who may need to jump out of the crazy "fishbowl of life" from time to time and jump into an alternate storyline. That, and to provide a playground (or swimming pool) for Little Miss Muse lest she go rogue once again...

* * *

The image for this was of a gorgeous orange goldfish jumping from his tiny fishbowl into a much wider body of water. More options, so to speak.

I told Little Miss I feared the Sultan was way too old for her. Then she schooled me on the eternal, ageless nature of all Muses and that, in their realm, age isn't a thing.

Then she denied ever having been in any relationship with the Sultan and she was just yanking my chain.

Well, slap me relieved.

I think... She's grinning again.

Clearly, I've once again lost control of my muse.

Lesson Learned: For any aspiring writers that may be reading this: Don't pick an imp for your muse. Get a bluebird or a butterfly or a bat, for that matter. Not a purple-winged imp.

90. THE ASSIGNMENT

Over the last few months, the creative Little Miss Muse left for a sabbatical. She's returned. The writing has started to trickle a bit. And the good news is, so far, none of it is in the style of COVID-flavor-of-the-month.

The gnawing craving comes next. I know this from past "sabbaticals" of life. That deep-down itch to go sit in a room alone and make stuff up. I know it's started when I'm in the company of others (my poor husband, what he puts up with) and I see their mouths moving, but the dialogue doesn't match the setting, and instead the words match more closely the characters' lines in my stories.

Then the cleaning and purging of the office.

Then the butt finally situates in the chair.

Then the popping and cracking of knuckles (and, if I'm honest, the kneecaps as I sit) and off we go. Little Miss Muse and me. In *hopefully* some sort of rhythm. I want a fantasy adventure. She wants a fantasy adventure. We hold hands. Purple sparks fly.

Then, before you know it, that trickle turns into a torrent. Soon I'll be setting timers at forty-minute increments lest I sit for too long and undo everything my Back Guy just put into alignment. Bless his heart.

I've also been submerging myself with classes earned during that 52 short stories in 52 weeks challenge. I'll turn my teacher on in the background and let him beat me up and direct and guide and dump wisdom. Mostly listening to the ones about fear and production and what he calls The Critical Voice. That nag of all nags that ties up muses of all styles and shapes — Little Miss included — and zaps the fun and life and sparkle out of the writing process. And brings in fear and "danger signs" everywhere.

And if you're thinking of writing, are a writer hiding in a closet or under a bushel somewhere, or you're thinking of exploring the creative process, Dean Wesley Smith's site gives a list of his upcoming workshops. Have a look over there and get ready to learn a new way of thinking about your art.

One assignment was to write a defense in *favor* of the critical voice, as if we were in a courtroom. I actually had fun with it. And when the "excuses" were down in black and white I could see how ridiculous they are. Some of the fears I've worked through already, but I added them into the narrative for "flavor." Some fears are works in progress — areas where I still struggle with that Madame Nag.

I've seen these assignments in other classes (I can remember one in Health Psychology where we had to pick an ailment and write a speech from the point of view of the illness) and therapists assign similar exercises to their patients — write a letter to your fear, write a letter to your past trauma, etc.

Below is the assignment, tweaked for the blog.

Ladies and gentlemen of the jury, my name is Giv Vitup, and I'm the defense attorney for Madam Critical Voice in this case. Over the course of the trial, you'll hear the prosecution for Little Miss Muse's attempt to annihilate my client with unfounded claims of uselessness, intent to do harm to Writer Beth's creative process, and aiding and abetting procrastination on works in progress.

However, the prosecution has no hard evidence for any of their claims, and reasonable jurors that you are, I don't have to tell you that the burden of proof rests with the prosecution. I'm confident that by trial's end, they will fail to prove these charges beyond a reasonable doubt.

On the account of uselessness, I intend to show that Madam Critical is quite necessary for the proper execution of manuscripts. I's must be dotted. T's must be crossed. All commas and periods and quotation marks must be in their proper positions or the manuscript will fail miserably. It's Madam Critical's highest honor to point out these things to Beth as she composes her stories. To ensure no embarrassing typos exist. To ensure a perfectly polished piece.

We'll enter evidence of past manuscripts showing instances where Madam Critical Voice was, indeed, squelched at times by Little Miss Muse, and those demonic dangling participles and unfinished thoughts were left hanging out for the world to see, bringing great harm to Beth's process. We can show hard-and-fast evidence that, in the absence of Madam Critical, Beth allowed Little Miss Muse to send her readers to the Analog Couch! I ask you to ponder ahead of this evidence: Is a critique of a manuscript a useless endeavor? I think not.

On the charge of intent to do harm to the creative process, we will call witnesses including family and friends who will testify under oath that a good, stern look at flights of fancy and whimsical story telling may indeed bring harm to Beth's relationships with them— and even God himself—if she should let a manuscript out of her grasp that even remotely hints at a real-life human in her world.

And finally, good people of the jury, on the charge of aiding and abetting procrastination, the defense intends to show, in detail, Beth's process. Learning is not procrastination, and, Beth will learn and learn and learn and in the end, produce more meaningful and powerful stories. Learning is forward progress, not procrastination.

We also intend to show that the mastery of all publishing platforms is necessary prior to completing manuscripts. If Beth can't publish her work perfectly in all markets, what's the point of finishing? We further intend to argue that Madam Critical's role in producing covers, writing back matter on unfinished pieces, and discussing all aspects of writing with other authors and her family improves the quality of Beth's work, if not the speed. Little Miss Muse, however, would rather Beth spend time in the chair concocting imperfect sentences and digging plot holes than for Beth to take the time to dust her office, purge the kitchen cabinets of stale food, and weed the roadside ditches—all necessary activities to clear Beth's mental space for Little Miss Muse to do her work in the first place.

We'll also provide time-stamped evidence that Little Miss, indeed, has been given time to work throughout Beth's week. Madam Critical ensures that all schedules are clear, that every cat and adult in Beth's life is fed, cared for, doctored and will cause no interruption. Because interruptions of any sort will derail Little Miss Muse, and Madam Critical is sooo careful to block out the perfect amount of time and space for her to work. I don't know about you, but that doesn't sound like procrastination to me; that sounds like sound planning.

Make no mistake, ladies and gentlemen, this will be a long and arduous trial. The prosecution will try to trick you into believing that Little Miss Muse's new words of fiction are far more valuable than any service Madam Critical provides. This is untrue and deserves a long, careful look at the evidence. Take your time. Examine every angle. Extrapolate every negative outcome that has the tiniest possibility of happening to our dear writer, Beth, if Madam Critical Voice were to be cuffed and jailed. Don't let Little Miss Muse rule in the author's roost.

And there it is. Ridiculous, yes? But it worked to shake loose some stuck-on fears and plow forward.

What's holding you back from what you want to do? Most likely the only thing hindering you is hanging between your ears.

* * *

On procrastination: An author friend posted this on her Facebook a while back. I don't know the original author. The quote isn't mine, nor was it hers. Google attributes it to a lady by the name of Bishop Rosie O'Neal:

346

"Procrastination is the arrogant assumption that God owes you another opportunity to do what you had time to do."

Ouch. That smarted.

Lesson Learned: What do I need to do? Do it now.

91. THE RETURN OF THE DUCKS

2020 hasn't exactly been our year. Yet. Maybe things will change.

(Insert huge rolling-on-the-floor-laughing gif here. Imagine one. Any gif with mass hysteria will fit.)

Realistically, though, we'll likely be stuck with the upheaval from a dozen arenas worldwide, and the news cycles will not settle until this time next summer.

I've been taking some time to realign our family's new reality with the very shaky reality outside our walls.

Namely, I've no day job to structure my days around. That's been interesting. And a little terrifying from a "what now?" standpoint.

Appointments and events that were canceled are gearing up for some modified version of rescheduling from social stuff to doctor-ish happenings. My pretty spiral-bound calendar for 2020 ain't so pretty looking anymore. Scratch out, rewrite, remove, and erase. Repeat.

And how do you plan a vacation or anniversary celebration when you're unsure which cities will be "open" and "safe" and which state parks will be overrun with those who can't do their typical vacations in said cities. Yes, I'm likely over-thinking this one, but I don't want to bring home the virus, nor do I want to dodge thousands of protesters, peaceful or not, when I'm trying to relax. I'd rather stay hunkered between the surrounding cornfields with the cats if that's to be the case.

Then there are those blasted ducks. The ones that left, went webbed-feet-up, left for brighter and bluer ponds, and that one that waddled drunk in the daffodils. They're slowly coming back. There may be a goose in the mix, but we'll deal with him later.

On one hand, it feels good. I'm quite accustomed to the disorder that disorderly fowls create. That feels normal.

On the other hand, I know there's that one dumb duck that'll always be off-kilter, doing as it pleases with no regard for schedules or timing, and generally driving me insane.

Such is life.

At any rate, I've taken time to realign my writing "ducks" into bite-sized goals. I've begun the process of publishing some of my short stories into collections. Those will be done by end of summer, hopefully.

Accountability is also a big issue for me now. I don't have that external weekly deadline from the writing challenge to keep me on track. I'll likely play around on the Facebook feed with some sort of "word count of the week" update. Just so some imaginary person out there will see it and go "Yay. She's writing."

And that will make Little Miss Muse, the drunk duck, the new goose, and me very happy.

* * *

Turns out, in that muddled state I was in and as things were gearing up for the ladies I take care of to head back to their regularly scheduled "doctoring," that I only had brain cells for one activity or the other: write or publish.

I did get some lines down. I got more books published, though, and there was a huge learning curve on the software for me. For whatever reason, I just didn't take to InDesign's platform so well. We're becoming better friends though, InDesign and I—or at least familiar acquaintances.

And thennnn... one of my ladies fell off a ladder. Then one's pancreas and another's kidneys, and off to the crazy Covid-riddled medical facilities we go.

It's been fun (insert huge eye roll here).

Lesson Learned: Roll with the punches. One webbed and waddling foot in front of the other.

92. WHO'S COUNTING?

A long time ago, I bought one of those variety cat toy packs with fuzzy mice, tinkle balls, pompoms, and a few plastic springs. All eventually gobbled up by the couch, the loveseat, or some other piece of furniture with more than an inch of clearance underneath.

So I bought another pack.

Then another.

I've lost count of how many value-packs-of-happiness have made it home from the grocery store.

But who's counting? Because these rescue kitties have had a tough go of it, and they need their pretties. And they had not one pretty left anywhere in the house. Or so we thought.

Then we moved the couch to clean and found a hundred or so of the "lost forever, buy us new ones, please" toys.

Stella, our mini-Maine Coon girl, prefers one toy for independent play: a chirpy cardinal bird—a hand-me-down from the Great and Glorious Cosmo, may he rest in peace. And for some reason, this noisy thing is NEVER gobbled up by those invisible tongues under the furniture. And its battery never dies. Stella keeps track of her cardinal so she can chant and sing to it. Loudly. Every. Single. Morning. Three a.m. to be precise.

And if, per chance, the bird is missing because one of the other kitties dared stuff it somewhere (or Mom found it and put it away), she will resort, albeit begrudgingly, to the tiny chirpy blue and white narwhal that's not nearly as loud.

Then she gives me *that look,* and I fear for my eyelids while I sleep —and I give her the cardinal back.

Malachi, our not-coloring-with-a-full-crayon-box boy, plays with whatever you're playing with. He's not picky. And he still can't work his toenails properly, so playing becomes a frustrating chore, one razor claw after another hopelessly entangled in a fuzzy mouse's tail or the hide of a catnip chipmunk or the even the carpet. The rest of his day is slotted for deep, comatose sleeps and begging food, the more Italian, the better—though Mexican is high on his favorites.

And until the great couch clean-out after Christmas, Amara, our boss-of-them-all lady who bullies and brutes her way through life, would busy herself with the bullying and the brute-ing and was generally too dignified to play.

Until she discovered the tiny, plastic spirals that came in one of those variety packs but were, unfortunately, greatly outnumbered by fuzzy mice and tinkle balls (which clearly are for dork cats, and she'd not stoop so low as to chase a tinkle ball).

Amara carries these springs in her mouth.

She plays fetch with the springs.

She sleeps with a spring.

She bats and races them down the hallway so hard her paw beans squeak on the hardwood floor.

She loses the coils under closed doors and then screams for us to open the doors (I think this started out as accidental, then she realized she had control over the humans and the opening of doors and now does it on purpose just to be a bossy brute).

She hides them on purpose.

She stores them.

She talks to them. About them. Sings like a dove, even, as she carries them from one end of the house to the other.

Then goes back to being a bully when she runs out or can't reach her stash deep under the loveseat.

So we bought Amara a bag of bulk springs, 66 in the pack. Sixty-six, in addition to the random ones from other packs and the smaller pack of ten. Over 80 now, but who's counting?

Why keep her in such a supply? We were getting desperate.

Because when Amara wears herself out with springs, she doesn't rip out Stella's tail feathers or bloody Malachi's ear lobes nearly as often.

I've never cleaned under a piece of furniture so often in all my life —all my cleanings put together. Every few days we're pulling out the loveseat so Amara can retrieve and reorganize her plethora of plastic coils.

(And, yes, we've tried to block the loveseat's "tongue" with bumpers of all sorts, but Malachi gets his toes stuck in them as he plays and pulls out whatever we've stuffed under there to prevent spring loss. Then the springs get lost AND we have a mess of foam or blankets littering the room.)

Stella and Malachi give Amara a wide berth and watch her respectfully as she goes about her spring dancing lest they lose fur and one of their nine lives (Not sure of Stella's life count, as she was three years old when we got her. Malachi, poor thing. Given his tendency for the innocently idiotic, that boy's got no more lives to lose).

I feel like Amara these days.

I've got 82 short stories to bat around and do something with. I know because I've counted them.

I'm turning into a grumpy bully. I need solitude and quiet to do my thing lest someone's willing to give their left eyelid to be in my space.

I have a plethora of short stories to edit, format, make covers for, and put somewhere. They're everywhere. Some piled under the desk. Some waiting in cyberspace. Some waiting on answers from the market.

I've fallen asleep editing them.

I've nearly lost a couple, those tech glitches (or operator error??) gobbling up formatting and fonts with giant invisible tongues lurking behind the computer screen.

I've stashed most all of them in one form or another onto an external hard drive and stashed the hard drive in a fireproof safe.

Some stories I've hidden in a drawer—on purpose—because of timing or because what the actual heck was I thinking when I wrote *that* one?

I'm talking about them. To them. Pacing with them up and down the hall, keeping an eye and ear out for Amara doing the same, lest we trip each other up and have a heap of manuscript pages flying and springs twirling in all directions—and then enter Little Miss Muse, and well, what chaos would ensue.

I haven't resorted to singing to the story pages yet, that's not the mood I'm in. But the crazy is settling in behind my eyeballs and showtunes could be on the horizon.

Perhaps I'll save the one-woman, one-muse, three-cat chorus line for when I finally learn InDesign well enough to not lose my religion over it. I can't help but think my younger self would've learned the program more quickly. The old me is plodding along much too slowly for my liking.

Bleeds and Margins and Gutters. Oh. My. Word!

I've been desperate enough to consider a consult with this high-tech toddler I know. See if he could lend a hand. He'd likely be faster if he could stay focused with all of Amara's spring shenanigans going on around the office—

And now I hear the cardinal chirping.

Stella's running through her vocal cord warmup—about fifteen hours early. And, unfortunately, I know this performance isn't taking the place of the one scheduled for the wee hours of tomorrow morning.

Amara has lost her 79th spring to the giant tongue living under the hall closet door. She informs me there's just one more spring left—she IS counting—and when the remaining coil is lost or stashed, someone may lose a body part.

And Malachi wants some spaghetti, but he says we can always order Mexican and he'd be fine with that...

He flicks his tail at me and walks out of the office, one page of a manuscript punctured by three toes of his left hind foot. He drags the page out of the room like toilet paper stuck to the bottom of a shoe, shaking his leg as he steps along.

Time to switch the Cardinal out with the Narwhal, pull out the loveseat for the third time in a week, and order Mexican.

Also for the third time in a week.

But who's counting?

* * *

We've since ditched the loveseat and replaced that piece with a futon with clearance enough for Amara to slide her whole body underneath. Which, evidently, is no fun. So, we're finding springs in a plethora of new locales (bathtub, folded bedspreads in the linen closet, under the stove, in my shoe) and she's yet to decide which location is worthy of a go-to hiding spot.

Part of the reason for doing this compilation was to remind myself where I've been and plan out/dream about where I'm heading with my writing.

And I'm sensing a pattern (several, actually, but this one popped out at me tonight). Margins, gutters, and bleeds. They seem to be my "Achilles heel of the moment." Not to be confused with our town's new frozen yogurt shop's "flavor of the month."

Lesson Learned: Find a master teacher on margins, bleeds, and gutters and shut up about them already. Also, remember to try that new frozen yogurt place this week...

93. SCI-FI JULY

If you'd asked me in 2019 my favorite genres to write in, dystopian would've been at the top—if not the very top—of that list.

Enter 2020 where the wide, wide world of social media memes have taken over:

"You've been 2020'd."

"Toilet paper apocalypse."

"Roll the dice and finish the dumb game." (Jumanji)

Scowling cats reclining in skillets on gas stoves begging every Linda, Karen, and Frank to "light it up already."

And that's just virus-related stuff.

I'll not touch on memes that featured protests, politics, handy-dandy face masks, or burning cities.

One of those cities we were to fly into for our 25th wedding anniversary prior to a cruise. Bahahaha. And I'd been worried if our marriage—25 years strong, mind you, love my man—could weather a tiny cabin on those couple of "at sea" days with no Andy Griffith and the hubs up to his eyebrows with rich buffet food. Let alone if we got "quarantined" at sea should one rogue passenger spike a fever or sneeze.

I'll let your imaginations take that image where it wants to go.

At any rate, living through the first few months of 2020 felt like a terrifying stroll down Dystopian Drive or Horror Hallow or Thriller Court. Though I doubt those that lost lives and/or livelihoods would categorize this year's entertainment selection as "thrilling."

At any rate, now that we've passed the midpoint—

Wait.

Wait.

Midpoint? Just past the midpoint in typical story form is where most of the action picks up.

Picks.

Up.

And then, just a chunk of pages further, it really picks up.

Like.

All.

The.

Way.

Up.

And then there's the climax at the end.

The end.

Which is a good five-and-a-half months from now. *Hang on while I have another stress-sigh-eye-roll-and-grab-another-Reese-Cup moment.

Ok.

I'm back.

Dabbed the eye leakage while I was at it, too.

Unlike tidy fiction tales, I doubt that any would agree our world's issues will be wrapped up in a neat, shiny bow on December 31st before the ball drops (will there be a ball drop?) and 2021 welcomes us all with a tall glass of (insert your most favorite comfort beverage here), fresh-baked cookies (choose your own flavor complete with the aroma filling the house), a giant hug from wrinkled, grandmotherly arms, and a "There, there. Tell me all about it, it'll be okay" sit-down at an antique table covered in lace doilies.

So, dystopian isn't something I've touched since this thing ramped up in March. I feel like I'm living in such an existence. But I did write a dystopian tale back in the fall of 2019 for the Vegas Work-shop when I actively enjoyed such things.

Set in future Earth way, way after we humans royally screwed it all up—the planet, the infrastructure, and each other. It was fun to write with just a tiny bit of hope sprinkled here and there. Hope that someone would get a clue and change their thinking.

A fellow author liked it. She asked me if she could put it in an anthology of other such Future-Earth Techy-stories.

A book of short sci-fi stories aptly named "Future Earth Tech".

I was honored. I met some of these author folks last year, and I'm stoked to see my little "B.A. Paul" in a list with their names!

My paperback version came. Hot off the press. Hot out of the mailbox in our current 99-degree heat index (seriously, Indiana is about to boil itself out of existence). So hot, actually, that Mr. Malachi Maxwell gravitated toward it and before I could even gander a peek at the contents, he splayed his hairy body on top of the book and soaked up all its fresh-from-the-sauna warmth. (And for those new to the blog, Malachi is a cat. Nothing too funky going on here...)

The book is available through a gob of online outlets, so take your preferred source for reading material: https://books2read.com/sci-fi3

Now, I know what you must be thinking. With such a gloomy lead-in, leaving us all longing for our grannies and warm cookies and hugs, would anyone really enjoy such stories now?

Well. Yes.

This is fiction, dear hearts. With time travel, space punk, mind uploads, and various and sundry human augmentations.

We don't have those things yet—at least not much of it. I, for one, have misplaced my magic wand which allows me to time travel, and I'm really bummed about it.

Enjoy the book.

Escape.

Then leave a review. Support these author folks who provide much-needed distractions from our current "tell it to your grandkids, uphill all the way" real-life dystopia.

* * *

In rereading these blogs since the February post date, sometimes I literally fall back in my office chair, run my hands over my face and wish I could time travel back to January 2020 and give myself a few fair warnings.

Just saying.

It gets worse, sweetheart...

Lesson Learned: Find the big-girl panties. Yank 'em up real high. You can't go back, may as well go forward.

94. QUIZ TIME!

Let's have a little fun. School is fun, right? Tests, quizzes? Well, maybe not. But those teeny-bopper magazines sure drew their young readers (and the dough from all the vacuumed floors and birthday money from grannies galore) with multiple-choice "tell me about yourself and we'll tell you what your future holds" quizzes.

I remember them from middle school. Quite the page-turning reads depending on whether you wanted to know if you were in the "in crowd" (I flunked those). Or whether you'd be cut out for celebrity-hood (flunked those too). Most of those quizzes I came across were of the choose-your-own outcome variety. I guess I had no need for celebrity status or in-crowdedness.

Now I think those writers' offspring must've grown up to write quizzes for Facebook and such. Polls for the youngers. Ones that start fights and create "my life is totally ruined" meltdowns all across the globe.

So, here we go…

What fresh catastrophes did July 2020 bring that posed challenges in the B.A. Paul household?

1. Laptop crash

2. Tornadic winds
3. Post-concussive syndrome from a ladder fall
4. Thyroid crash
5. All of the above.

The answer is e, all of the above. Though I wasn't the one to personally suffer post-concussive syndrome, that was a dear family member. Stressful, nonetheless. Folks, don't let your loved ones climb ladders unattended when they have no business climbing ladders unattended.

And folks, if you can get away with never having thyroid fog, I'd highly recommend any option other than that. Detrimental to mental capacity and productivity. All you want is a fuzzy blanket and a cat. And the cats are over cuddling in the heat, even with the air on.

Tornadic winds (some called them straight-line. Not sure officially. I'm calling it The Great Wind Event, as it was definitely not in the "warm summer breeze" category) downing my ancient, twisted, giant glories. Yeah, let's do something else next July. That was no fun. And this week will be very loud and tumultuous as the trimming crews come to clean up the mess. Nonetheless, we were very blessed that it only did damage to the trees. We were out power for a bit, but others got it worse. I didn't hear of any injuries. It was a close one.

Laptop? Well, my poor old Lenovo had one digital foot out the door for quite some time. Slower and slower by the week. My dear, sweet hubs bought me a new setup for our anniversary—quite the surprise, but very much appreciated. We'll have been hitched 25 years next month. We were to fly into Seattle. Seattle. Have a gander around the city for a couple of days. Get on a boat. A boat. To Alaska. On a boat.

Nope. We canceled our trip when the virus ripped through the states. Then the cruise company canceled our trip on top of us canceling our trip. So, a laptop it is, and I'm very grateful. I'm still searching for ideas for him, which brings me to question #2:

What should Beth do for her husband for their 25^{Th} wedding anniversary?

1. Nothing. Her love is enough.
2. Reschedule the boat for a future year and hope for a different outcome.
3. Yard knick-knacks (he's got a thing for benches and swings...)
4. Compose a short story and dedicate it to him.

e. Jury's out. We shall see.

E. That would be E. Likely not D. I've got a week or two. There's time. And had I bought the swing, The Great Wind Event would've toppled the tree onto it. So there's a wee, bitty, bitty bright spot. We did not suffer the loss of a swing that I did not buy yet. We'll hang onto the bitty bright spot, since this year is so 2020...

Setting a weekly, public writing goal is just the push Beth needed to

a. Worry about writing.

b. Find reasons to push the writing to the end of the week, then panic.

c. Get words down on the page.

d. All of the above.

If you chose D, you'd be correct. Funny what thinking about others "knowing" what you're supposed to be up to does to the mindset. I've gotten words down that I wouldn't have otherwise, so I'll keep posting the weekly goal until it doesn't work.

How does B.A. Paul feel about learning a new program designed to make her publishing life easier?

1. Great. Learning is fun. She wishes to learn all the things!
2. Mediocre. Thyroid fog, crashed laptop, and The Great Wind Event have hindered the progress.
3. Chin up, dearie. It'll come. Beth's brain isn't as young as it used to be. But it still works...occasionally.
4. Little Miss Muse would rather be writing, causing Beth great anxiety over time spent floundering on the program vs. time spent on getting new words done.

5. Beth is about to mortgage the house to pay someone else to do the dumb program.
6. All of the above.

Yup. You guessed it. All of the above. Sometimes I rip through all five choices in the span of two-hour time chunks.

What will be the title of B.A. Paul's next release when she finally masters (read "masters" as "good nough") the publishing program?

1. Spunk and Spice
2. Out There
3. Mystery Minutes
4. All the Feels
5. Just a Tick of Whimsy
6. All of the above. She's obsessed with releasing them all at relatively the same time.

You ought to know by now. I'm leaning toward F. Maybe one a day or something, but out they'll go to the big, wide world, hopefully starting next week. Next week! The end of July 2020.

Announcing the release of her short story collections by the end of July 2020 is just the push Beth needs to:

1. Worry about it.
2. Find reasons to maneuver the work to the end of the month, then panic.
3. Get the collections done and out the door already.
4. All of the above.

I likely already know the answer to #6. Hopefully, though, I can break the "last one is always the right one" pattern and choose C. This week, I'll aim for C.

Let you know in a week or two.

In the meantime, enjoy the rest of July, 2020.

And I'm laughing all the way out of the room as I hit save.

July 2020.
2020.
Enjoy.
Hahaha...

Bonus Question: To enjoy the rest of what 2020 has to offer, one should:
Turn off the news
Take a blessing tally
Take a social media hiatus
Take a walk
Take a chill pill (or a nap or another walk)
Take up a new hobby
All of the above.

This one's a choose-your-own outcome deal. Pick one. Any one. Or a combination. You'll not be wrong...

* * *

We did end up going on a small one-night trip away from the house for our anniversary (See Blog 97). That was a slightly bad idea, though there were enjoyable moments. And I guess it's a trip we'll never forget... and we were welcomed home by one of our ladies being admitted to the hospital (a different lady than the one who toppled off the ladder).

Lesson Learned: Take the enjoyable moments because there's always another round with an old woman in some hospital... And Little Miss tells me I could very well be the next old woman in the hospital.

95. TOAST, JAM, BASEBALL, AND BOOKS!

I spent a good part of last week's "working hours" churning out blurbs for short stories, tweaking covers for upcoming releases, and *finally, finally* getting the hang of InDesign.

I hope.

We shall see when my proof copies start sneaking into my mailbox.

Hand-held evidence of my efforts—both a year's-worth of writing a short story a week and the learning curve of publishing in general. More than likely, though, these little paperbacks will show me what I've not yet learned, let alone mastered.

New titles include Mystery Minutes, Spunk and Spice, Out There, All the Feels, and Just a Tick of Whimsy. All are collections of six short stories... What a project!

I also spent a good deal of last week's "working hours" watching that little gray loading circle twirl and spin and jiggle as it toiled with my uploads—both the manuscripts and the cover designs.

More than once, Amazon's platform told me to go get a cup of coffee. That it could take a minute. Or longer.

Twice it told me to just leave and get a sandwich.

Not kidding.

A sandwich.

It was kind about it. Not in a huffing, eye-rolling sort of way. Not like, "Quit hovering, you moron. I'm working here."

More like. "Perhaps you should consider some strawberry jam with your toast..."

To amuse myself, I imagined that coffee/sandwich notification box reading aloud to me in a British accent. Hence the toast and jam.

A couple of times, I had to shut down the browser and reload everything... My errors clogged up the works good and proper. I could've baked bread from scratch and smashed great vats of strawberries into gallons and gallons of jelly BY FOOT before the issues were sorted out...

But the last time the platform's little gray circle spun and twisted and told me it was checking margins and bleed lines, and that I should take a hike, I did. I hiked to the living room and watched three innings of baseball.

Yup.

Real, live baseball.

Now, I'm not a sports person, but I don't mind having a baseball game on in the background. I don't mind attending a Major League game once every three years or so if the weather isn't sweltering and someone gives us free tickets. But I flat don't care who wins. I can enjoy the experience for a moment, then I'm on to the next thing.

But today? Watching the game today was just odd. As odd as if a thick-accented Brit spoke directly to me through my computer screen about jam and toast. That kind of odd.

And, I had toast and jam instead of popcorn. So...

With no fans in the stands, you'd have thought it was a televised warmup/training session. And when the ball snapped into the catcher's glove or cracked off the end of the hitter's bat — you know? You remember? How balls snap and crack when there *are* fans in the stands? With the appropriate cheering crescendo and explosions of excitement from the crowd?

Well... those snaps and cracks sounded much like when I drop cookie sheets in the kitchen. Smashes and clangs. Because the echo...echo...echo...

And the piped-in-through-the-loudspeakers cheering didn't do the job of warm-blooded bodies, absorbing the sound waves... I guess I miss those snaps and cracks. I bet the players do too. I bet they dearly miss the sound of a well-hit ball in a too-full stadium.

The league tried to mimic that sound, best as it could. But that piped-in stuff was very well timed. Too well timed. Gone are the days (at least this season) of the seemingly random massive cheering starting with four drunk dudes at one end of the stadium growing and swallowing section after section. Rising and falling back and forth, round and round.

Spinning and cheering from one section to the next until some bat made contact with that little round orb and... magic. And real cheers and moans and boos and whatever else the crowd felt like throwing out. Magic.

Magic. Like that Amazon circle...loading. Round and round. Waiting until something happens in cyberspace with 1s and 0s and code...

Waving and spinning...

And the announcers. Oh my. I think they were bored. The last comment I heard before I ended my three-inning stretch:

"You know. If they want to keep the ball in the park, they have to pitch so that the batter doesn't make contact with the ball."

Oh my.

And, lest my blog post devolve into meaningless fluff (because I would NEVER do that) ... Back to the point.

While I wait for the mail truck to deliver my first-try paperbacks, you can check out the links to the electronic copies. A sneak peek, of sorts, for hanging with me on the blog.

A more formal "Yippee!" dance-and-jig Facebook announcement post will be forthcoming once I'm happy with the paperbacks and once the blog page has been updated with the links.

Happy reading.

Happy baseball watching, for what it's worth. What a year.

Maybe grab some toast and jam while you watch the game. Yours doesn't have to be strawberry. Peach preserves are nice this time of year, too.

* * *

Seems I always manage to sneak into the living room while the hubs is watching (or sleeping through) some game where the announcers get bored and state the obvious.

Lesson Learned: Edit the fiction for stating the obvious. It's quite off-putting.

96. THEY'RE HERE

Crazy, crazy, hectic couple of weeks. Summer has a way of swallowing time and spitting back at you in useless, sweaty chunks. At least in our neck of the universe.

Then add in 2020's kick-butt karma along with Murphy's Law Grand Revival, and there's no end of the day-bumping chaos.

At any rate, I've slacked on the new word count drastically, but ramped up in the production arena. Because Little Miss is sweltering in the corner, complaining of missing days gone by and she's no idea where to take the work in progress.

I swear, that little imp is going to be the death of me...

But... She did help out on a couple of the covers for the short story collections. Seven of them!!!

These nifty titles are comprised of tales I've written over the last couple of years. And no sense in leaving them rattling around on a disk drive somewhere.

So, check out the book tab above to see the details in one clean place. Or, you can see them directly on Amazon. Other outlets to come, but for now this is your link to buy these titles, either electronically or paperback. The blog's book tab links will take you directly to the titles, as well.

Buyer Beware, though: Some of the singles you see on Amazon are short stories that are included in these collections. Read the contents and make sure you're not purchasing the same title twice. (Or go ahead and purchase the same title twice. Or three times. Or twenty. I'll be sure to buy Little Miss Muse her favorite purple soda, and maybe some grape bubblegum, and we can finally bribe her into getting off her plump purple..., well, you know.)

Have a great week. Happy browsing!

* * *

The plan is to clean up the Amazon page so that only the collections remain. Or to brand the singles' covers differently—I've not decided yet.

Lesson Learned: Decide already and get it done.

97. TRAIL 8

A couple of weeks ago the hubs and I got away on a mini 25th anniversary trip.

Mini. Small. Quick.

Because COVID and various political mayhem canned the previously planned and looked-forward-to Alaskan cruise. We toyed with flying somewhere for a long weekend. Then those "somewheres" didn't want Hoosiers in their states without negative COVID tests and a fourteen-day isolation. That's not a long weekend. That's stress wrapped in possible divorce court proceedings. And for our 25th? If we want 25 more, we'd have to figure out something else.

Other drivable trips were downgraded to a 160-mile round trip, one-tank, one-night getaway to a state park we've never been to and a quaint town with tourist-ish shops and "art district" venues.

Now, before my rant, I want to be clear: We did enjoy our time together, which was the whole point. Enjoyable moments. Making memories. Reminiscing. All of that stuff that we try to do regularly, but the 25th poured on extra pressure. (And we were supposed to be on a boat, doggonit!)

Because with the pandemic, travel plans even just a few counties from home are complicated. One must pack for the unexpected. Will the restaurants be open for dine-in or open at all? What time will they be open? Will we be dining in our front seats, air conditioner blasting with a grand and glorious view of the restaurant's parking lot? If so, make sure the SUV is stocked with utensils, salt packets, napkins, etc.

Do things board up early in this small town we're visiting to allow for deep cleaning of the facilities? Uh-oh. In the event we stayed out too late in the state park, we could end up eating dinner from a vending machine.

So pack the dollar bills and quarters—

But wait! There's a coin shortage. Will the machine even take quarters, or will we be required to "round up" our $2.75 Snickers bar to an even three bucks?

And don't forget to pack the masks. Disposable or cloth? Gaiters or tie-ons? Should I pack the same number of masks as underwear? Is that the general rule of thumb? Or double? Maybe double the masks—

But wait! I've experienced a grand, out-of-nowhere, no-warning-given sneeze in one of my masks during a grocery run. Now *that* was unpleasant, being stuck without a backup mask and other patrons looking at me like I'm Typhoid Mary. Really, it's allergies—or more likely single, rogue mask fiber made its way up a nostril and tickled just right.

Then what? What if our seasonal allergies kick in and we each sneeze once an hour? Inside our masks? Factor in migrating mask fuzz and fibers, and who knows what could happen. Pack every mask in the house and buy a box of disposable ones to cram into our pockets.

Hand sanitizer? Check. Some in the car door (it hasn't exploded in the heat yet, I'll count us lucky on that front). Small bottles for the purse, backpack, and pocket. And I've had a container of Clorox wipes (brand name, even, pre-pandemic purchase) rolling around in the SUV since February.

Patience? Is our one suitcase for our one-night trip big enough for all the pandemic patience needed? Probably not. Because we have to save room for flexibility too. Can't plan anything for sure—and I like my plans and ducks to be in nice neat rows... Oh, well.

We arrive at the state park.

A too-cheery gatekeeper told us a few of the most sought-after areas had been closed due to too many people gathering in one spot. Well great.

But no worries. Trail 8 loops around from a lookout tower to the lake. And we should try out this Trail 8.

Now, loop implies circle and the trail map said 3.5 and "moderate." Not being hikers or trail people for the most part, we thought, cool. A few miles. A tower. A lake. Moderate.

And hardly anyone around.

My kind of trail.

Well. There was a reason no one was around.

They lied. The paper map with its impossible-to-follow dots and lines. The cheery gatekeeper at the front entrance. The fading sign at the lookout tower. They all lied. Trail 8 is not 3.5 miles. And it's a figure-eight with a line through it. So what about that is 3.5 miles? The whole loop? The cut-through to the lake? There and back again, and you don't even see Hobbits in the Shire?

And the mud. Oh, my, the mud. It was a single trail, not wide enough to walk side-by-side. Lined with poison ivy (hubs has an awful reaction should he get into that mess). Briars reached out to greet around some turns. Dense, lush forest trapped in more heat and humidity the further we went, and me in front as the unofficial "poison ivy pointer outer."

Now, we did enjoy bits of it. Streams, little footbridges. Fungus groupings of all shapes and shades where my Little Miss Muse started to dance and chant, "Fairies, and Gnomes and Elves! Oh, my!" Beds of ferns as far as you could see. So that was cool.

The mud, though, caused us to walk the trail straddled most of the time, grasping branches and each other as best we could so as not to wipe out. With all those masks, we had to pack light and would've required purchasing a new change of clothes for each of us for the return home.

We met a few folks here and there who said they'd been traipsing through mud and ivy forever and never saw a lake (one red-faced, gasping lady had *two* hiking poles, so she had to know more about these things than us small-town newbies). Another couple said yes, there's a lake, but their dog rolled his eyes at us and gave us an over-the-shoulder plea to go no further as they tugged his leash and they walked off.

We reached the water. Finally.

When I say "Lake" every one of you pictures in your mind some sort of hole in the ground with water in it, most likely. The lake in my mind's eye is big enough for hundreds of boats and jet skis and has nooks and crannies for fisherman to feed their families. Maybe I can see the other bank, but its blurry and the people and boats over there are a fraction of a millimeter tall.

Your lake may be bigger like Lake Michigan or smaller, like a 50-boater.

"Lake" was a bit of a reach for this bit of contained liquid. There was water. And people fishing. But I could read the brand name of the tackle box next to the gentleman casting his line from across this "lake."

Now I know why the dog was so disappointed. That look was "Don't waste your time, lady. More mud and no lake."

Back at the car, drenched and weary, we wiped our legs down with Clorox wipes. Yup. In a pinch, it was worth the sting not to have to go to the ER and get hubs shot up with Benadryl and Prednisone.

I hope I don't lie to my readers. If my "trail guide" blurb on the back of the book says the story promises a cozy mystery that pulls the heartstrings, I hope I don't "Trail 8 Lake" it and give you an epic space saga clocking in at 100K that leaves you muddied down and itchy.

We made memories, though. And we can check "travel during a pandemic" off our 2020 bucket list.

And we both bought new tennis shoes after Trail 8. I made sure mine had a tick of purple trim for Little Miss.

Thanks, nature, for the anniversary gift.

* * *

Some friends of ours asked about going to this same location shortly after we returned home. I did them a favor and, like the dog pleading with us about what's to come, I just shook my head. "You'll make memories, I just can't guarantee what kind."

Lesson Learned: Even the muddiest of memories, when given enough weeks and mental space, can be cherished cautionary tales, at the very least.

98. THE CARD

This, quite frankly, is the most "risqué" blog I've ever concocted. Maybe ever will unless my life takes some strange, unforeseen twist. And after 2020, well... I'm actually eagerly awaiting the Mother Ship to come and suck us all away and drop us into *OUR* 2020, not *THEIR* 2020.

But anyway...

My intention isn't to be insulting, offensive, or judgmental. I try to keep my writing somewhere between PG and PG-13. But this content might, for some more fragile spirits, dip its toes into the R-rated realm. Just a dip, though.

Others, I hope, will find the true heart of the blog and think it funny (And *that's* my intention: Funny, a break from the mundane and chaos for just a minute). So fair warning: If you're easily offended, had some embarrassing round of bad luck, or perhaps you've been a little too risqué yourself at some point in your life, just stop reading.

And you don't have to tell me you stopped reading. Please, for the love of all things wise and wonderful, just don't tell me anything.

At all. Ever. About this blog and whether you stopped or not. I don't want to know. I've stuffed my index fingers deep into my ear canals and I'm singing "LALALALALALALALA" as loudly as humanly possible.

I. Don't. Want. To. Know.

For those of you thick-skinned enough to read on, things will become clearer as we go.

So, easily offended? Right now, just click elsewhere. If you do not heed my warning, read ahead like the stubborn person you are, and then scold or shun me later, I'll kindly remind you that you failed to follow the directions clearly outlined above...

Seriously. You were warned.

Got your big-girl panties, everyone?

Here we go.

Last year about this time I ran out of greeting cards. I don't send many, but I do take spells where I'll send "real" mail. I was in one of those moods and a good friend was about to go in for surgery, and Walmart's selection of sappy, run-of-the-mill cards just wasn't doing it for me. I like the snarky cards. Ones with a little spunk and spice. (Imagine that!)

So I went to Etsy and browsed the one-of-a-kinds there. Support the creatives directly. Cut out the big-box middlemen. (Seriously, please do that. Small businesses, artists, musicians, *ahem* authors...)

I ran across a shop that specializes in snarky-on-the-outside, blank-on-the-inside cards and filled my cart. She offers some straight-up cute ones, pretty and proper ones, too, but I bypassed those because I was in full-on snark mode.

And I like the blank ones. It's a rare day when a stranger writing canned sentiments for the Greeting Card Company knows anything of how *my* particular people operate...

I scored the perfect surgery card.

Stocked up on birthday cards for my gang, who are equally snarky and enjoy a good laugh. You know. The kinds of cards you wouldn't send to the typical grandmother in your life who'd declare, "Well, for Heaven's sake!" and then give you a lecture on appropriateness.

Found some cheer-up cards. Because even before the Grand Virus of Dismay, people needed cheering.

I came across a card that doubled me over laughing. Not just a smile. But a doubled-over belly laugh with a dose of "I can't wait to send this to someone." I put two—TWO—of that design in my cyber shopping cart, paid the bill, and eagerly awaited my very own "real mail" package full of "real mail."

The cards didn't fail in quality. Nice designs, bright colors. Good, sturdy envelopes. Very pleased.

The surgery card was a big hit. Had just the effect intended with the right amount of "I really do care about you" mixed with a fitting, friendly level of humiliation.

The birthday cards, likewise.

And I eagerly awaited the perfect recipients for my snarky cheer-and-encouragement cards. It didn't take long, because, well, even in 2019, life happened.

I brought the card out. Enjoyed the artwork again. Smiled again.

Uncapped my pen.

Opened it to the inside to write something personal and relative, and...

I froze. The logical, think-it-through-stupid part of my brain that had turned off during the greeting-card shopping spree came back online, and I saw my purchase in a whole new light.

The front of the card holds a jar of yellow daisies on white background. In fancy black lettering, the greeting says: At least it's not herpes.

Herpes.

Then the brain buzzing "What Ifs" started.

Oh. My. Goodness.

What if the recipient (who I think is snarky like me, but maybe not) finds this offensive? What if *gasp* they *have* herpes?

Then, not only have I failed to cheer up my friend with a fitting, friendly level of inappropriateness that says "I really do care about you," but I've also insulted, enraged, and dredged bad memories from the miry clay.

What if there's a detail of this particular friend's life that I know nothing about? Because which of you in casual, friendly, or even best-friend conversations would bring up a medical diagnosis of, well, a rather embarrassing nature? Not many—like not a single one—in my circle would.

What if they *do* find it funny, they *don't* have herpes, but they show it to someone who *does* have herpes? Then the vicious circle starts again...

What if this?

What if that?

To be clear: I don't think the recipient I had in mind for this card has/had herpes. But I don't KNOW one way or the other.

I capped my pen.

I put the card away. Tucked it next to its twin, because I bought TWO.

I turned myself into that Greeting Card Company writer with the canned sentiments. I sent the intended recipient a text that said I was thinking of them. To hang in there.

Because it was the safe thing to do.

No way.

No way am I sending this to TWO people I know and care about and hope that:

They'll find it funny, because they're screwed up like me.

Neither of them has herpes.

The roommates/spouses, etc. of the recipients find it funny (not that many people are screwed up like me).

The roommates/spouses, etc. of the recipients also don't have herpes.

Now, I could write a story with this scenario and not give it so much consideration (and I might use it in a small scene someday far off, but if you'd like the dilemma to use in one of your story scenes, go right ahead, I'll not mind). The characters would be humorously offended, life would go on, and you, my dear readers, would close the book and go about your day.

Even if you have herpes.

Because it's fiction. And coincidences happen all the time in fiction. And I didn't write the story personally to you or about you. It was written to the masses, so to speak.

However, holding a card delivered by your trusty mail person, signed by someone close to you, baring the name of a *mostly* sexually transmitted disease would likely cause a different response. Because this is real life. *Especially* if you have herpes and now believe that I have inside access to your medical file.

Or your ex.

Or your exes.

See? This is why I don't want to know. "LALALALALALA..."

Don't email me. Don't message me.

I'll be too busy searching the electronic White Pages for two complete strangers five or ten states over to send these cards to—without a return address. (Wouldn't that be a gas!)

But do check out this shop on Etsy. Stone Donut Shop. From courteous to slightly-more-than-irreverent, her cards will make you smile. Even her tag line says "We make cards that don't suck."

I agree. They certainly don't suck.

I may go get myself into some more trouble over there today. I'm almost out of "give-them-a-stroke" cards...

* * *

Update: I did send ONE of the cards. Then didn't hear anything for a day. Then two. Then three.

Then panic sat in and I dreaded the first face-to-face encounter with the recipient.

Then I got the text that the card was absolutely perfect.

Oh, thank goodness.

Now, what to do with that last card...

*Lesson Learned: Think it through, stupid (stupid me, not you, dear reader.
Because you, dear reader, always think things through).*

99. SMALL, BUT MIGHTY

The last couple of blogs, and the ones for the next couple of weeks, have been prepped/written and contemplated ahead of time. Historically, summers have been intense for our family—no matter what the rest of the world is going through—and this one is no different.

High-stress situations.

Lots of health issues in lots of folks.

Lots of hours logged on the road and in the waiting areas of hospitals and doctors' offices. Lots and lots.

So, in anticipation of my "predicted life-on-hold roll," I'm writing ahead. So, if the content doesn't seem to match what you know about my "real-time life," this is why.

Earlier this summer, the hubs and I managed some time to hunt around at a few garage sales. Problem: In early summer, my allergies are still an issue, and, given everyone's fear of sniffles, sneezes, and flushed faces, I did manage to scare a few folks—no matter my twelve-foot distance from everyone I came across.

One such allergy spell crept up on me in a stranger's driveway, and, as it would happen, I did find a singular item of interest. It cost a whopping 25 cents. One whole quarter.

In between sneezes, I shoved the item and the quarter into my husband's hands, demanded he pay for it, while I ran back to our vehicle lest someone chase me down the drive and bathe me in Lysol while calling in the nearest HazMat team.

"Really? Are you sure you need this?" He called after me. Desperation tainted his voice.

I shot him that over-the-shoulder-glare-with-head-tilt that only 25 years of marriage to the same human can produce. I didn't need to use my words. He understood completely my desire for that 25-cent object.

His shoulders slumped, and I continued to the car as he tromped back to the checkout gal who likely would have rather us rob her of the item as opposed to touch our filthy coin.

Back in the car, air conditioning blasting, allergy leakage properly taken care of, and breath caught, hubby opens the door, slides in, and hands me my prize. "You've no idea the looks I got. I can't believe you made me do that."

I grinned. "I can only imagine. They likely believe you live in your mother's basement."

Then I placed the 10.5-inch-tall cardboard standup cutout of my childhood hero above the sun visor and we took off.

Wonder Woman.

In this instance, she's small, but mighty. Mighty enough to bring a grown man to embarrassment at a garage-sale checkout.

A small, but mighty image powerful enough to conjure up many happy memories of childhood playdates with imaginary friends, golden lasso of truth and bullet-proof bracelets and boomerang tiara. Well. The adventures were endless.

My Little Miss Muse, also small but mighty, now sits in the corner more than a tick miffed as I position my little hero's cutout next to the monitor. I explain to my Muse about the ins and outs of jealousy. Of envy. "No, Little Miss. She's not taking your place as my muse. She's just a reminder."

"She doesn't even wear purple." Swirls and puffs of grape-scented glitter fall from Little Miss's arms as she throws them up in exasperation. "Nothing about her is purple. I don't see a lighter, either." She squints at the cutout.

"That's why you're my Muse and she's just a small reminder."

"What can she possibly remind you of?" Little Miss takes a gulp of her lavender lemonade as she twirls a bottle rocket in the other hand. I must tread carefully now... she's about to pull out her amethyst-bedazzled lighter—and we're sitting indoors.

I think for a moment. Of all those invisible adventures as a child and the break they gave me from real life. Of the real-life adult "adventure" I'm on now with family and responsibilities and the world drowning in uncertainty...

I form the words carefully. The lighter is out and Little Miss is flick, flick, flicking the flame very close to the tip of the fuse.

"That she's Wonder Woman... and I am not," I say softly,

I'm not Wonder Woman. Not even close.

I don't have to be everything to everybody all the time.

I don't have to discern whether someone is telling the truth.

I don't have to stop flying bullets.

And though I would like to take off in an invisible jet, I don't *have* to travel to and fro fighting forces of evil, apathy, or stupidity, either.

"She's Wonder Woman. I am not." This time with a little more force. And I actually believe it.

So does Little Miss, who sets her bottle rocket aside and pulls out the sparkler that she uses to keep her purple curls in a bun. Her hair spills over her shoulders in violet waves, her little imp wings wriggle behind her. She flicks the Zippo one last time. The spark takes and she aims the spitting wand at me. "You ready to get to work? I've got a great idea..."

A big smile winds up her cheeks. It's contagious. I smile now, something I've not done nearly enough of lately. A glorious scene, faint at first, then as crystal clear as an Amazonian lake, floods into my mind. My fingers fly over the keyboard while my small—but mighty—Little Miss Muse plays conductor, waving her sparkler from the top of my monitor.

P.S.

Sorry, DC Comics, for taking your copyrighted character on so many adventures and never giving you nor the original creator due credit.

I'm giving credit to you now.

Thanks, Mr. William Moulton Marston. Your 1940's creation gave a tiny, fragile little kid in the 1980's something powerful to hang her daydreams on.

And that's no small feat.

* * *

Malachi Maxwell and Stella Marie HATE my Wonder Woman cutout. More specifically, I believe they hate her position on my desk. Since placing her near the monitor, they've knocked her over, drug her off, and sat their nasty rear ends on her face.

Well, then.

I've moved and rearranged and now poor little Wonder Woman has to peek her head from a stack of file folders at me, lest the rogue cats chew off her lasso and at least one red boot.

I think Little Miss may have something to do with this.

Lesson Learned: When you have kids, kits, or Little Miss Muses, you can't have anything nice.

100. 100 LITTLE REASONS

Today marks the 100th blog post. One hundred! Some were short. Some were sweet. Plenty were snarky vents.

Many featured Little Miss Muse in all her purple, glittery glory. Though now she's in the corner, flicking her Zippo at me, declaring that I still haven't given her due credit. Muses are such egotistical creatures...

To celebrate, I've decided to list the top 100 reasons I love writing. Keep it positive. Keep it sparkly.

And mostly keep away from the negativity bender I've been on lately (when surrounded by such a massive amount of worldly downers and family drama, one tends to muck about in one's own negative attitude).

But, today? I'm celebrating! In no particular order (except maybe that very first one—holding tight to the number-one spot is an intro-vert's absolute dream):

1. Alone time.
2. My office supply fetishes are tax deductible.*
3. Cheaper than a therapist.
4. Anger management.

5. Imaginary friends still talk to me.
6. Author friends from around the world.
7. Playing with cover designs.
8. Brainstorming a thousand possible outcomes that I can control.
9. The learning never ends.
10. Holding a book in my hands that was only in my mind a few months ago.
11. Cats are mandatory sub-muses, it seems.
12. Going for a brisk walk counts as "work time."
13. Napping counts as "work time."
14. Going for a drive counts as "work time."
15. Going to a movie counts as "research."
16. Meandering the library shelves is "research."
17. Meandering Half Price Books is "research."
18. Half Price Books can sometimes be tax deductible.*
19. Writing goes with me, laptop or not.
20. Those missing chunks of time when Little Miss Muse and I are in complete sync.
21. Those moments when the characters speak so loudly that they take over the scene.
22. When the ideas fly so fast, the fingers can't keep up.
23. Venting/planning/dreaming "in public" on this blog.
24. Planning/dreaming/plotting scenes when I'm stuck in boring social situations.
25. Little Miss's muse-bomb-drops at three a.m.
26. Ah-Ha moments when a "stuck" character figures his own way out of his problem.
27. Obtaining a workable knowledge of a complicated-to-me program to publish the paperbacks.
28. Finding an amazing piece of advice and slapping it on the wall above my computer.
29. Replacing that amazing piece of advice with a new one when a cat tears the other one down.

30. Sending off half-a-dozen short stories at once to publications that might like them.
31. Personal rejection letters from publications that "never give personal rejection letters, but..."
32. Acceptance letters.
33. Finding contributor copies in the mail.
34. Finding checks in the mail.
35. The little bar graph growing on the sales reports.
36. Comic Conventions count as research and are possibly tax-deductible.
37. The thrill of that first professional sale.
38. The thrill of the second professional sale.
39. And the next...
40. Being asked to be in an anthology out of the clear blue sky.
41. Red marks and purple Post-Its on my drafts mean my proofreader saved me embarrassments.
42. I love my first readers and their eye for even more embarrassing blunders.
43. I love all my readers.
44. My Web Guy relieves me of tech-y-ish duties that I'd likely screw up.
45. Creating a character that makes me laugh.
46. Creating a character that gives me nightmares.
47. Creating Little Miss Muse (though she believes she's *always been*).
48. Chasing Little Miss.
49. Bribing Little Miss.
50. Sourcing grape-flavored bubble gum and purple high-heels for Little Miss.
51. Stocking up on Little Miss's bottle rockets, sparklers, and lighter fluid.
52. Begging Little Miss to let me sleep one more hour before she begins her playtime.
53. Returning to the keyboard after a "life roll."

54. Making publishing to-do lists longer than this list.

55. Marking off those tasks in great sweeping chunks.

56. Brainstorming titles.

57. Listening to writer podcasts.

58. Reading other authors' blogs.

59. Loving some podcasts/blogs enough to schedule them in my calendar.

60. Taking online writing classes that kick my butt.

61. Watching Little Miss laugh herself stupid that the writing class kicked my butt.

62. Conquering 30 short stories in 30 days.

63. Conquering 52 short stories in 52 weeks.

64. Writing that first novel.

65. The elbow to the ribs when something funny happens and a friend declares "Story fodder!"

66. "You should write about that" comments after every comical/dramatic/untoward real-life event.

67. Smiling, knowing I'll never "write about that."

68. Two-hour Facetime calls to France to discuss life and publishing.

69. Sharing a table of contents in a professional publication with people I've met.

70. Watching other author friends have great success.

71. Cheering on other author friends in their goals.

72. Making the 20th "NO, Just DON'T" do-not-disturb sign for my door when I'm writing.

73. Turning down social events to sit alone in a room and make stuff up.

74. Making stuff up in the sunroom with the windows open.

75. Making stuff up under the giant maple tree in the front yard.

76. Making stuff up at someone else's house while I dog/cat/plant sit.

77. Being okay with liking unicorns because it's "inspirational" and "research."

78. Being okay with liking all things '80's child because it's "research."
79. Being okay with talking out loud to myself... *ahem* I mean to Little Miss.
80. Enjoying the giant framed Big Bird on my office wall because he's imagination inspiration.
81. Ditto on the imagination fodder for the framed: Ewok,
82. Kermit, Willy Wonka,
83. The tiny blue embroidered bunny patch from my deceased grandmother's jewelry box,
84. ET, and Gizmo.
85. Turning a 25-cent, ten-inch-tall Wonder Woman cut-out into a meaningful blog post.
86. Turning mower lines, ducks, cat toys, and banana stickers into meaningful blog posts.
87. Being better at something than I am at cooking. Much, much better.
88. Being better at something than I am at cleaning house and fashion choices.
89. Being okay with sucky fashion because that's my "work uniform."
90. Respecting the amount of work that goes into any published book.
91. My name is now floating around somewhere in the Library of Congress database. Ha!
92. Finding story inspiration at the bottom of the kitchen utensil drawer.
93. Finding story inspiration in a stranger's landscaping.
94. Finding story inspiration in a funeral home museum.
95. Those moments where I have to stop a chore and go write down that "aha" moment.
96. The moment I realize I never went back to that chore.
97. The look on someone's face when they don't believe I really write, then I hand them my novel.

98. Having to set the timer to get up and stretch because the writing "stretch" is going so well.

99. Showering Little Miss with praise and adoration for providing #98.

And, #100:

Not to be insulted, neglected or otherwise outdone by any other item on this list (even though I believe she was credited and mentioned an appropriate number of times), I love my Little Miss Muse in all her purple, glittery glory. Where would I be without her?

(And that got her out of the pouting pose. She's putting the lighter away, and her chubby rump is wriggling with excitement... I sense we're about to go on an adventure!)

In the meantime, she sends violet glitter-caked high-fives and hopes you all—whether writers or golfers or violinists or professional banana-sticker collectors—find a hundred little reasons to celebrate the joys in life.

*I am not a tax accountant. So don't try to tax-deduct your own hobby/fetish/fun-time expenses without consulting a professional.

* * *

I can think of a hundred more reasons, but I'll save that second batch for Blog Post 200.

Let's see. This posted the second Monday of September 2020, so 100 weeks past that (and factoring in the free fiction Mondays), so that should put the 200th right at the beginning of 2023.

Oh, my. 2023. What will our world look like then?

Who will be president? Will we even know?

Weather events? Civil unrest?

How many of my aging ladies will make it that far? How much more time does our family have to spend with them?

How many more precious memories can be made?

Tragedies overcome?

Adventures taken?

How many words can I write between now and then?
How many titles published?
How many new skills can be learned?
How many more antics will Little Miss engage in before 2023?
Only time will tell.

Lesson Learned: Do what you can today. Tomorrow isn't promised.

LINKS AND WEB ADDRESSES

Chapter 1: Tim Hawkins, comedian: timhawkins.net

Chapter 6: Dean Wesley Smith (mentioned throughout the book)
His personal blog: www.deanwesleysmith.com
WMG Publishing, where you can find workshops and high-end fiction: www.wmgpublishinginc.com

Chapter 9: Steven James Author: www.stevenjames.net

Chapter 10: "Cockatoo Loves Elvis" on YouTube: https://www.youtube.com/watch?v=CEQuDyuQFKE

Chapter 15: NaNoWriMo.org

Chapter 32: Bubble Wrap Day: https://nationaldaycalendar.com/bubble-wrap-appreciation-day-last-monday-of-january/

Chapter 62: Brian Tracy's book: My Book

Chapter 74: Ellery Queen Mystery Magazine: https://www.elleryqueenmysterymagazine.com/

Chapter 77: Heinlein's Rules from Dean Wesley Smith: https://www.deanwesleysmith.com/tag/heinleins-rules/

Summary of info: https://en.wikipedia.org/wiki/On_the_Writing_of_Speculative_Fiction

Chapter 86: Explaining the Pandemic to My Past Self on YouTube: https://www.youtube.com/results?search_query=explaining+the+pandemic+to+my+past+self

Kristine Kathryn Rusch's Blog: https://kriswrites.com/2020/05/06/business-musings-schrodingers-future/

Chapter 89: Stephen King interview: https://www.npr.org/2020/04/08/829298135/stephen-king-is-sorry-you-feel-like-youre-stuck-in-a-stephen-king-novel

Chapter 93: Future Earth Tech
https://books2read.com/sci-fi3

Chapter 98: That amazing Etsy shop (as of December 2020, she's still in business):
https://www.etsy.com/shop/stonedonutshop

ABOUT THE AUTHOR

Beth enjoys chucking words into sentences then standing back to see what magic—or mayhem—falls out, crafting tales in mystery, sci-fi, fantasy, and general "slice of life" fiction. She couldn't accomplish this without the help of her tutu-clad Little Miss Muse and Trudi the Concrete Office Goose, who's partial to superhero capes.

Her stories have appeared in multiple publications, including Pulphouse Fiction Magazine and Ellery Queen Mystery Magazine, and in multiple fiction anthologies. She's received several Honorable Mentions from Writers of the Future. Her lighthearted blog peeks into the writing life as she pokes fun at herself and her circus of a life.

Follow the antics of Little Miss Muse and Trudi, read Beth's blog (she might have burned down her kitchen last week), and discover the stories at bapaul.com.

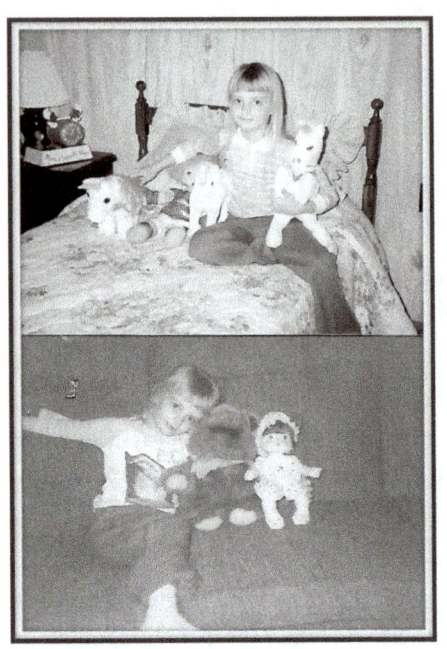

ALSO BY B. A. PAUL

Short Story Collections

Spunk and Spice, Volumes 1 and 2: A Collection of six short stories celebrating timeless wit and wisdom.

Out There, Volumes 1 and 2: A Collection of six short sci-fi and speculative tales.

Mystery Minutes, Volumes 1 and 2: Six short mystery stories

All the Feels, Volumes 1, 2, and 3: Collections of inspiring short stories

Just a Tick of Whimsy, Volumes 1 and 2: Collections of fantasy shorts.

Hijacked Holidays: Definitely not your warm-and-fuzzy winter tales.

Dark Minds: Toe-curling twisted mysteries.

Blog Compilations: Slices of the writing life with lots of laughs and bumps in the road.

Life Along the Way

Life All Over Again

Novels

Triage

Young Adult (or Young at Heart) Books

Switch: Book 1 in the Oliver Andrews Trilogy

STAY IN TOUCH!

BAPAUL.COM

Take a glimpse into B.A. Paul's writing journey, including the ups and downs of managing family, "real jobs," ducks in wobbling rows, and chasing down her Little Miss Muse. New blog posts go up Mondays, with the first Monday of the Month reserved for a free fiction short story available on the blog for a limited time.

Newsletter Signup!
Click here to sign up for the newsletter and receive a free exclusive short story!
Get the latest release information, author updates, and exclusive content.